Machine Vision

Algorithms, Architectures, and Systems

PERSPECTIVES IN COMPUTING, Vol. 20

(Formerly "Notes and Reports in Computer Science and
Applied Mathematics")

Machine Vision

Algorithms, Architectures, and Systems

Edited by

Herbert Freeman
The Center for Computer Aids for Industrial Productivity
Rutgers University
Piscataway, New Jersey

ACADEMIC PRESS, INC.
Harcourt Brace Jovanovich, Publishers

Boston   San Diego   New York
Berkeley   London   Sydney
Tokyo   Toronto

ACADEMIC PRESS, INC.
1250 Sixth Avenue, San Diego, CA 92101

United Kingdom Edition published by
ACADEMIC PRESS INC. (LONDON) LTD.
24–28 Oval Road, London NW1 7DX

Library of Congress Cataloging-in-Publication Data

Machine vision: algorithms, architectures, and systems/edited by
  Herbert Freeman.
     p. cm.—(Perspectives in computing : vol. 20)
  Proceedings of a workshop "Machine vision: where are we going?",
organized in April 1987 at the Hyatt Regency Hotel in New Brunswick,
NJ, by the Rutgers University CAIP Center.
  Includes bibliographies.
  ISBN 0-12-266720-4
  1. Computer vision—Congresses. I. Freeman, Herbert.
II. Rutgers University. Center for Computer Aids for Industrial
Productivity. III. Series.
TA1632.M335 1988
006.3'7—dc19   88-6320
                                                                  CIP

88 89 90 91   9 8 7 6 5 4 3 2 1
Printed in the United States of America

Contents

Preface   vii

'Smart Sensing' in Machine Vision   1
    Peter J. Burt

Introducing Local Autonomy to Processor Arrays   31
    T. J. Fountain

Integrating Vision Modules on a Fine-Grained
    Parallel Machine   57
    James J. Little

Computer Architectures for Machine Vision   97
    Azriel Rosenfeld

Machine Vision Architectures and Systems — A Discussion   103
    T. J. Fountain

Industrial Machine Vision — Is It Practical?   109
    Joseph L. Mundy

A Perspective on Machine Vision at General Motors   149
    Wayne Wiitanen

Industrial Machine Vision: Where Are We? What Do
    We Need? How Do We Get It?   161
    Mark A. Lavin

Bottlenecks to Effective Application of Machine Vision —
    A Discussion   187
    J. Sklansky

Inference of Object Surface Structure from Structured
    Lighting — An Overview   193
    J. K. Aggarwal and *Y. F. Wang*

Range Image Segmentation   221
    Paul J. Besl and *Ramesh C. Jain*

Learning Structural Descriptions of Shape   257
    Jakub Segen

Machine Vision as State-Space Search   273
    Steven L. Tanimoto

Directions for Future Research - A Panel Discussion   299
    Herbert Freeman

Preface

In April 1987 the Rutgers University CAIP Center organized and hosted a workshop in machine vision at the Hyatt Regency Hotel in New Brunswick, NJ. The theme was "Machine Vision: Where Are We and Where Are We Going?" The objective of the workshop was to assess the current state of the art of machine vision and set a course for future research.

The workshop drew some 75 attendees, and was purposefully limited to achieve an environment that would be conducive to free interaction and exchange of ideas. Participants came from all over the United States as well as from some foreign countries, and collectively represented a major fraction of the leading researchers in machine vision in the world. Representatives from industry and academe were present in nearly equal numbers. The two-day program consisted of 12 formal presentations of 40 minutes each, two one-and-one-half hour panel sessions, and three evening open-discussion forums. This book, though assembled subsequently, represents, in effect, the proceedings of that workshop.

Machine vision is concerned with achieving electronically what the human eye does so masterfully: visual perception. It involves image sensing, image processing, pattern recognition and image understanding. In the industrial sector the promising applications are in the areas of materials handling, autonomous vehicle guidance (with collision avoidance), inspection, continuous-process control, and surveillance, with inspection looming as the application with the likely greatest payoff.

Research on machine vision has been in progress for over 25 years, yet practical accomplishments have been modest. To date most installed machine vision systems are relatively simple and involve only simple computer processing. In most cases, only silhouette images are utilized and frequently the illumination is specially structured to reduce the burden on the pattern recognition computations. The installations often are in hazardous or extreme clean-room environments where the high cost of such systems can be more readily justified. Generally, the difficulties in bringing machine vision systems to the market place have been both technical and economical - current performance is still very much limited and their costs compare unfavorably with the same task performed by humans.

It has been stated that "...the best vision system is a solution that avoids the need for it." This may have some validity today; however, it is not an inherent truism. Vision is by far the most powerful and versatile sensing mechanism in the animal kingdom. This is true for direct human vision as well as in those cases where human vision is enhanced through the use of microscopes or telescopes. There is every reason to believe that once we achieve machine vision with a capability even modestly approaching that of human vision and at competitive cost, the installation of machine vision systems will virtually explode - not unlike the explosion of computer graphics systems once these reached acceptable levels of performance and cost in the late 1970's.

The prevalent opinion in machine vision today is that any significant increase in processing complexity for industrial applications must await the arrival of new special-purpose, parallel-type computer architectures. There are projects underway today in virtually every machine vision laboratory in the world to develop "machine vision engines", that is, special- purpose computers that will have the requisite capabilities at affordable costs. Rapid progress is being made, and new exciting developments are surfacing almost daily.

The workshop, and thus indirectly also this book, were made possible through the generous support of the New Jersey Commission on Science and Technology. This support is gratefully acknowledged. The editor would also like to express appreciation to Ted Wu for his painstaking efforts in formatting the manuscript with LaTeX.

Herbert Freeman

Contributors

Numbers in parentheses indicate the pages on which authors' contributions begin.

J. K. Aggarwal (193), *Computer and Vision Research Center, The University of Texas at Austin, Austin, TX 78712*

Paul J. Besl (221), *Computer Science Department, General Motors Research Laboratories, Warren, MI 48090-9055*

Peter J. Burt (1), *David Sarnoff Research Center, Subsidiary of SRI International, Princeton, NJ 08543-5300*

T. J. Fountain (31,103), *Department of Physics and Astronomy, University College London, London WC1E 6BT, England*

H. Freeman (299), *CAIP Center, Rutgers University, CN-1390, Piscataway, NJ 08855-1390*

Ramesh C. Jain (221), *Electrical Engineering and Computer Science Dept., University of Michigan, Ann Arbor, MI 48109-2122*

Mark A. Lavin (161), *Automation Research Department, Manufacturing Research, IBM Research Division, Yorktown Heights, NY 10598.*

James J. Little (57), *Artificial Intelligence Laboratory, Massachusetts Institute of Technology, Cambridge, MA 02139*

Joseph L. Mundy (109), *Artificial Intelligence Branch, GE Corporate Research and Development Center, Schenectady, NY 12305*

Azriel Rosenfeld (97), *Center for Automation Research, University of Maryland, College Park, MD 20742*

Jakub Segen (257), *AT&T Bell Laboratories, Holmdel, NJ 07733*

J. Sklansky (187), *Department of Electrical Engineering and Computer Science, University of California at Irvine, Irvine, CA 92717*

Steven L. Tanimoto (273), *Computer Science Department, University of Washington Seattle, WA 98195*

Y. F. Wang (193), *Computer and Vision Research Center, The University of Texas at Austin, Austin, TX 78712*

Wayne Wiitanen (149), *Computer Science Department, General Motors Research Laboratories, Warren, MI 48090-9055*

'Smart Sensing' in Machine Vision

Peter J. Burt
David Sarnoff Research Center

Abstract

In human vision, sensing is a distinctly active process: the eyes continually move to explore the visual world, and to locate and gather specific visual information. Similar 'smart sensing' strategies may be essential for practical computer vision systems. Through intelligent selection of data at early stages of analysis such systems can reduce the data and computations required to perform many tasks by three or more orders of magnitude. Modest vision systems can then perform challenging tasks in real time.

Smart sensing places particular demands on the architecture of computer vision systems. These should support multiresolution, pyramid processing and pipeline data flow. We have designed and built a system of this type, the Pipeline Pyramid Machine.

1 Introduction

Images contain vast amounts of information, enough to challenge the processing capabilities of even the most powerful computers. Yet only a small fraction of this information may be relevant to a given task. It is expedient, often essential, that a vision system avoid or discard excessive detail at the very earliest stages of analysis, at the sensor itself.

Still there is a tendency among system designers, at least in the research community, to develop vision systems that process images in full detail through the early stages of analysis, and only begin to distinguish between useful and extraneous information as objects are identified, at a relatively late analysis stage. How, it may be asked, can a vision system determine that particular image information is unimportant until it has completed at least rudimentary analysis of that information. Besides, the initial stages of analysis involve only iconic processing. While such operations are data intensive and time consuming in present computers, they are amenable to implementation in special purpose hardware. Once such hardware is available, it is argued, there will be little need for concern about efficiency.

A closer examination of the nature of visual information and the requirements of early vision suggest, however, that it is possible to identify certain generic strategies for selecting salient information at the sensor. These 'smart sensing' strategies lead to very significant improvements in the speed of a vision system, or reductions in its cost, that are critical in practical applications. These strategies are the subject of the present paper.

It is also possible to determine essential architectural features of a computer system for smart sensing. For example, such systems must be capable of processing image data at multiple resolutions and within restricted windows, or 'regions of interest'. Considerations of such requirements lead to a proposed pipeline, pyramid architecture for smart sensing.

2   What is Smart Sensing

Smart sensing may be defined as the selective, task oriented, gathering of information from the visual world. The viewer, be it man or machine, takes an active role in the sensing processes, probing and exploring the environment in order to extract information for the task at hand. This active approach to vision is already quite familiar to us from our own visual experience, for the human eye is the preeminent example of a smart sensor.

Imagine, for example, that you are driving a car down a country road. Your visual task as driver is to locate and follow the road, observe oncoming traffic, and detect and avoid any unusual objects in the road. At the same time you look for signs or other landmarks that indicate progress towards your destination. However you do not examine the world in uniform detail. Rather your eyes fixate in turn on certain critical patterns, an oncoming car, the center line, an object in the road, a sign, devoting perhaps a quarter of a second or a second to each fixation.

The eye is capable of gathering detailed information about a scene only in the small region centered on the fovea. Its resolving power falls rapidly outside this region, towards peripheral vision. Thus while you fixate the road, you hardly notice individual leaves, or even trees by the side of the road, or objects in the fields beyond. What is remarkable is the skill with which your visual systems locates and extracts just that visual information required to drive the car, while it ignores the vast flow of information not relevant to this task.

What are the essential elements of smart sensing? In the case of human vision three elements are apparent. First there is the concentration of resolving power within the fovea. This serves at once as a probe by which the visual system can explore the visual world and as a device by which the system can limit the amount of detailed information it must process at any moment in time. The second is the broad field of view provided by peripheral vision. This serves an alerting function; while sensing the world at much reduced resolution it detects unexpected objects or events. It also provides a guidance function, directing the fovea for close object examination or tracking. Finally there is high level cognitive control of eye movements. As a viewer performs a task such as driving, he understands the requirements of this task and moves his eyes to meet its needs.

These three features of human vision, the fovea, the periphery, and high level control, are essential for smart sensing in computer vision as well. These and several other basic elements of smart sensing will be examined more closely below.

3   Why Smart Sensing

It can be argued that selective information gathering, smart sensing, is both necessary and sufficient for most vision tasks. It is the nature of the physical world that objects are localized in space and events are localized in time. When performing physical tasks a person or an autonomous system interacts with only one or a few objects at a time. It follows that at any moment in time a vision system need only gather information from a small region or a few regions of the visual field. Selective, smart sensing is sufficient.

That smart sensing is necessary follows from the practical and economic realities of vision applications. Full, uniform sensing and analysis is prohibitively expensive in hardware and analysis time, and offers too little benefit over selective sensing. This is true for natural as well as computer based systems. Consider, for example, a task in which a system must continuously monitor activity over a wide field of view, such as automated surveillance. The pattern of light entering the camera represents a three dimensional signal in space and time. This volume must be sampled by the camera with sufficient spatial and temporal resolution to detect all events of interest, and to distinguish between important and uninteresting events. The resolution required will clearly depend on the particular surveillance task (it will be different for an SDI sensor and a parking lot monitor) but a typical application might need 512 by 512 samples per frame and 30 frames per second. Raw image data then emerges from the camera at a rate of 8M samples per second. If selective sensing is not employed, and this data is processed uniformly, then the number of elementary operation required per second just in the initial stages of analysis could number in the billions. This far exceeds the capabilities of even today's super-computers. Yet a practical and marketable automated surveillance camera can cost only a few thousand dollars. Such practical surveillance cameras are possible, but they must rely on highly selective processing, smart sensing, to reduce the camera data in the first stages of analysis. Here, clearly, smart sensing is necessary.

Similar data rates and computing demands arise in industrial vision tasks. And in industrial application there are always practical limitations on the computing resources that can be made available. Again selective, smart sensing is essential.

4 The Elements of Smart Sensing

While vision tasks may vary considerably in the information they must extract from a scene, there are just a few smart sensing techniques that can serve most tasks. Seven general and powerful techniques are listed in Table 1. The first four of these relate to the way in which image data is represented, while the remaining three relate to the way in which data processing is controlled.

- Representation

    Controlled Resolution: Use the lowest resolution sufficient for the task.

    Restricted Windows: Restrict high resolution analysis to windows of interest.

    Integrated Measures: Represent feature measures at reduced positional resolution.

    Compressed Range: Represent samples with few bits.

- Control

    Peripheral Alerting: Monitor the full field at low resolution to detect critical events.

    Model-Based Guidance: Direct foveal analysis to resolve ambiguities and verify hypothesis.

    Coarse-to-fine analysis: Compute rough estimates at low resolution, then refine at higher resolutions.

Table 1: The Elements of Smart Sensing

4.1 Controlled Resolution

The resolution, or detail, of raw image data as it is obtained from the camera is determined by physical characteristics of the camera itself, which in current designs are fixed and unchanging. The resolution required to perform a task, on the other hand, is not fixed, and may vary from moment to moment and from region to region over the scene. In some cases only coarse pattern structure needs to be measured over a relatively broad area of the visual field; in others precise details are required in small patches of the field. In a computer vision system it is generally necessary to use a camera matched to the highest resolution required for the task (both in space and time), but then to reduce resolution through filtering and resampling wherever possible for subsequent analysis. Such resolution reductions are not only important for efficiency; excessive detail in the data can actually confound analysis. A vision system can easily become mired in irrelevant detail, 'missing the forest for all the trees'.

The pattern detection task shown in Figure 1 demonstrates the importance of matching image resolution and sample density to the scale of relevant information. The task is to locate a target pattern, T, in this case a car, wherever it may occur in a source image, I. The target can occur at any scale.

Assume for simplicity that detection is based on template matching. (While this is a crude approach to pattern analysis it will demonstrate issues that hold for more sophisticated techniques.) Suppose the source image measures N by N samples, while the target template measures M by M. The cost of a correlation match is then on the order of N^2M^2 operations, the number of match positions examined in I, times the number of samples of T contributing to each match.

Now suppose we wish to increase the size of the target by various scale factors, s. Two approaches may be considered, as illustrated in the figure. In the first the target is increased in size by s, while in the second the source image is decreased in size (and sample density) by the same factor. The correlation match is then repeated. Both methods yield equivalent results. (Assume the original M by M target array is sufficiently large and detailed to unambiguously define the target pattern.) But the cost of the match process when target size is increased is order $N^2(Ms)^2$, while the cost of the process when the image is reduced is order $(N/s)^2M^2$. The difference, a factor of

Method 1: Target size increased by **s**

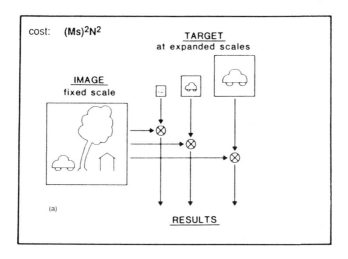

(a)

Method 2: Image size decreased by **s**

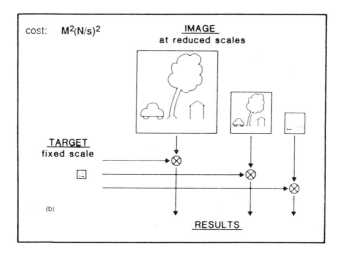

(b)

Figure 1: Two Methods for Detecting Targets Patterns over a Range of Scales.

s^4, demonstrates the importance of reducing source image resolution to match that of the information salient to the task at hand. This can indeed be large considering that scale changes of target patterns within a scene are often by factors of 10 or more, due to variations in viewing distance!

More generally, objects in a scene may appear rotated and partially occluded, as well as shifted and scaled. It can be shown that the advantages of matching image data to minimal target scale, controlled resolution, are even greater in this general case.

4.2   Restricted Windows

The maximum resolution, or sample density, required to perform a given task is determined by the scale of salient information in the scene. But this maximum resolution is generally required only in limited regions. Thus in representing and processing image data the maximum resolution can be restricted to 'windows of interest' that contain critical patterns, while the remainder of the scene is represented at reduced resolution. In this way data samples are treated as a limited resource that should be distributed in a non-uniform fashion to match the distribution of salient information in the scene.

For convenience of implementation we assume that windows of interest are rectangular, but their size and sample density may vary. Often there is a reciprocal relationship between window size and required sample density: fine detail typically needs only to be examined in small regions of a scene, while coarse, low resolution features must be examined over correspondingly larger regions. As a result, the number of samples within a window of interest tends to remain fairly constant, regardless of window size or resolution.

The use of multiple windows is illustrated in Figure 2. Here an object, a face, is recognized through a hierarchical matching technique based on decomposition of the target into subpatterns. The process begins at low resolution, using a correlation search or related technique to locate the head roughly within the field of view. Once the head is located a search is begun for the eyes. This requires higher resolution, but the search region can be restricted since the approximate position of the eyes relative to the head is known. Once

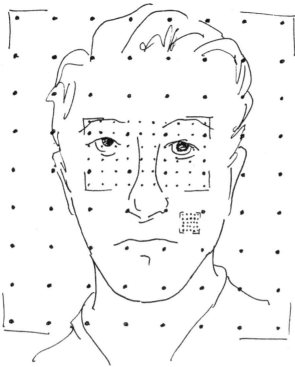

Figure 2: Pattern Recognition as a Sequence of Fixations over Multiple Resolutions.

the eyes or other comparable features of the face have been located the search may go to a higher level of detail within a still smaller search area, perhaps to find distinctive features that distinguish one person from another. In this way pattern recognition is formulated as a sequence of match operations, beginning at low resolution and proceeding towards ever greater detail. At each step the match process refines information obtained in proceeding steps.

We use the term 'foveation' to refer to an analysis operation performed within a selected window of interest and at a particular resolution. The task of recognizing a typical object might required 10 to 30 such foveations, each involving the examination of perhaps a 10 by 10 array of samples. The full recognition process then entails examining on the order of 1k samples. This is a small fraction of the samples required to represent the object at uniform high resolution, which may be 100k or more.

4.3   Integrated Measures

Frequently pattern information has two characteristic scales, or resolutions: the first, higher resolution is that required to detect the pattern in the source image, and the second, relatively lower resolution is that required to specify the location of that pattern in subsequent stages of analysis. For example, details of texture, once detected, may be converted to local statistical or energy measures represented at lower spatial resolution. Similarly motion or stereo estimates may require an analysis of image detail followed by local integration. In hierarchical object recognition, the positions of component patterns often need not be specified precisely once it is established that these patterns occur in the image.

Two distinct processing steps are required in forming such integrated measures. In the first, a filter is applied to the image to detect or enhance a particular pattern element. In the second, local integration is used to group or sum occurrences of the pattern element within small neighborhoods. Local integration is equivalent to a low pass filter, and the sample density of the integrated measures can be reduced accordingly.

Integrated measures in computer vision are analogous to information encoded by complex cells in the human visual system. This is suggested in Figure 3. The computation of a given measure can be performed by two arrays of simple units, as shown in Figure 3a. Image samples are examined first by an array of feature selective units, then the output 'response' values of these units are summed locally by the second array. Individual elements in the summing array will then have a non-zero response when the appropriate feature occurs anywhere within its summation region. In an analogous fashion a complex cell responds to a particular feature, such as an edge element, wherever it occurs within a larger receptive field, Figure 3b.

Integrated measures are selective in the pattern information they encode, and they yield data reduction through subsampling at the integration step. A typical reduction factor is perhaps 4 to 1 in each signal dimension, or 16 to 1 total for the two spatial dimensions.

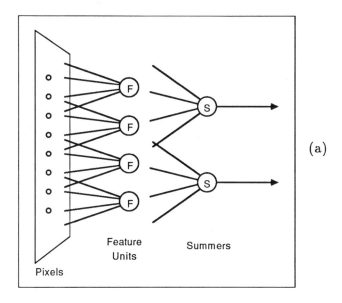

(a)

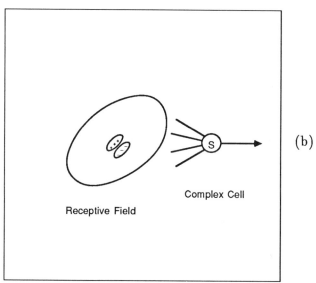

(b)

Figure 3: Formation of Integrated Image Measures.

(a) By Arrays of Computing Elements.

(b) By Complex Cells.

Further reductions can often be obtained when integrated measure are combined and integrated again to form more complex compound measures.

4.4   Compressed Range

Image data in computer vision are typically represented with 8 bits per sample. This standard reflects the limited capabilities of current sensors and A/D converters, as well as the cost of storing large image arrays. It can be argued that larger data words, perhaps 12 or 16 bits, should be used. Certainly the human visual system can operate over a range of image intensities that is orders of magnitude greater than can be represented directly by 8 bits. On the other hand, it may be questioned whether visual data is represented within the neurons of the visual system with greater than 8 bits accuracy. And, using standard image compression techniques, it is possible to represent image data within a computer with well below 8 bits per sample without loss of salient information. This reduction in the dynamic range is achieved through intelligent encoding of the intensity data. Neurons in the the human visual system, for example, are sensitive not to absolute image intensity but to local changes in intensity. And these local difference measures are normalized through gain control to further restrict the dynamic range.

Similar encoding is possible in computer vision. For example, the Laplacian pyramid represents an image as local difference measures much like coding in the early stages of human vision. Each pyramid sample is formed as the difference between local averages computed within two Gaussian weighting functions, one of which is twice the size of the other. The resulting code is complete (the original image can be exactly reconstructed) and it can achieve data reduction to one or two - bits per pixel (Burt and Adelson, 1983). Using a simple version of this encoding technique, just 2 or 3 bits per pixel have been shown to be adequate for tasks such as motion analysis (Burt, et. al, 1984).

In sum, an increase in the dynamic range of image data at the sensor over the current standard is desirable for computer vision. But once an image is represented in digital form, this extended range can be encoded with 8 bits or fewer per sample to achieve data reduction without loss of information.

4.5   Peripheral Alerting

Smart sensing relies on control strategies as much as on data reduction techniques to achieve efficiency. The first of these strategies is peripheral alerting. While small portions of the visual field are singled out for detailed analysis it is often necessary to monitor the remainder of the field to detect critical events when they occur, and to provide necessary guidance for positioning the analysis windows.

While the periphery of an image can be represented at reduced resolution, extensive use of integrated measures may be essential to retain sensitivity to small objects or brief events. Peripheral alerting must often be particularly sensitive to temporal change. For example, systems designed for surveillance and target tracking should respond to events anywhere in the field of view, but once detected the system can foveate and track targets, thus allowing the more detailed pattern analysis to take place over an extended period of time. This division of alerting and analysis functions between peripheral and foveal vision is a highly effective and general expedient in vision.

4.6   Model-Based Guidance

I have defined smart sensing as the selective gathering of scene information, and have suggested that this is largely a matter of locating critical regions in an image and concentrating the data gathering resources in these regions. Sensing becomes a sequence of foveations through which the system explores the visual world. This search is most effective when it is guided by knowledge of what objects may occur within a scene. Then the sequence of foveations can be structured to optimally verify and discriminate between objects. The process begins with low resolution measures in peripheral vision, and fragments of detail provided by initial foveations. The high level analysis system then forms an hypothesis about object identity, and directs subsequent foveations to points in the scene that may be expected to contains confirming information. When initial data suggests several alternative hypothesis, sensing can be directed to gather additional evidence at those points in the scene that are expected to most directly distinguish between these hypothesis.

This type of efferent control of sensing by higher level vision centers plays an important role in human vision. Vision is a dynamic process in which information gathering and interpretation proceed together, each directing and following the other. Similarly smart sensing in computer vision is carried out by sensing and analysis processes that are tightly coupled. For such a system to be effective the high level analysis component must work rapidly on partial information even as it is being gathered, while the sensing component must accommodate high level guidance, particularly in the selection of appropriate resolution, analysis windows, and integrated measures.

4.7   Coarse-to-Fine Analysis

A general strategy for constructing fast algorithms in machine vision is to begin analysis at a low (coarse) resolution, obtain a first estimate of the measure of interest, then to progressively move to higher (fine) resolution while refining this estimate. The cost of the computation is minimized at low resolution through subsampling, and remains small at successive refinement stages because only first-order adjustments are required. Coarse-to-fine search in pattern or motion analysis can yield three or more orders of magnitude speed-up over searches performed at a single resolution.

Suppose, for example, we are searching for a particular pattern that is known a priori to lie within a search area measuring 2^n by 2^n in a larger image. The coarse-to-fine search could be carried out within a pyramid structure, beginning at level $n - 1$, where the position of the target is known to within plus or minus a single sample distance. A correlation search over a 3 by 3 area then should suffice to detect the target. The precision with which the target is located need only be plus or minus half a sample distance at this level. The search can then move to level $n - 2$ with a priori knowledge of the target position again within plus or minus 1 sample distance. The search is repeated within 3 by 3 neighborhoods at successive pyramid levels until full resolution is reached. In this way the final search at full resolution is restricted to a 3 by 3 neighborhood rather than the original 2^n by 2^n search area. Searches at lower resolutions contribute little to the overall computation cost because they are carried out with subsampled target arrays. For typical values of n (eg. 5 or 6) the resulting computational savings is 2 or 3 orders of magnitude over fixed resolution search. Efficiency could be further improved by decomposing the target into subpatterns, as in in the hierarchical pattern matching procedure described earlier.

It is not always appropriate, or possible, to implement coarse-to-fine search within a pyramid representation of the intensity image itself. A small target against a cluttered background may not be detectable at reduced resolution. But this does not necessarily preclude a coarse-to-fine search. It is often possible to enhance features of the target at full resolution through appropriate filter operations, then perform the coarse-to-fine search on a pyramid representation of the feature image.

To support coarse-to-fine search the sensor and early processing stages of a vision system must generate multiresolution representations both of the intensity image and of various feature images and measures.

5 The Benefits of Smart Sensing

How important is smart sensing? What improvements in efficiency can the selective, task oriented, gathering of scene information be expected to bring? This will depend of course on the particular vision task at hand, but savings in excess of three orders of magnitude will be typical when compared to uniform processing at full resolution. I base this factor on qualitative estimates of the contributions to efficiency for the first four elements of smart sensing listed in Table 1:

Controlled Resolution: Assume a 64 to 1 reduction. In general, analysis will need to be carried out at many resolutions, but relatively few operations will be performed at full resolution. If we assume the balance of processing can be carried out with a reduction of scale by a factor of $s = 4$, pyramid level 2, then the reduction in data due to subsampling will be $s^2 = 16$. But as discussed previously, the advantage in computation will often be $s^4 = 256$ or greater. The assumed factor, 64 to 1, is a combination of these contributions.

Restricted Windows: Assume 16 to 1 reduction. Windows of interest typically represent a small fraction of the image domain, but the size generally increases in inverse relation to resolution. As a rough estimate, a typical window at pyramid level 2 ($s = 4$) might measure 1/8 the dimension of an image. If four such windows are required for analysis at that resolution then 1/16 of the image domain will be examined.

Integrated measures: Assume 16 to 1 reduction. This figure assumes that integration is followed by 4 to 1 subsampling in each spatial dimension. Larger factors would be obtained if temporal integration were included, or if multiple integration stages, compound measures, were considered.

Compressed range: Assume 4 to 1 reduction. With careful encoding of image data it should be possible to represent images with 3 or 4 bits per sample. If this is obtained from a full range 12 or 16 bit source image, then the reduction factor is 4 to 1.

These four factors combine to yield reductions in data and computation by 2^{16}, or between 4 and 5 orders of magnitude. This assumes the four elements of smart sensing make independent contributions to the overall system performance. However the contributions are not entirely independent, so I take four orders of magnitude to be a reasonable estimate of the benefits that can be achieved through smart sensing. Three orders of magnitude should be relatively easy to obtain.

As a second measure of the benefits of smart sensing we may attempt to estimate the data rate at which a human processes visual information when driving a car. First we need to determine the amount of information available to the driver. To put an upper bound on this data rate, suppose the driver views the road with a video camera and display rather than directly through the car's windshield. The display must have high resolution so that the driver can read signs at a distance and perceive nuances in the motion of oncoming cars, just as if he viewed the road directly. Suppose, in particular, that the display measures 1k by 1k pixels, and that 32 frames are presented per second. The overall data rate available to the driver is then 2^{25} samples per second.

Of course the driver cannot assimilate all of this information and he must sense and process information selectively. If the display is mounted at a distance from the driver at which he can just resolve its pixels, then his fovea will subtend an area measuring about 32 pixels across. He is capable of making at most 4 foveation per second to view and track different regions of the scene. The total data gathered by foveal vision is then 2^{12} samples per second.

I assume that the driver's peripheral vision processes data at about the same rate as his fovea. This could represent integrated measures at significantly lower spatial resolution but higher temporal resolution. For example, the peripheral vision portion of the display might be represented with 16 by 16 sample arrays, generated at the rate of 16 per second, to account for another 2^{12} samples per second. Thus the driver senses only 2^{13} of the available 2^{25} samples, for a reduction of 2^{12}. Again the benefits of smart sensing are a reduction in data and processing of between three and four orders of magnitude.

These estimates are admittedly crude. In some cases it may be difficult to achieve such improvements in efficiency, but in others far greater improvements will be possible. The important point is that smart sensing techniques yield very significant increases in the efficiency of vision systems. Such techniques must be considered as an integral part of almost any practical system. In addition to increased processing speed, they may bring very substantial reductions in equipment cost or an increase in the sophistication of the analysis that can be performed.

6   Architectures for Smart Sensing

What computer architecture is best suited for smart sensing? To answer this question we should again examined each of the elements of smart sensing to identify the basic computations that they require. We can then determine the computing hardware and data flow that can best serve these computations.

Table 2 summarizes the elementary computations required in smart sensing. For each of the four data representation related techniques, left column, the required computations are shown, center column, along with possible hardware implementations, right column. We assume that raw image data from the camera is represented by regular arrays of discrete sample. The computations listed act on this signal to extract useful information.

Controlled resolution: The system should have flexibility to select a wide range of new rates. The computations required are a discrete low pass filter with controlled band limit and a resampling process. Both operations can be implemented in hardware with dedicated computing modules.

Restricted windows: This involves no computations, but does have implications for hardware. The system must be able to effectively address regions of interest anywhere within a larger image buffer. It must also be able to treat boundaries of these regions appropriately when performing filter or other neighborhood operations.

Integrated measures: The basic computations are:

   1. a filter to select or enhance a feature,
   2. a rectifying process such as sample by sample square or absolute value,
   3. local integration, and finally
   4. sample rate reduction.

The window used in the integration stage should be adjustable over a wide range of sizes. The hardware required for these operations includes a unit capable of general filter convolutions for feature selection, a look-up table (LUT) for point operations, and a low pass filter with appropriately adjustable kernels for local integrations.

Compressed range: This requires a high pass filter and a compressive function, such as a log transform. In hardware these operations may be performed in a filter unit and a look-up table. In addition, an ALU or large LUT is required for division.

Function	Computation	Hardware module
controlled resolution	filter decimate	• low pass filter • decimator
restricted windows		• 'region of interest' • addressing
integrated measures	filter point operations local integration	• band pass filter • oriented filters • LUT • low pass filter
compressed range	filter point operations division	• filter • LUT • ALU

Table 2: Smart Sensor Computations

Of the operations listed in Table 2 the most demanding by far are the low pass filters used in controlled resolution and local integration. If directly implemented these would require extremely large filter kernels, making them both costly to compute and impractical to implement in hardware. It is essential that the filter operations be performed with a fast hierarchical algorithm, such as that used in Gaussian pyramid generation. Large kernel filters are then achieved as a cascade of small kernel filter and decimate operations. By limiting sample rates to powers of two, it is possible to implement such operations at low cost.

All of the operators listed in Table 2 are 'iconic'. That is, the basic data objects are sampled arrays, and operations on these arrays are homogeneous and local. This fact, along with the requirement for controlled resolution and analysis within windows of interest, have strong and specific implications for the computer architecture used in smart sensing systems. In particular, it should be based on pyramid computation and pipeline data flow.

Iconic operations can be performed effectively by SIMD mesh-connected processor arrays, and by pipeline arrays of specialized function modules. However, the mesh array is not well suited for performing these operations when sample rates and analysis windows change dynamically in the course of analysis. Such changes necessitate frequent transfers of data within the array and poor utilization of processing elements. The result in both cases is a substantial loss of efficiency. A pipeline architecture, on the other hand, can accommodate such changes in a natural way. Data flows though the processing elements in raster scan order while subsampling and windowing take place during data transfer. The time required to perform an operation is directly proportional to the size of the image array.

7   An Implementation

Pipeline data flow and pyramid computation have been identified as central elements of a vision system designed for smart sensing. Other features, such as high level analysis and control, are also essential. We have designed a flexible, modular system, the Pipeline Pyramid Machine (PPM), that implements these features (Burt and van der Wal, 1987). We have also constructed a prototype machine, the PPM1, that can perform pyramid and other iconic operations at video rates (van der Wal and Sinniger, 1985). Here I give an overview of the PPM design, then describe two applications of PPM1 that illustrate smart sensing.

7.1   A Two Stage Vision System

Figure 4 illustrates how smart sensing may fit into a general purpose vision system. Distinct components with different architectures perform iconic and symbolic processing. Computations related most directly to smart sensing take place in the iconic component, the PPM. The architecture here supports pipeline flow of data through

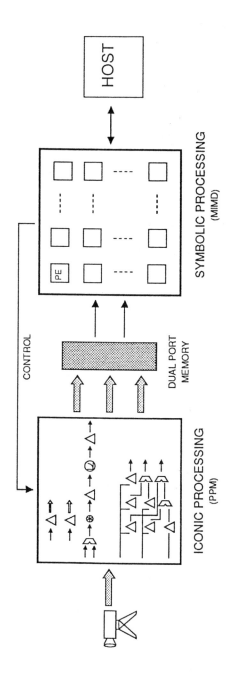

Figure 4: A Two Stage Architecture for Computer Vision.

iconic computing modules, including pyramid units. The symbolic component provides high level analysis and control. In the figure it is shown as an MIMD array of processing elements. These access iconic data generated by the PPM through a common memory area. Each processor could be responsible for a particular analysis window or analysis task. A host computer controls interaction of the MIMD processing elements and assigns tasks to these elements. Other architectures could be used at this level. Indeed the simplest and most common configuration is one in which a general purpose host, a von Neumann machine, performs all symbolic analysis.

7.2   The PPM

The Pipeline Pyramid Machine consists of a number of special purpose function units and a flexible interconnection network. The data flow may be a simple pipeline, with data being passed from module to module, or it may consist of several such pipelines running in parallel. Thus parallel processing takes two forms, simultaneous processing at the various stages of a pipeline, and the simultaneous flow of data through multiple pipelines.

More generally these pipeline pathways may intersect, with convergent and divergent data streams. The computations then may be represented as graph structures with the computing elements as nodes and data paths between elements as graph links. If data flow is restricted to be in one direction on each graph link, with no loops, the computation is said to implement 'flow through' image analysis. We refer to the resulting flow pattern as a 'lattice pipeline'. This type of analysis is important when processing a continuous sequence of image frames in real time. Once a flow pattern is set up, data can enter and exit from the system at fixed rate, without interruption.

Smart sensing also requires changes in the computations performed in the PPM as the system isolates and homes in on critical regions of a scene. The network of interconnections in the PPM can be dynamically changed in the course of analysis under control of the high level system.

The PPM design is modular, and in principle, is completely extendible: an arbitrary number of function modules can be added, and the data flow through the modules can be arbitrarily complex. In particular implementations there will be limitations of course. Still it is possible to implement 'virtual' lattice pipelines of considerably greater complexity than can be configured directly on a given machine. Only a sub-graph is implemented at any moment in time, and data is stored as it emerges on the output lines of the sub-graph. Processing shifts to other sub-graphs as the required input data and processing modules become available. A microsequencer within the PPM is in charge of setting up the segments of the flow, maintaining integrity of the overall lattice pipeline so that the computation looks continuous to higher level systems.

The PPM can perform only a restricted class of operations, the hierarchical iconic computations required for smart sensing. This restriction has the advantage that the architecture and hardware are simplified, while it seldom imposes any limitation on analysis. The modular hardware design is compact and expandable. Individual processing modules can often be implemented as single chips. A systems for a special application, such as automated surveillance, can be housed in a small package, possibly as part of the camera itself. Systems with 10 or so modules can be assembled for demanding applications such as real time motion analyst, with prodigious processing power again in a modest machine.

Although operations in the PPM are iconic, and hence homogeneous over sample arrays, sequences of such operations can implement what would seem to be non-homogeneous computations, including local adaptive gain control. They can also process irregularly sampled data, or irregularly shaped image segments (Burt, 1987).

7.3   Surface Flaw Detection

Two examples will illustrate the basic elements of smart sensing and the power and flexibility of the PPM. Consider first an inspection task in which flaws are detected in the phosphor coating of CRT screens. This is a vision task currently performed by humans during the manufacture of television sets.

Flaws occur is several forms. One type, called a water mark, is shown in the left panel of Figure 5 This appears as a small region that is slightly lighter than surrounding regions. While the flaw is relatively easy for humans to locate, it can be quite difficult for computer systems. Flaws of this type have low contrast, here only 4 gray levels, or 2% relative the the surrounding region. And other features of the CRT image tend to mask the flaw, including a fine grain texture and a gradual but significant gradations in brightness over the CRT screen. The presence of these background patterns precludes the use of a simple threshold to detect the flaw. Other pattern selective operations, if applied at pixel resolution, inevitably respond to texture grain but fail to locate the flaw.

A practical constraint on an industrial inspection system is that it perform its task rapidly and at low cost. Images with sufficient resolution for CRT inspection, including the detection of other types of flaws, must be at least 1k pixels on a side. Only a few seconds can be allowed for the inspection of each screen.

Figure 5 shows stages in a simple procedure based on smart sensing that can perform this inspection task. The procedure has four steps, which may be represented schematically as in Figure 6.

The image is first decomposed into band pass components through Laplacian pyramid construction. The band best matched in scale (resolution) to the class of flaws of interest is then selected for further processing. In this case pyramid level L_2 is used, Figure 5b. (The L_2 array is 1/4 as large in each dimension as the original image due to subsampling. However it and other images in Figure 5 are shown expanded to full size to aid in comparison.) Since the texture has energy predominantly at higher frequencies (smaller grain) and the gradations in illumination have energy at lower frequencies, these are largely eliminated in this image.

As a band pass image, L_2 has both positive and negative values, and a mean of zero. The next processing step rectifies the signal by squaring each sample. The image is passed through a point operation module, possibly implemented as a look-up table, Figure 5c. The resulting values are then integrated locally, step 3, by constructing a Gaussian, low pass pyramid. Integration blurs then subsamples the image. Any isolated large values in the squared image, that may be due to residual texture or noise, are reduced by the blurring

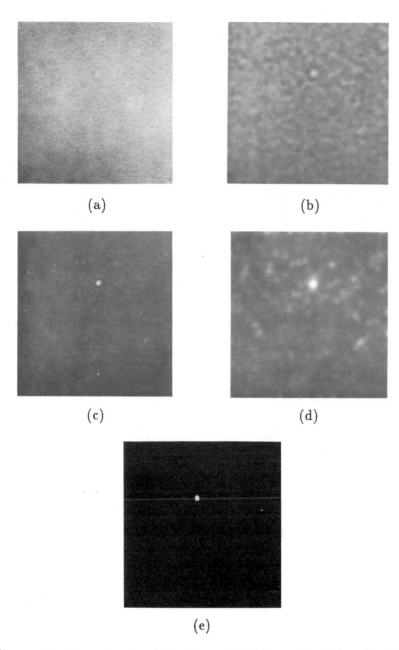

Figure 5: Steps in the Detection of Surface Blemishes in CRT Screens.

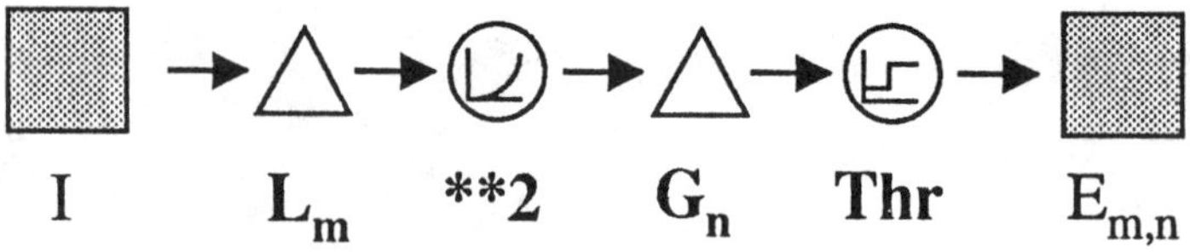

$$I \qquad L_m \quad **2 \quad G_n \quad \text{Thr} \quad E_{m,n}$$

Figure 6: Sequence of PPM Computations Used in Blemish Detection.

process, while groups of such samples associated with flaws are enhanced. Subsampling then limits the number of integrated samples that must be passed to the remaining stages of analysis. The flaw in the example now has 400% contrast, and a simple threshold can be used for detection, Figure 5d.

This example, as described, does not involve windowing or close examination of suspected flaws, but it does illustrate the other three elements of data reduction in smart sensing. The first step, generation of the second level band pass Laplacian image, is an example of controlled resolution, while the third step, construction of the first Gaussian level, generates integrated measures. It might be said that the final step, the threshold, reduces the dynamic range of the data to just one bit per sample. The overall process not only isolates critical information used for flaw detection, but yields a data reduction of 512 to 1. (64:1 reduction in samples, 8:1 in bits per sample.) These computation would require about 1/2 second for a 1k by 1k image in PPM1.

7.4   Smart Surveillance

Windowing strategies are illustrated in a second example of smart sensing. The objective in this case is to provide security around a building. A 'smart surveillance camera' is required that can automatically detect certain types of activity, such as people or cars moving in a parking lot, while ignoring other activity, such as the movement of leaves, birds and clouds. Furthermore, detection and discrimination have to be carried out continuously, in real time, on full video (30 frames per second). Only modest computing resources can be used, such as a microprocessor, so that the system can be marketed at relatively low cost with the camera.

A procedure very similar to that described above for flaw detection can be used in surveillance. This is shown schematically in Figure 7. A sequence of image frames arrives from the camera. The first analysis step is to form the difference image between successive frames. If there is no motion or change in the scene, this image will be uniformly zero. When there is activity, this will be evidenced by non-zero difference values. The difference image is then decomposed into a set of spatial bandpass components through Laplacian pyramid construction. Spectral energy will fall into different frequency bands depending on the size and surface pattern of moving objects, and their velocity of motion. For example, small objects such as moving leaves, may appear predominantly in the highest frequency band, while changes in illumination due to passing clouds would appear in low frequency bands. Objects of interest may have predominant energy in an intermediate band. This band is selected for further processing. Its values are squared (a LUT operation) and integrated locally through Gaussian pyramid construction.

The final Gaussian pyramid, representing 'change energy' integrated within windows of various sizes, is passed to the microprocessor for analysis. In our implementation using PPM1 the original image measured 256 by 256 samples. The microprocessor, however, can detect events of interest by monitoring a level of the integration pyramid that measured only 16 by 16 samples (256 to 1 data reduction). Any activity in the entire scene and within the selected frequency band can be readily detected at this pyramid level. However, once detected, it is generally necessary to isolate and examine the moving object in greater detail. The microprocessor then 'homes in' on the object by moving to progressively higher resolution pyramid levels in successive frame times. Only a 16 by 16 window of samples is examined at each level, but detection of the object at one pyramid level directs placement of the window at the next. In this way the system can detect even small objects or brief events while monitoring the full field of view at low resolution, and can then examine any suspicious activity at full resolution (Anderson, et. al.,

1985, Burt, et. al, 1986).

This example demonstrates alerting and foveation strategies in smart sensing, as well as data reduction through controlled resolution (choice of appropriate Laplacian pyramid level) and the computation of integrated measures (Gaussian pyramid construction).

The PPM1 can perform the required iconic operations at a rate of 15 frames per second. A practical system might required a larger field of view (512 by 512) and higher frame rate (30 or 60 frames per second). And it might also require additional filtering stages so that the change energy measures are more precisely tuned to targets of interest. Such systems can be readily implemented in modest hardware using the modular PPM approach. But without smart sensing the same task would probably exceed the computing power of even large mainframe computers.

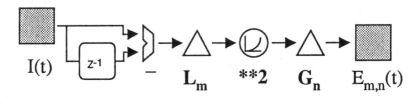

Figure 7: Computing 'Change Energy' Measures for Automated Surveillance.

8 Summary

Smart sensing is a style of image analysis in which the gathering and interpretation of visual information proceed in concert with one another. The sensing process gathers scene information selectively, thereby greatly reducing the data that must be processed at later stages, while the analysis process directs sensing to regions of the scene that may be expected to contain critical information.

Smart sensing is important. It can lead to improvements in system efficiency of three or more orders of magnitude. Such improvements are essential for practical application of vision, such as in industry.

There are certain generic strategies for smart sensing. These include the careful control of the resolution and sample density at which image data is processed, the restriction of analysis to windows of interest, and the further reduction of data through the generation of integrated measures.

These general strategies lead to a specific computer architecture for smart sensing. Pyramid processing is required to perform resampling and local integration efficiency, while a pipeline data flow is required to perform iconic operations effectively given that sample density and windows of interest change continually in the course of analysis.

We have developed a computer vision system, the Pipeline Pyramid Machine, to support smart sensing. The system is modular and extendible, making it well suited for a wide range of applications. Modest hardware provides considerable power and flexibility. Individual function modules can often be implemented as single chips. Small sets of modules can then perform demanding tasks, such as flow field motion analysis, in real time.

Components of this type, and smart sensing in general, are likely to play an integral role in practical vision system of the future.

Bibliography

[1] C. H. Anderson, P. J. Burt, and G. S. van der Wal, *Change detection and tracking using pyramid transform techniques*, Proc. SPIE Conference on Intelligent Robots and Computer Vision, Boston, 1985, p. 72–78.

[2] P. J. Burt. *Hierarchical linear fit filtering: a method for processing image segments*, Fifth Workshop on Multidimensional signal Proc., IEEE-ASSP and EURASIP, Delft, the Netherlands, 1987.

[3] P. J. Burt and E. H. Adelson, *The Laplacian Pyramid as a compact image code*, IEEE Trans. Communications, COM-31, 1983, p. 532–540.

[4] P. J. Burt, C. H. Anderson, J. O. Sinniger, and G. van der Wal, *A pipelined pyramid machine,* in Pyramidal Systems for Computer Vision, V. Cantoni and S. Levialdi, Eds., NATO ASI Series, Vol. F25, Springer-Verlag Berlin, 1986.

[5] P. J. Burt and G. S. van der Wal, *Iconic image analysis with the Pipeline Pyramid Machine (PPM),* IEEE Workshop on Computer Architectures for Pattern Analysis and Machine Vision, Seattle, Oct., 1987.

[6] P. J. Burt, Xinping Xu, and Chinsung Yen, *Multiresolution flow-through motion analysis,* RCA Technical Report PRRL-84-009, 1984.

[7] G. S. van der Wal and J. O. Sinniger, *Real time pyramid transform architecture,* SPIE Proc. Intelligent Robots and Computer Vision, Boston, 1985, p. 300-305.

Introducing
Local Autonomy to
Processor Arrays

T. J. Fountain
Department of Physics and Astronomy
University College London

1 Introduction

Flynn's classical taxonomy of computer architectures [1], embodying
the ideas of singular and multiple instruction and data streams, is
widely used as the basis of a convenient shorthand method of classifying multi-processor architectures. Two of the principal categories
of classification are SIMD, generally used to refer to architectures
of the CLIP4 [2] type, and MIMD, which is used as a catch-all category covering any assembly of processors which act autonomously
for some or all of the time.

From the differing degrees of success with which the two types
of systems have been employed, and from a consideration of the
types of algorithms which can be most effectively applied to each,
it is apparent that a wide conceptual gulf exists between the two
categories. The CLIP7 programme at University College London
[3] is attempting to bridge this gulf by constructing systems which
embody increasing degrees of autonomy for each processor, whilst
achieving a complete understanding of the operation and application
of the system at each stage.

This paper addresses the question of how this process should
proceed, by analysing the types of autonomy which processors in an
array can embody, and by seeking examples of the operations which
each step allows to be more efficiently executed. In the following
sections a progression from pure SIMD to complete MIMD is de-

31

rived which, although it may not be complete, nevertheless provides a conceptual framework around which subsequent parts of the CLIP7 programme can develop. As a corollary to this process, an analysis is attempted of the hardware penalties which are incurred by increasing autonomy. This process is facilitated both by considering real examples of variously-autonomous devices, and by developing an idealised circuit design from a non-autonomous starting point through the various stages of increasing autonomy.

One further point should be considered before any details are discussed, and that concerns the differentiation of data and control in a processor. Figure 1 illustrates the point. Each part of the figure shows a quite general processor/memory unit. Part (a) is a non-autonomous processor, where an external instruction stream operates upon locally-stored data. In part (b) the external control stream is modified by the locally-derived data, giving one type of local autonomy. However, for the two examples to be different in reality, data and control must have a different significance. If it is argued that no such difference exists, then Figure 1(c) can represent either of the other parts of the diagram. If this line of argument is pursued, qualitative differences in types of autonomy disappear and only differences of degree remain.

From the above it is apparent that, in order to make meaningful differentiations between types of local autonomy, the author must contend that there is a real difference between data and instruction in a general processor. This viewpoint is supported by the experience of any user of a computer. The program which is written to control the computer has a quite separate existence, and a different significance, from the data upon which the program operates. Although it is quite possible to regard any processing element as a black box with inputs which could interchangeably be called 'data' or 'control', such a level of abstraction only serves to obscure the desired functioning of the box and will therefore be avoided here.

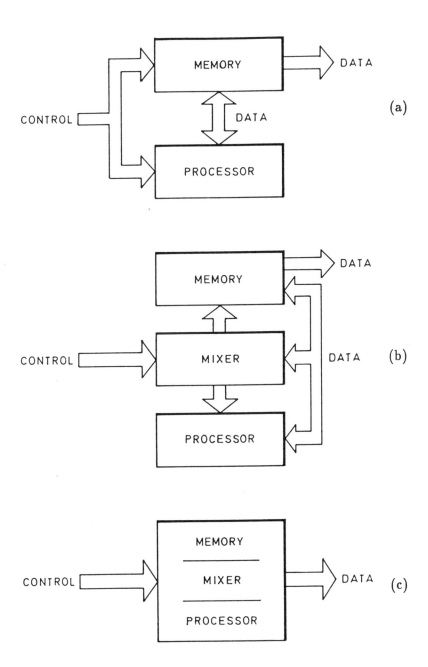

Figure 1: Non-equivalence of Control and Data.

2   Degree of Local Autonomy

The first, necessary step in the process set out in this paper is the identification, in general terms, of the various levels of autonomy available to each processor in an array of elements which are acting in concert upon some problem. No matter how much independence each element is allowed, some degree of global control will remain. In the following it is assumed that an appropriate global control is provided and that, usually, control of the locally-autonomous aspects can be either global or local as required.

2.1   No Local Control

In order to develop a progression of autonomous systems, we should first define a starting-point. Although it ought to be rather easy to propose a processor which embodies no local autonomy, it is, in fact, more difficult than might have been supposed. One example which the author can adduce is that of a single-function systolic array, for example a convolution device [4]. Not only is no local autonomy permitted, but the global function cannot be changed.

2.2   Local Activity Control

Most of the so-called SIMD processor arrays (CLIP4 [2], DAP [5], MPP [6] etc.) do in fact embody very simple local autonomy, namely the ability to locally determine whether or not each processor in the array is active. This can be easily achieved by a variety of means and leads to substantial improvements in performance.

2.3   Local Data Control

Processors which embody this type of autonomy allow the source and destination of the data used by a globally-determined process to be locally selected. This can be achieved either by calculating a local address (or offset) for the local memory, or by local control of the neighbourhood connectivity functions. In either case the processor function is under global control.

2.4 Local Function Control

The elemental processors in an array can be regarded as consisting of two sections, one part concerned with movement of data around the processor, the other part executing some function upon that data. The function generator may be singular (a single-bit ALU) or multiple (ALU, barrel-shifter and multiplier). In either case the next stage of local autonomy allows each processor to select which function is to be performed, data movement being under global control. This can be achieved either by storing a previous result and using that to control the function, or by local addressing of a look-up table of functions.

2.5 Local Algorithm (Operation) Control

In this mode of local autonomy, each processor in the array is provided with a section of program control store. However, the sequencing of these stores is under global control, thereby ensuring synchronous operation of the array. The size of the program store may be small, in which case only a single algorithm is stored at each processor. The processors can have different algorithms and synchronous operation is ensured by appropriate padding, all algorithms comprising the same number of microinstructions. The same is true if the program store is large, but in this case a library of algorithms can be stored at each processor, selection being by local addressing.

2.6 Local Sequencing Control

Each processor in this type of array not only has local selection of algorithm, but is also able to sequence its own program memory. This in turn implies that synchronism over the array is no longer automatic, but must be ensured by appropriate handshaking operations. At this level, only data needs to be passed between processors.

2.7   Local Partitioning Control

At this highest level of local autonomy, processors not only autonomously manipulate data which may be passed between them, but can alter the placing of program segments within the array, presumably on the basis of load equalisation or as a result of sequencing a complex program of the expert system sort.

3   Examples of Autonomous Processors

In this section an attempt will be made to develop a coherent series of circuit designs which embody the various degrees of autonomy. Each processor will incorporate:

1. Programmable functions

2. Local memory

3. The ability to communicate with eight neighbours

4. Global selection of local or global control

5. A consistent set of design principles

At each stage of the process the circuit will embody the level of complexity required by the relevant degree of autonomy, and the quantity of memory which is appropriate to the degree of complexity. As far as is possible, each processor will be a development of its predecessor in the sequence.

The purpose of this exercise is as follows. It is a truism that, once a computer has reached a certain minimal level of complexity, it can be programmed to perform operations of any degree of complication. The reason for introducing added complexity is to improve the efficiency of execution. In order to determine whether such an improvement is being obtained, it is necessary to determine the cost of increased complexity as well as the effects on performance. In a preliminary paper of this sort, the benefits of increased autonomy can only be roughly estimated, but it should be possible to quantify the costs quite accurately. It is to permit this to be done fairly that the exercise described in this section is carried out. For some of the levels of autonomy considered, it will be possible to give examples of existing circuits. However, because the technologies, intended uses and design philosophies of these vary widely, comparisons between them are meaningless in terms of assessment of the value of architectural differences.

The process commences with a consideration of single-bit processors, as these are widely used at the low-autonomy end of the scale.

3.1 Single-bit Circuits

The circuit shown in Figure 2 incorporates a processing element which is both a full (1-bit) adder and a dual minterm generator. This circuit will be used as the basic processing element for subsequent levels of autonomy. The arrangements for neighbour connections include the use of one of the outputs of the processor as an output to neighbours, and the provision of a multiplexer to select one of the eight neighbour inputs at any time. The amount of memory which is provided is chosen so that its complexity (in terms of number of transistors) is approximately the same as that of the other elements of the circuit combined. This principal will be used consistently at each level of autonomy and, in the present case, results in a 256 × 1-bit store.

This single bit circuit is the non-autonomous basis of the hierarchy which will be developed. It embodies about 1000 transistors in CMOS technology. The changes required to incorporate the first level of autonomy, activity control, in such a circuit are minimal and are indicated by the dashed lines in Figure 2. They involve provision of a 1-bit storage element and the use of the output of this element as a control to determine whether a 'load memory' instruction will be executed. The additional circuitry required amounts to about 10 transistors, i.e. 1% of the original circuit.

Almost all of the processor arrays usually thought of as pure SIMD fall into this autonomous activity category. It will be argued here that this is the only degree of autonomy which is worthwhile

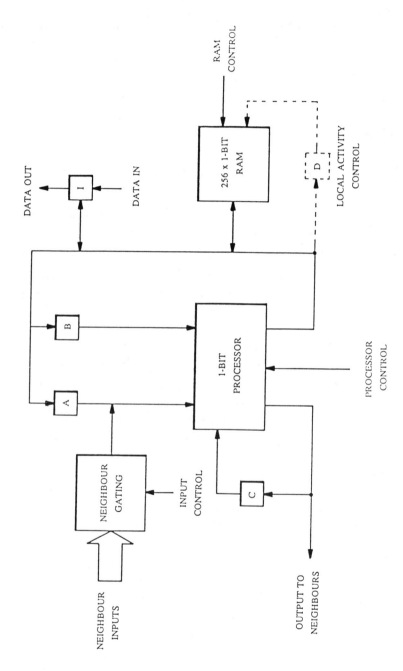

Figure 2: Basic Bit-serial Processor Circuit.

in a single-bit circuit. This is principally because subsequent levels require the generation, storage and use of multi-bit entities for use in local control, and it seems much more appropriate to manipulate these with multi-bit circuits. Since proportional increase in complexity will be the measure considered here, this introduces no lack of consistency. The next sections, therefore, will consider multi-bit circuits.

3.2 Multi-bit Circuits

The basis of this section will be a 16-bit development of the processor introduced in section 3.1, and this circuit is shown in Figure 3. The principal exception to the 16-bit scheme lies in the activity control, which is still single-bit. We may therefore calculate that such a circuit embodies about 16,000 transistors.

The first enhancement to local autonomy concerns data control (section 2.2). In the case of an array processor such as this, there are two main sources (and destinations) for processor data; the local memory and the neighbours. To permit local control of the first, i.e. local addressing of memory, a 16-bit adder and a 16-bit register are needed, plus some means of selecting either local or global address. It can be calculated that such additional circuits require about 1000 extra transistors, i.e. about 6% additional circuitry. To embody local control of the neighbourhood connectivity, it is only necessary to provide a 3-bit register and local/global switching for the resulting control lines to the multiplexer. These elements make a negligible contribution to the circuit complexity. The circuit resulting from these changes is shown in Figure 4.

It should be borne in mind, however, that the overall complexity of the circuit has been increased by a factor of 16. If this additional complexity cannot be utilised (in, for example, multi-bit arithmetic) then the cost of incorporating this degree of autonomy has been high indeed.

At least two systems are being developed which embody this type of autonomy. They include CLIP7A [3] and the GF11 [7], although neither of these is implemented in an optimum manner. In the first

T. J. Fountain

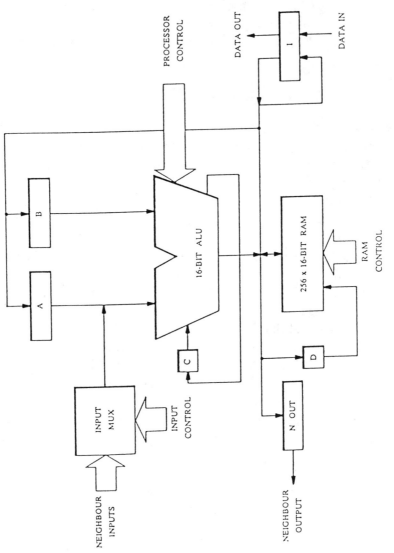

Figure 3: 16-bit Processor Circuit.

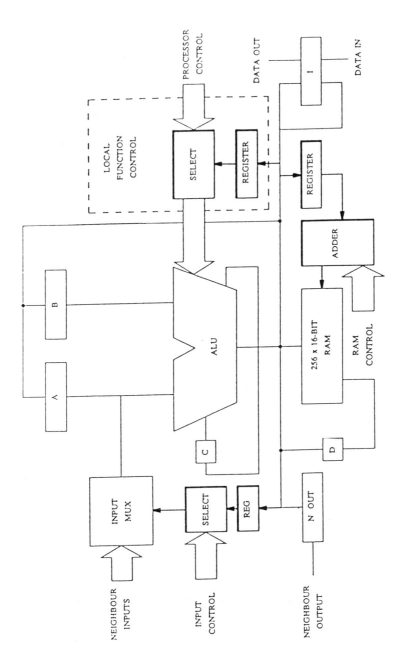

Figure 4: 16-bit Processor with Local Autonomy (Bold Outlines).

case this follows from the use of a general-purpose circuit as the basis of the system, and in the second case from the incorporation of high-complexity floating-point multipliers in the processor.

The next stage of local autonomy, that of controlling the function to be performed at each processor, is more difficult to define in hardware terms because of the variety of possibilities which are available. At its simplest, a system of this type which embodied only an ALU as its function generator would simply require an additional 16-bit register, whose inputs could be derived either from a previous result or from global control , and whose outputs would determine the function to be executed. Such an arrangement, shown inside the dashed outline in Figure 4, needs about 200 transistors, about 1% increase.

At the other end of the scale, it might be argued that, for this type of local autonomy to be worthwhile, much more flexibility of function should be permitted. As an example, a processing element could embody an ALU, a multiplier and a barrel shifter as alternative functional elements. In such a case, the control of the choice of function need be no more complex than that described for the simpler circuit above, but the overall complexity of the circuit would have increased by about 100%. Almost all of this increase, however, has resulted from increasing the functional effectiveness of the circuit in an attempt to improve the utilisation of the local autonomy.

Any decision about the effects of introducing this type of local autonomy to a circuit would have to be very carefully argued in the light of the preceding paragraphs. Perhaps partly for this reason, the author knows of no systems which incorporate precisely such arrangements.

The introduction of the next type of autonomy, that of local control of the algorithm to be executed, involves a number of significant changes. The processing element now incorporates a block of microcode memory. In the example shown in Figure 5, the 64 words, each of 32 bits, which are included require about 4000 transistors, an increase of 25% over the circuit shown in Figure 4. The function of the global controller is now twofold. First, it must distribute to each processor the required microcode and second, it must supply addresses to sequence the microcode for all processors in synchronism. The arrangements for the distribution of microcode should be reasonably efficient lest time spent on this operation should become the determining factor in circuit performance. This probably implies a dedicated input channel for the microcode and a corresponding increase in input pins and circuit complexity which together are equivalent to a further increase in silicon area of perhaps 10%.

A natural progression from the degree of autonomy described above is to make each processing element responsible for sequencing its own microcode memory. The implementation of a complex sequencer, such as the Am29331, would require vast numbers of transistors and would be inappropriate to this type of circuit. That more modest sequencers are adequate is indicated by, for example, the transputer [8], whose 16-bit version embodies about 150,000 devices in total, including 2 kwords of memory. In the case of the circuit considered here, 5000 transistors would probably be sufficient to implement a suitable sequencer, and this corresponds to an increase of about 25%. However, a further consideration must be taken into account. In order to make local sequencing a more worthwhile option, the sequencer should be allowed to select from a variety of algorithms. This in turn implies that a considerably larger microcode memory should be provided. A 2000 microword memory would allow selection from about 32 algorithms, but would require an additional 128,000 transistors, according to the design assumptions made throughout this paper. This is a massive sixfold increase in complexity over the previous circuit. Compared to this, the additional circuits needed to implement the necessary handshaking with the eight neighbours are negligible. The complete circuit required for this level is shown in Figure 6. Each section of the circuit is marked with the number of transistors (T) needed for its implementation. The total number required is about 160,000.

One final degree of autonomy is proposed in section 2.7, namely the ability to determine locally the partitioning of an overall task. For the previous level described, this function is invested in the global control, partly because large quantities of software are required to balance the necessary factors, but perhaps mainly because of the

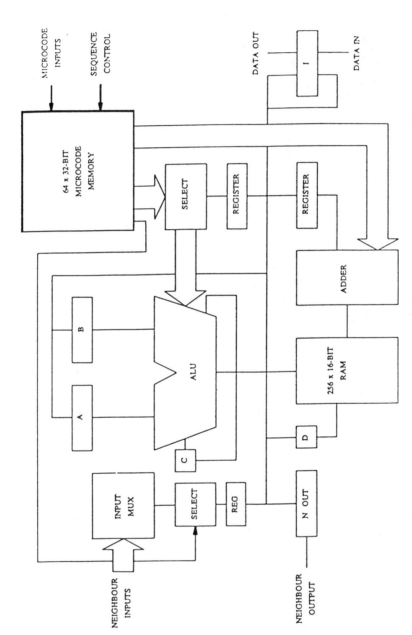

Figure 5: 16-bit Processor with Local algorithm Control (Bold Outline).

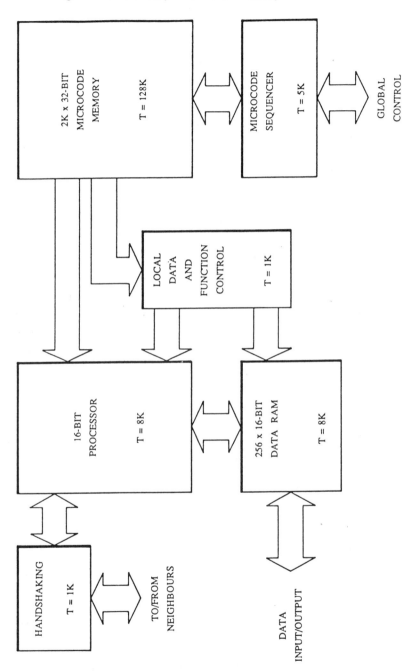

Figure 6: 16-bit Processor with Autonomous Sequencing.

Type of autonomy	Increase in complexity over previous level
Activity	1%
Data	6%
Function	1%
Operation	30%
Sequencing	25–600%
Partitioning	100%?

Table 1: Proportional Increase in Circuit Complexity

conceptual difficulty of allowing a number of processors control over the same function, which may affect them all. It is probable that, for such an arrangement to operate successfully, every element of the array would need the complexity of a minicomputer, with the added requirement to communicate appropriately with its neighbours in the network. In the estimation of the author, this would imply at least an order of magnitude increase in complexity over the previous level, principally because of the additional memory requirements.

The figures derived in this section concerning the increases in costs associated with increasing levels of local autonomy are summarised in Table 1. The second part of this exercise, the determination of the likely benefits at each stage, is begun in the next section, where examples of algorithms suitable to each type of autonomy are given.

4 Algorithms

The exercise of assessing the benefits of including various levels of autonomy in arrays of processors is relatively easy for the early stages of the sequence, and becomes progressively more difficult as the complexity of autonomy increases. One of the main uses of the CLIP7A system will be to emulate the various degrees and thereby generate experimental figures for the improvements in performance under var-

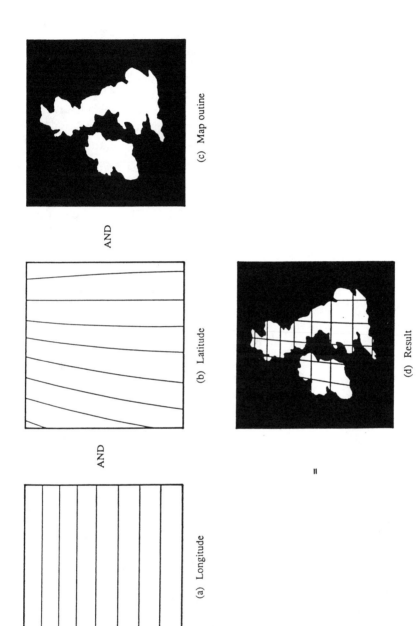

(c) Map outine

AND

(b) Latitude

AND

(a) Longitude

(d) Result

=

Figure 7: Calculating a Result within a Specified Area.

ious conditions. At this stage, however, it is possible to suggest some
of the areas where benefits will accrue, and in some cases to estimate
the likely degree of improvement.

For the case of local activity control, the implications are simple
to analyse. The desired end is that a specified process should take
place in a particular set of processors, and not take place in the
remainder. As an example, consider the sequence of images shown
in Figure 7. It is intended that the OR of images (a) and (b) should
be constructed, but only within the white area in image (c). In a
non-locally active array, this could be achieved by first computing
the OR of the two principal images, then ANDing the result with
image (c) - a total of two operations. In a locally-autonomous array,
the processors would each perform the OR of (a) and (b), but image
(c) would be applied as the activity mask at the same time, giving
the result in one operation. In either case the result is image (d).
This seems to imply a 100% improvement in performance but, of
course, this is only true for those functions where the activity can
be used. In the type of binary processing usually implemented with
such processors, it may be estimated that this occurs more nearly
10% of the time than 100%, so the true improvement in performance
is likely to be about 10%.

The second level of local autonomy involves the control of source
and destination of data. Where this concerns the connections between neighbours in the network, as, for instance, in the operation
of mapping an arbitrary graph onto a regularly-structured array, it
may be estimated that the ability to set up different local connection
directions simultaneously, rather than have to operate sequentially
for each of the specific directions, offers an improvement by the same
factor as the number of directions (usually either four or eight). The
operation is illustrated in Figure 8 but, as well as the usual fact that
the improvement only applies for the particular class of operations,
it is unlikely that the maximum theoretical improvement would be
achieved in any real case. A more likely level of improvement would
be the maximum number of offspring of any node in the graph.

A second area where data autonomy might be used in a rather
more straightforward way involves the processing of sequences of im-

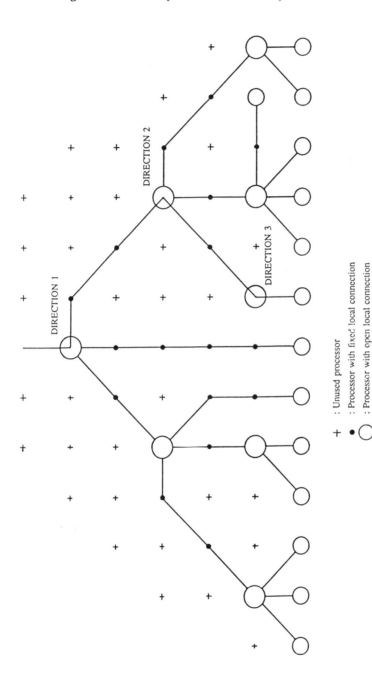

DIRECTION 1

DIRECTION 2

DIRECTION 3

+   : Unused processor

•   : Processor with fixed local connection

◯   : Processor with open local connection

⬡   : Processor with variable local connection

◯   : Leaf

Figure 8: Mapping an arbitary graph onto a mesh.

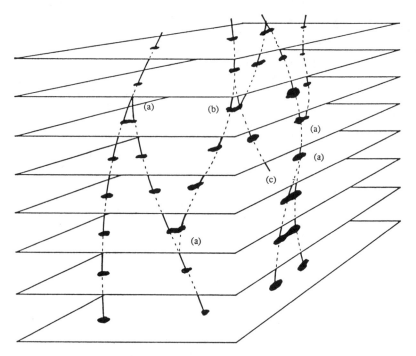

Figure 9: Reconstructing Connectivity Through a Series of Micro-
tome Slices.

      (a) Simple branch.
      (b) Complex branch.
      (c) Vessel end.

ages. Figure 9 illustrates an example taken from the analysis of the
vascular structure of the carotid body. At the stage shown, the positions of blood vessels have been determined in each of the sequence of
images, and the requirement is to determine connected sets through
the sequence, indicated by dashed lines. Given a number of starting
points in an arbitrary image, connectedness for each may be up, down
or both. After a number of steps in the search, the current points of
interest on different paths may be in widely-separated images. Such
a situation could be conveniently dealt with if each processor in the
array could fetch information from whatever image it wished. The
search could then proceed simultaneously over many tracks. Conver-

gence and divergence would be dealt with automatically.

The implications of the change from single-bit to multi-bit circuits have also to be taken into account. Single-bit processors permit computation at any desired precision (provided only that sufficient memory exists), the decrease in performance which accompanies increasing precision being exactly pro rata. A multi-bit circuit such as that considered here gives the same performance for a range of precisions, whilst decreases in performance when the precision eventually exceeds the processor word-size are quantised.

The succeeding levels of local autonomy all involve, to increasing degrees, differing functions at each processor. It appears to the author that it is at this stage that a qualitative difference appears. It is difficult to devise many worthwhile algorithms based on image (iconic) operations which utilise this type of autonomy. It may be that, in general, such levels are more suited to symbolic operations such as database searching, or functions in the general area of artificial intelligence.

Within this context, then, it remains to suggest how the varying levels of functional autonomy might be utilised. One simple use of functional autonomy in an image context would be in the normalisation of arrays of floating-point numbers. In this case, each processor can determine whether the mantissa should be shifted left, shifted right or remain unchanged, and also whether the exponent is incremented, decremented or unchanged. In a typical case this would lead to a twofold improvement in performance for the normalisation operation. Since, in floating-point arithmetic, normalisation is a frequent occurrence, the overall improvement in floating-point routines might be close to 100%.

At the next stage, and for the first time in this sequence of increasingly autonomous processors, decisions must be taken either consciously or automatically, concerning the spatial placement of algorithms over the array of elements. In some cases, for example where the peripheral elements of an array execute one operation whilst all others execute a second, such placement is quite easy. The only implemented example which approximates this type of autonomy, the Programmable Systolic Chip [9], can be used in this mode because of the particular requirements of systolic array operations. These frequently require incoming and outgoing data from the array to be specifically-formatted on input and reformatted on output. An array of processors embodying algorithmic autonomy could be readily programmed to perform such operations. The likely benefits in such a case would accrue because no specialised hardware need be provided to perform the specialised peripheral function. It is difficult to see how more general distributions of different algorithms could be usefully achieved without some individual feedback from processors to controller, indicating status or next required algorithm.

At this point the author will introduce an example from the field of computer-generated graphics. One method of calculating the perceived view of a volume containing objects whose positions and shapes are known in terms of cartesian coordinates is to use the technique known as ray tracing, illustrated in Figure 10. In one embodiment of this technique, the three-dimensional volume of space is divided into a uniform grid, and one processor is assigned to each volume. Each processor then calculates the intersections between the rays which pass through its volume and any objects (or partial objects) which reside in the volume. Processors must receive information from, and pass information to, neighbouring elements concerning ray paths and intensities.

This problem could obviously be programmed onto (three-dimensional) arrays embodying differing degrees of functional autonomy. For the type of array just described, having sufficient autonomy to choose and execute selected algorithms, which are sequenced in lockstep mode, there would be a number of areas of inefficiency. First, the lengths of algorithms required to calculate intersections with different types of objects would vary considerably. Second, some processors would have more intersections to calculate than others. Third, because the global sequencing would require data passing between elements to be coordinated, many processors would be idling for a considerable part of the time.

The next stage of autonomy, where local sequencing and local control of handshaking is allowed, would mitigate one of these areas of inefficiency. Each element along the path of a given bundle of

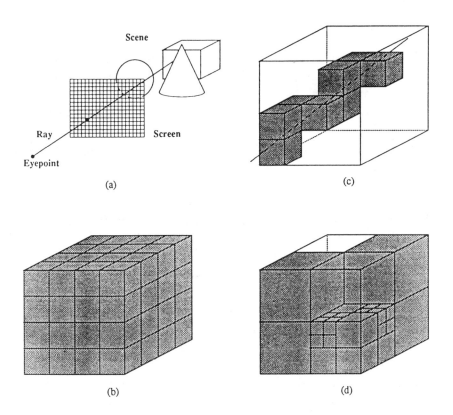

Figure 10: Generating Computer Graphics by Ray-tracing.

(a) Conceptual technique.
(b) 3-D space divided into equal volumes.
(c) A ray traverses a contiguous set of elements.
(d) An altenative subdivision of space.

rays could pass data onward to the next element as soon as calculations were complete. Since, on average some elements along any path would have heavy computational loads, whilst others would be lightly-loaded, the average performance of the assembly would be improved. The degree of improvement, though, is difficult to calculate with any precision. One method to estimate an upper bound is as follows. Assume that the largest ratio of maximum to minimum computational load is 10 : 1. If the numbers of high-load and low-load elements along each bundle of rays were to be exactly equal, whilst at every plane of elements along the paths at least one element has the maximum load, the improvement in performance gained from autonomous sequencing and handshaking would be rather less than 2 : 1. In most real cases, of course, the improvement would be rather less than this figure.

The introduction of the next degree of local autonomy, dynamic local load balancing, would appear to guarantee that this upper bound of improvement could always be achieved, because the computational and data-passing loads on the elements could (theoretically) be exactly balanced. However, the very process of load balancing might require such substantial amounts of computing time that possible improvements would be overwhelmed.

It is likely that the facility of load balancing is only worthwhile in situations where the time taken for processing on a given task outweighs significantly the time taken to pass the combined programs and data for the task between processors. It would presumably be possible to estimate these factors for each task and append the information to the task, thereby allowing such an exercise to be carried out, but the circumstances under which the process would be required to proceed dynamically are at present obscure to the author. For this reason no such algorithm will presently be proposed.

5   Conclusions

This paper has presented the results of three exercises, two of them consequent upon the first. In the first instance, a hierarchy of local autonomy has been developed which spans the range from pure

SIMD to arrays which require no separate global control at all. The levels of autonomy described comprise Null, Activity, Data, Function, Operation, Sequencing and Partitioning. The second result concerned the development of a series of circuit designs which embody the increasing degrees of autonomy within a consistent set of design principles, each circuit evolving from the previous one. This has enabled the cost of each increment in autonomy to be estimated with reasonable accuracy, although some external factors such as a change from single-bit to multi-bit processors complicate the issue. Third, a series of algorithms have been considered which allowed the benefits of each increasing stage of autonomy to be estimated. An important proviso at this stage concerns the frequency with which the chosen classes of algorithm might be encountered in any real application. A more important point concerns the type of algorithm considered in this paper. In most cases these are the types of algorithms which might have been implemented on a normal SIMD array. Local autonomy is used 'merely' to improve the efficiency of execution. It is expected that, during the CLIP7 programme, new categories of algorithms will be developed which will further extend the area of use of such partially autonomous arrays.

Because this exercise is a preliminary to carrying out experimental measurements on CLIP7A, it would be inappropriate to draw any but the most general conclusions from the estimates presented in this paper. It would be reasonable at this stage to conclude that a variety of degrees of autonomy are available to the processing elements of arrays, and that these are likely to lead to improvements in the performance of a variety of classes of algorithms. Any assessment of an optimum degree of autonomy at an acceptable cost must await the empirical results from this and other programmes. At the moment it appears likely that a law of diminishing returns may be operating, partly caused by the overheads involved in distributing large control programs to arrays of processors and partly caused by the duplication of costly control circuits and program memory at each processor.

Bibliography

[1] M. J. Flynn. *Very high speed computing systems.* Proc. IEEE 54, 1966, p. 1901–1909.

[2] T. J. Fountain and V. Goetcherian. *CLIP4 parallel processing system.* IEE Proc. 127E, 1980, p. 219–224.

[3] T. J. Fountain. *Processor Arrays: Architectures and Applications.* Academic Press, London, 1987.

[4] J. V. McCanny and J. G. McWhirter. *On the implementation of signal processing functions using one-bit systolic arrays.* Electron. Lett. 18, 1982, p. 241–243.

[5] S. F. Reddaway. *DAP - a distributed array processor.* 1st Annual Symp. on Computer Architecture, Florida, 1973, p. 61–65.

[6] K. E. Batcher. *Design of a massively parallel processor.* IEEE Trans, C29, 1980, p. 836–840.

[7] J. Beetem, M. Denneau and D. Weingarten. *The GF11 super-computer.* Proc. 12th Ann. Int. Symp. on Computer Architectures, Boston, Mass, 1985, p. 108 et seq.

[8] S. Brain. *The transputer — exploiting the opportunity of VLSI.* Electronic Product Design, Dec. 1983, p. 41–44.

[9] A. L. Fisher, H. T. Kung, L. M. Monier, H. Walker and Y. Dohi. Design of the *PSC: a programmable systolic chip.* Proc. 3rd CALTECH Conf. on VLSI, 1983, p. 287–302.

Integrating Vision Modules on a Fine-Grained Parallel Machine

James J. Little
Artificial Intelligence Laboratory
Massachusetts Institute of Technology

Abstract

Integrating the modules of early vision, such as color, motion, texture, and stereo, is necessary to make a machine see. Parallel machines offer an opportunity to realize existing modules in a near real-time system; this makes system, hence integration, issues crucial. Effective use of parallel machines requires analysis of control and communication patterns among modules. Integration combines the products of early vision modules into intermediate level structures to generate semantically meaningful aggregates. Successful integration requires identifying critical linkages among modules and between stages. The Connection Machine[1] is a fine-grained parallel machine, on which many early and middle vision algorithms have been implemented. Several communication patterns typically arise in implementing and combining modules on such machines. Schemes for integrating vision modules on fine-grained machines are described. These techniques elucidate the critical information that must be communicated in early and middle vision to create a robust integrated system.

[1]Connection Machine is a trademark of Thinking Machines, Incorporated

1   Introduction

The architecture of fine-grained parallel machines is well suited for exploring issues both in vision and biological implementation of vision modules [28]. Many early vision modules, for example, use only local communication in their computation, which maps directly onto fine-grained mesh-connected architectures, and onto biological wetware. As much as possible, methods which have a plausible projection onto mechanisms which have local or bounded communication structures will be preferred. The following discussion examines the advantages of the fine-grained architecture as a flexible testbed for realizing vision systems, without depending upon the particulars of the target architecture, the Connection Machine.

The goal of the vision system is to compute properties of the scene for recognition. Recognition is a demanding high-level visual task – requiring the full range of visual capabilities, from shape computation to structure identification to model matching. The needs of all vision tasks are not the same; sometimes navigation needs only simple quantities such as time to collision. In this view, navigation is obstacle avoidance. However, a broader interpretation of navigation as route-planning and location identification includes more high-level visual processing such as landmark recognition.

Our working hypothesis is that discontinuities of all types are critical in vision; there are several instances of methods which directly produce these evidence of boundaries, such as motion [29], texture [55], as well as edge detection. Discontinuities in several modules provide a rough segmentation which leads to the first stages of recognition, where the structure of the image elements and their character helps index stored models.

2   Motivation

Vision is computationally intensive. The prospect of near real-time vision has only recently been raised by the introduction of fast, highly parallel computers. At the same time, our knowledge of the independent behavior of vision components has rapidly advanced. The combination of knowledge and expanded capabilities increases the pressure to construct working systems. Individual components of a vision system are not robust, but their combination, through integration, can be robust, from the synergy of the information in multiple image modalities. A central issue for implementation is the form of data communication among the subcomponents of the vision system.

Most early vision modules produce a dense map of depth values. Interpreting this map is again an image analysis problem, but simpler, with much ambiguity removed. Discontinuities in depth, orientation and curvature provide a compact description of the depth map; an example of a system for computing this segmentation of the depth map is the Surface Primal Sketch [5]. It is simpler, instead, to detect discontinuities in the various modalities which produce the surface, to perform the analysis as early as possible.

The underlying hypothesis of the system described here is that the first stage of vision derives image structure, and produces a rough description of boundaries and cues to surface shape. Each boundaries is labeled with its likely physical cause. Intensity edges can arise from a variety of physical causes:

- Occlusion – depth discontinuity – where the surface turns away either smoothly, or abruptly, coincident with an orientation change

- Shadow – change in illumination

- Specularity – special configuration of surface orientation, illumination, surface properties

- Orientation – change in surface orientation, a roof edge

- Albedo – change in the reflectance properties of a material

Intensity edges that correspond to discontinuities in other modalities are more likely to be caused by object boundaries.

In the Vision Machine [40], Poggio suggests that the output of early vision modules is a set of edge-assertions, identifying rapid changes (at current scale) in some quantity. Each module independently produces these assertions. The goal is to construct a sufficiently rich description to permit fast recognition and to identify the physical cause of boundaries. The Eye/Head system [8], with two cameras, is the input device for the Vision Machine. The camera platform in the Eye/Head can pan and tilt. In addition, the pointing direction of each camera can be controlled with 3 degrees of freedom. Finally, lenses with controllable zoom, focus and aperture will soon be added. Then, the Eye/Head will be able to explore the scene actively. For the moment, the system description restricts itself to a static sensor.

2.1 Recognition

Recognition is often posed as matching image features, chosen from a vocabulary of primitives, to features of models stored in a library. Primitives for matching in recognition include a wide range of image features from edge fragments to corners to region attributes. The actual features types are chosen to be quasi-invariant, i.e., to be affected as little as possible by differences of position, lighting, or imaging geometry. In practice, recognition demands some type of segmentation of the image. Edges are minimal constituents of a segmentation, representing fragments of boundaries. When recognition uses isolated contour fragments, without notions of connectivity and higher-order clustering, it must rely on extensive search [16].

Grouping is essential for high-performance matching; richer features lead to a smaller vocabulary, and faster, more focused search. Middle vision processes are essential for aggregating image events into larger structures for rapid indexing. Also, real images generate broken, partial contours which must be completed into closed, connected contours. Grouping and completion are both essential processes for a vision machine. Recognition also depends on uncovering structural and spatial relations among features. For example, recognizing that a figure represents a face is likely to need only identifying the compact blobs, representing the eyes, and their symmetrical position. However, more detailed recognition, identifying whose face it is, needs more attention to shapes of features and their relative sizes and positions.

2.2   The Structure of the Vision Machine

The Vision Machine is composed of multiple processes computing separate maps from the image. Each map, or layer, is the output of an individual early or middle vision process, or module, such as color, motion or texture. The maps inherit a shared retinotopic mapping from the image coordinate system to their own coordinate system. For simplicity, this mapping may be the identity. Computationally, each processor in the fine-grained machine contains all elements in these maps (layers) for a particular location. Constraint computations among modules at a point are thus internal computations in a processor. Since each processor is mapped to a point in the image, only one module computes at a time. Certain processes, such as intensity edge detection, generate outputs which are the input to other modules, such as texture, and so must precede others. The relation among these subsystems is left unspecified, since the relation is complex, and its discovery is part of the research goal.

Middle vision determines the location of significant changes in the contents of the maps, and constructs extended image structures from them; it needs extensive non-local communication. Processes make the system adaptable, using computations requiring a high degree of fan-out, which is simulated using general, non-local communication on a fine-grained machine. Boundary elements constructed by middle vision, with their structural relations, feed upward to recognition processes, which do not necessarily operate in the image coordinate frame. Constraints among modules operate at boundaries, where there may be only a loose registration in the retinotopic coordinate system, across modules; registering misaligned boundaries is a task for intermediate vision. This discussion considers only up to the level of aggregation which is input to recognition.

Questions of organization and communication are of paramount importance. There are several goals of this system: rapid recognition, robustness, and adaptability. Integration of modules can provide the last two properties, while structural computations can lead to rapid recognition. Structural issues arise in computing blobs, lines and regions. There is a layer to implement structure finding, such as visual routines [52] and chunking [31]. Adaptability arises from a sensitivity to image content, which necessitates analysis of statistics such as signal-to-noise ratio.

The system computes at multiple scales, but, in contrast to pyramid systems, successive scales do not have fewer sample points. This configuration provides overlapping coverage, so that elements at coarse scale have overlapping support. The structure of the target fine-grained machine, the Connection Machine, does not confer any advantage on reductions in processors in coarser scales, since different scales are processed at different times. A lower sampling rate at coarse scales produces many idle processors. For an $m \times m$ system, the pyramid uses $4m^2/3$ data elements, while a uniform scheme uses $m^2 \log m$. The number of wires is four times the number of elements; however, since each scale computes separately, the communication load is the same for the two schemes. Likewise, the memory load is well within the characteristics of target machines.

3   Modules

Modules are subsystems which can are distinguished either by the form their input and their output – *shape from x* descriptions [21]. They correspond to inherent modalities of vision, our capabilities to infer the shape of objects from a variety of visual cues, such as:

- Shading – variation in surface orientation

- Motion – variation in time

- Texture – variation in material reflectance properties

- Color – variation in spectral distribution of reflected light

- Stereo – variation in imaging geometry

Each module relies on the variation of some property of images to deliver cues on the shape of objects; where the depth function is discontinuous they indicate the boundaries of objects. Often included in the list of *shape from x* is shape from contour, but the interpretation of the geometry of boundaries is placed at a higher level, in the intermediate level in vision. These subsystems identified with these modules are nearly independent, so they have been studied in isolation. The resulting algorithms are only partially successful on natural images, where simplifying assumptions are frequently violated. Hence the need for integration.

4 Fine-grained Machines

Several existing architectures are termed "fine-grained": the central assumption is that there are enough processors so that the mapping from data elements to processors in the computer architecture is one-to-one, or some small ratio. Whether the processors are relatively simple of complex is unimportant. One result of this exercise of designing and implementing a Vision Machine is to discover how much complexity is needed in the processors. The Connection Machine is a powerful fine-grained parallel machine which has already proven useful for implementing vision algorithms. Among the existing vision systems on the Connection Machine are binocular stereo [10] and optical flow detection [29]. In implementing these systems, several different models of using the Connection Machine have emerged, using the different communication modes of the machine. The Connection Machine implementation of algorithms takes advantage of the underlying architecture of the machine in novel ways. Here several common, elementary operations are described which are useful in many parallel algorithms. The discussion avoids specifics of the communication capabilities of the Connection Machine. Other fine-grained computing systems which have high-bandwidth communication, such as versions of the Cosmic Cube [44], the mesh of trees [49], or systems based on fat-trees [26], permit the types of communication needed for effective implementation of vision.

4.1 The Connection Machine

The Connection Machine [19] is a fine-grained parallel computing machine having between 16K and 64K processors, operating under a single instruction stream broadcast to all processors (Figure 1). It

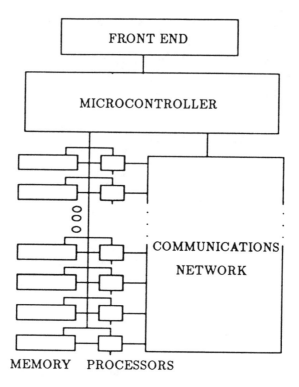

Figure 1: Block Diagram of the Connection Machine.

is termed a Single Instruction Multiple Data (SIMD) machine, because all processors execute the same control stream. Each of the processors is a 1-bit serial processor, with 64K bits of memory in the CM-2. There are two modes of communication among the processors. In the first mode, the processors can be thought of as connected by a mesh of wires into an $m \times m$ grid network (the NEWS network, so-called because of the four cardinal directions), allowing rapid direct communication between neighboring processors; m is variable. The second mode, the *router*, allows messages to be sent from any processor to any other processor in the machine. The processors in the Connection Machine can be envisioned as being the vertices of a 16-dimensional hypercube (in fact, it is a 12-dimensional hypercube; at each vertex of the hypercube resides a chip containing 16 processors).

In the CM-1, used presently in the AI Laboratory, NEWS communication is carried out on a separate set of wires ($m \times m = 128 \times 128$ for 16K); in the CM-2, those wires are gone, and NEWS accesses use the hypercube wires. Each processor in the Connection Machine is identified by a unique integer, its hypercube address. This address specifies the destination of messages handled by the router. Messages pass along the edges of the hypercube from source processors to destination processors. In addition to local operations in the processors, the Connection Machine can return to the host machine the result of various operations on a field in all processors; it can return the global maximum, minimum, sum, logical AND, logical OR of the field.

To manipulate data structures with more than 64K elements, the Connection Machine provides *virtual processors*. A single physical processor operates as a set of multiple virtual processors by serializing operations in time, dividing the memory of each processor accordingly.

The Connection Machine architecture permits useful primitive operations for early, middle and high-level vision. It is distinguished from mesh computers by its capability for general non-local communication among the processors, and from pyramid machines by its uniform bandwidth communication among all processors. Each processor in the Connection Machine is associated with a data element; in computer vision these elements, in early vision, are the pixels in the image. The style of computation appropriate to the Connection Machine is termed *data parallelism* [20]: parallelism is not over processes or functions, but over data. The model of computing for the Connection Machine is based on general, non-local communication among processors.

4.2   Powerful Primitive Operations

Many vision problems can be best solved by a combination of several communication modes on the Connection Machine. There are several common, elementary operations which recur throughout this discussion of parallel algorithms: routing operations, distance doubling and scanning. Routing implements general, non-local communication

among processors; distance doubling is a particular message-passing
strategy, made possible by the router, which permits communication
among n processors in $\log n$ message-passing cycles; scanning allows
certain fast computations on sets of processors in a communication
pattern dependent on their location in the machine. Because routing can re-organize information in one communication step, the Connection Machine encourages flexible data structures and algorithms
which take advantage of these different communication modes.

Routing

Memory in the Connection Machine is attached to processors; local
memory can be accessed rapidly. Memory of processors nearby in the
can be accessed by passing it through the processors on the path between the source and destination. This implements a mesh-connected
style of computation. The *router* on the Connection Machine provides parallel reads and writes among processor memory at arbitrary
distances and with arbitrary patterns. It uses a packet-switched message routing scheme to direct messages along the hypercube connections to their destinations. This powerful communication mode can
reconfigure completely, in one parallel write operation, taking one
router cycle, a field of information in the machine. The Connection
Machine can combine messages at a destination, by various operations, such as logical AND, inclusive OR, summation, and maximum
or minimum.

Distance Doubling

Another important primitive operation is *distance doubling* [59] [27],
which compute the effect of any binary, associative operation, on processors linked in a list or a ring. For example, using *max, doubling*
can find the extremum of a field contained in the processors. Using message-passing on the router, *doubling* propagates the extreme
value to all N processors in a ring in $O(\log N)$ steps. Typically, the
value to be maximized is the hypercube address of the processor. At
termination, each processor connected in the ring knows the label
of the maximum processor in the ring, which serves as a label for

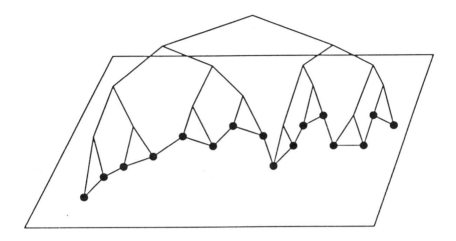

Figure 2: Tree Structure on a Linked Edge.

```
processor-number = [0   1   2   3   4   5   6   7]

A                 = [5   1   3   4   3   9   2   6]

Plus-Scan(A)      = [5   6   9  13  16  25  27  33]
Max-Scan(A)       = [5   5   5   5   5   9   9   9]
```

Figure 3: Examples of Scanning, Using the *Plus* and *Max* Operators.

the set of all connected processors. At the same time, the distance from the maximum processor can be computed in each processor. Figure 2 shows the induced tree structure associated with a linked set of processors.

Scanning

Another set of powerful primitive operations are the *scan* operations [4]. These operations simplify and speed up many algorithms. They directly take advantage of the hypercube connections underlying the router and can distribute values among the processors and to aggregate values using associative operators. Formally, the *scan* operation takes a binary associative operator $\oplus$, with identity 0, an ordered set $[a_0, a_1, \ldots, a_{n-1}]$ and returns the set $[a_0, (a_0 \oplus a_1), \ldots, (a_0 \oplus a_1 \oplus \ldots \oplus a_{n-1})]$. This operation is sometimes referred to as the data independent prefix operation [9]. Binary associative operators include minimum, maximum, and plus. Figure 3 shows the results of scans using the operators *maximum*, *plus*, and *copy* on some example data.

Scan operations can act of partitioned data; the beginning of a partition or *segment* is signalled by a processor whose *segment bit* is set. The *scan* operations starts over again at the beginning of each segment. The *copy-scan* operation distributes data over a set of processors which extends until the next segment begins, permitting local broadcast.

Versions of the *scan* operations also work using the NEWS coordinate system; these are termed *grid-scans*. Scans in grid directions can efficiently implement spatially homogeneous computations such as region summing [28], in which each pixel receives the sum of a field in an area surrounding it. Using NEWS communication, region summing takes time linear in the radius of the region, while, using *scans* it is independent of the radius. Blelloch [4] argues that *scan* operations can be efficiently implemented on many network topologies, and that existing parallel hardware, such as the Connection Machine execute *scan* operations at least as fast as parallel memory references. The *scan* model is useful for any situation where concentrated local communication can be uncovered in a computation.

5 Vision and Parallelism

Vision algorithms from early, middle and high-level vision place different requirements on a fine-grained parallel machine. Early vision modules, such as edge detection, optical flow, stereo, compute locally in the spatial domain. Middle vision (line following, image chunking, visual routines) has regular, but context dependent, communication. High-level processes, such as recognition, use arbitrary communication as described in [17]. Flexible communication is crucial to effective implementation of the variety of these communication patterns.

Early vision algorithms exhibit *spatial parallelism*; all pixels are processed in unison, in a spatially homogeneous computation. The classic example is filtering or convolution. A large class of regularization computations [3] can be cast in this framework, when the input data lie on a regular mesh. These spatially parallel computations are easily mapped into operations using only NEWS accesses. An important feature of *spatial parallelism* is the uniformity of the communication patterns involved in the computation.

Middle and high-level vision demonstrate many tasks requiring arbitrary, diverse communication which can utilize the power of the router. In middle vision, computing image features such as edge following utilizes communication patterns which depend on local image structure, for example, the direction of the gradient. Routing operations fit this task well, in addition to enabling efficient algorithms based on *doubling*. High-level vision tasks utilize more general patterns of communication. *Scan* operations are well suited to those problems in which processing elements can be grouped into sets which have concentrated communication activity. *Scans* distribute and collect information rapidly.

There are natural classes of operations which map easily into the different communication modes of the Connection Machine. In the following discussion, several algorithms from various levels of vision will be described, to explain the use of the Connection Machine. These algorithms assume an initial mapping of processors to pixels in the image array.

6   Early vision modules

6.1   Edge Detection

Edge detection is, in most, but not all, aspects, a spatially parallel operation. Edge detection is an important first step in many low-level vision algorithms. It generates a concise, compact description of the structure of the image, suitable for manipulation in image interpretation tasks. The edge layer has a special place in the organization of vision modules, since what it computes serves as important input to other layers. The first stage of all edge detectors exhibit spatial parallelism. The following discussion analyzes the Connection Machine implementation of the Canny edge detection scheme [7].

Filtering

A fundamental operation in vision processing is filtering an image. This both removes noise from the image and selects an appropriate spatial scale. Typically, filtering is accomplished by convolution with a filter of bounded spatial extent, often a Gaussian. Convolution in a fine-grained machine needs only spatially local, regular accesses, which in the Connection Machine are NEWS accesses. Convolutions are thus usually very efficient, on both mesh-connected and more highly-connected configurations. Early vision modules generally solve ill-posed problems, necessitating the use of regularization methods [3]. Regularization methods make algorithms robust against noise; they typically impose constraints on the smoothness of the solution. When the data lie on regularly spaced samples, as on a mesh, standard regularization methods can be implemented as filtering.

Canny Edge Detection

The Canny edge detector [7] combines several good features of edge detection schemes into an overall system which performs well on many images. In addition, it is supported by a thorough analysis with well stated goals. The edge detector has several stages:

1. Gaussian Smoothing $G * I$

2. Directional Derivative $\nabla(G * I)$

3. Non-Maximum Suppression

4. Thresholding with Hysteresis

Gaussian filtering and computing directional derivatives are local operations as described above. Non-maximum suppression selects as edge candidates pixels for which the gradient magnitude is maximal in the direction of the gradient, requiring only local operations, such as interpolation and comparison.

Thresholding with hysteresis eliminates weak edges due to noise. Two thresholds on gradient magnitudes are computed, *low* and *high*, based on an estimate of the noise in the image intensity. In thresholding, all selected pixels with gradient magnitude below *low* are eliminated. All pixels with values above *high* are considered edges. All pixels with values between *low* and *high* are considered edges if they can be connected to a pixel above *high* through a chain of pixels above *low*. All others are eliminated. This is a spreading activation operation; it requires propagating information along curves.

The noise estimation stage, for computing thresholds, is, at present, a global operation. The histogram is computed, by various global methods, and examined to set thresholds. Later discussion (see Section 10) will present several ways to improve the threshold determination stage.

Propagation

In thresholding with hysteresis, the existence of a *high* value on a connected curve must be propagated along the curve, to enable any *low* pixels to become *edge* pixels. This requires a number of operations depending on the length of the longest segment above *low* which will be connected to a *high* pixel. Only pixels above *low*, which survive non-maximum suppression, are considered. Each pixel can, in constant time, find the one or two neighboring pixels with which it forms a connected line, by examining the state of all 8 neighbors in the NEWS network. All pixels above *high* are marked as *edge* pixels. In the current implementation, the program iterates, in each step marking as *edge* pixels any *low* pixels adjacent to *edge* pixels. This uses NEWS connections. When no pixel changes state, the iteration terminates, taking a number of steps proportional to the length m of the longest chain of *low* pixels which eventually become *edge* pixels. *Doubling*, propagating a bit to indicate the *edge* property, changes this dependence to $O(\log m)$. For most practical examples, propagating in the NEWS network is faster than using the asymptotically optimal *doubling* procedure.

6.2   Optical Flow

Little, Bulthoff and Poggio [29] have implemented a fast, parallel optical flow algorithm on the Connection Machine; the input images are assumed to have been acquired at small time separation Δt relative to the velocities in the scene, so that most image displacements are small. The algorithm generates an optical flow field, a vector field which is an approximation to the projected velocity field [53]. The procedure can produce a sparse or dense field, depending on whether the input stage utilizes edge features or intensities. The algorithm looks for a discrete motion displacement $\underline{v} = (v_x, v_y)$ at each discrete location x, y in the image, to minimize:

$$\|E_t(x, y) - E_{t+\Delta t}(x + v_x \Delta t, y + v_y \Delta t)\|_{\text{patch}_i} \qquad (1)$$

where the norm is over a local neighborhood centered at each location x, y and $\underline{v}(x, y)$ is assumed constant in the neighborhood. Equation (1) implies that the algorithm should look at each x, y for $\underline{v} = (v_x, v_y)$ such that

$$\int_{\text{Patch}_i} |\tilde{E}_t(x, y) \tilde{E}_{t+\Delta t}(x + v_x \Delta t, y + v_y \Delta t)| dx dy \qquad (2)$$

is maximized. Equation (2) represents the correlation between a patch in the first image centered around the location x, y and a patch in the second image centered around the location $x + v_x \Delta t, y + v_y \Delta t$.

Consider a network of processors representing the result of the integrand in equation (2). Assume for simplicity that this result is either 0 or 1. (This is the case if E_t and $E_{t+\Delta t}$ are binary feature maps.). The processors hold the result of multiplying (or logically "anding") the right and left image map for different values of x, y and v_x, v_y. The next stage is for each processor to count how many processors are active in an x, y neighborhood at the same disparity. Each processor thus collects a vote indicating support that a patch of surface exists at that displacement. The last stage is to choose $\underline{v}(x, y)$ out of a finite set of allowed values that maximizes the integral. Membership in the finite set is dictated by the displacement range considered. This is done by an operation of "non–maximum suppression" across velocities out of the finite allowed set: at the given x, y, the processor is found that has the maximum vote. The corresponding $\underline{v}(x, y)$ is the velocity of the surface patch found by the algorithm. This algorithm is similar to the stereo algorithm implemented by Drumheller and Poggio [10] on the Connection Machine. The algorithm produces the optical flow, a vector field in the image coordinate system. Note that image intensities can be used in equation (2), as well as image features. In this optical flow, the well-known "aperture problem" [34] is solved in a local fashion. This is consistent with the overall philosophy of the Vision Machine, to find local methods, often iterative, which performs the same computation as existing methods which require global communication. Note that the summation over a patch can be efficiently implemented using region-summing based on *scans*. Figure 4 shows two images in a motion sequence taken by the Eye/Head system. Figure 5 shows the edges found the Canny edge detector on the second image. The man in the left is rotating leftward, away from the camera, while the man seated is stationary. In figure 6, the sparse output of the scheme, using edges only, is shown. At each point where unambiguous motion was found, a vector is drawn: a small blob identifies the point, and a line points in the direction of motion; its length is proportional to the speed of the motion. Finally, figure 7 shows the dense field resulting from minimizing sums of squared grey-level brightness values over local patches. The fact that two forms of computation produce consistent values for optical flow shows the robustness of the method. In the grey-level motion, boundaries are obscured, by using large patches, but all portions of the figure respond. The edge-based motion shows gaps along contours. Their combination provides both localization, along edges, and connectivity, since consistent motion in a compact region is a strong cue for an object.

There are several schemes for detecting boundaries of motion from the optical flow field: first, the voting scheme produces a scalar field, the sum of the votes, associated with the optical flow. At boundaries, the local votes will be divided among two or more optical flows associated with the motion fields of the two objects in the voting region. Inside the object, all votes will agree. As a result, at a boundary, the vote will be a local (spatial) minimum. A second

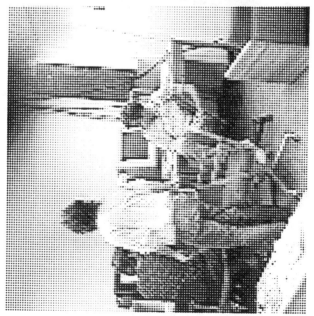

Figure 4: Two Images from a Motion Sequence: the First Image Is Shown on the Left.

Figure 5: Canny Edges for the Second Image.

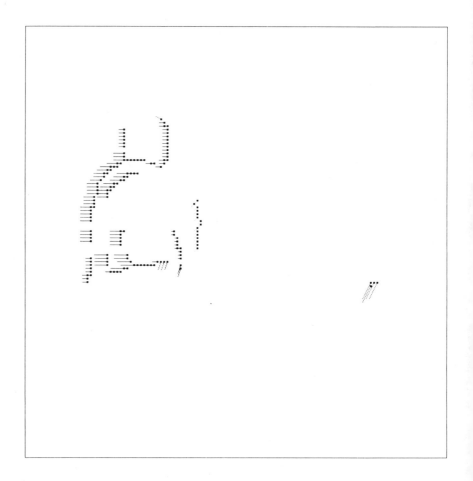

Figure 6: Sparse Optical Flow Field from Edges: only Moving Contours Appear.

Figure 7: Optical Flow from Grey-level Brightness

method implements the lobula scheme of the fly [41] and operates directly on the optical flow field to identify figure/ground relationships. The lobula scheme locates boundaries where the optical flow value divided by weighted local average, over a large region, is greater than unity. Examples of these schemes operating on synthetic images can be found in [29].

Finding Boundaries

The lobula scheme just described for identifying boundaries in motion uses a common scheme: the result of a regional summation is either compared with other local sums or suppresses or enhances the local value. Local prominence, where a region of an image "stands out" from the background [31], has also been explained by local differencing, to detect *odd-man out* properties. Local prominence may be a simple scheme for explaining the emergence of place tokens in the raw primal sketch [32]. Likewise, winner-take-all (non-maximum suppression) networks [24] have been suggested to explain shifts in attention – in such networks, the site with most activity (the winner) remains on, and all other sites in the group turn off. Simple neural mechanisms have been suggested to implement winner-take-all networks. The voting scheme described above for determining optical flow is an instance of this form of computation. Texture boundaries are perceived at changes in the distribution of textural features, *textons* [22]. Voorhees [55] shows how to use a simple statistic based on the local histogram of texton features, blobs, to account for many perceived texture boundaries. Again, the common feature of these methods is aggregation and simple analysis of data from a local support region.

7   Interconnecting Modules

An important question that arises during integration is the amount of coupling among the modules: to what extent are the modules independent?

Treisman's work [48] on "pop-out" phenomena suggests that the visual system has direct access to activity in individual modules that register color and shape, in parallel, but that conjunctions of particular color and shape are more difficult to computer. The data suggest that the computations for conjunctions proceed serially. Subsequent psychophysical investigations by Nakayama [38] demonstrate that conjunctions between modules, such as stereo/ motion and stereo/color are parallel. These psychophysical experiments serve to identify coupling among outputs of modules. The results suggest that there are, for particular module pairings, the layers or maps which contain the outputs of the pair of modules are more or less directly connected, and their joint activity can be inspected, on demand, by higher processes. Other pairings requiring attention, as shown by serial search for their conjunction, are presumably only indirectly communicating. The effect of such psychophysical research is to uncover connections; where they are found, later computational research can elucidate their role in vision.

Bülthoff and Mallott [6] investigated interactions between depth cues from shading and stereo. They list several possible forms of interaction, including accumulation, veto, cooperation, disambiguation, and hierarchy. A good system design requires incremental improvement and graceful degradation.

It has been suggested that the natural place to combine multiple sources of information is in computing the surface representation. This stage is usually cast as an interpolation problem from scattered points. Terzopoulos [46] integrates multiple sources of information in an extended energy term which governs interpolation. The energy terms represent smoothness of the interpolating elastic medium. But this level of integration ignores the interdependence of the sources of information. When outputs of multiple sources are combined by summation in an energy term, results of noise in one term are combined with noise in other terms, leading to deterioration in the output of all modules. The study of camouflage offers interesting examples of how the visual system can be misled; for example, the contours of a leopard are obscured by albedo changes which are unrelated to bounding contour. The slightest movement, however, of the leopard makes it immediately visible. It is not clear that a system which combines all information before boundary identification can respond well in such a situation. Engineering system principles, too, argue that system components should be loosely coupled, to reduce interference among the modules.

The stability of a system, in the numerical sense, composed of several subsystems is not simply the sum of the stability of the subsystems. It depends on the interdependence of the subsystems. If vision modules are independent, simple combination of modules will not introduce instability into the system. However, the information sources of most vision modules are not disjoint. Processes which work from brightness alone, such as texture, and simple brightness edge detection will likely encounter difficulties at the same location. The information sources are not independent, hence their results must be correlated, or at least susceptible to noise or insufficiencies under similar conditions.

In practice, each module is able to provide information for generating shape description, without necessity of reference to other modules. Thus there is an independent path to higher vision stages that does not pass through other modules. Integration is not necessary, but useful for robust behavior. When there is impoverished information for one module, there is impoverished information for all modules that depend on similar inputs. But independent modules provide data to bridge gaps that arise. Along a moving contour, where the motion is parallel to the contour, no motion is detected, but the intensity edge continues. Then, a theory such as Hildreth [18] can explain how a motion value is attributed to the contour, by determining the smoothest, defined appropriately, motion field on the contour. Intensity edges are combined with stereo and motion data in work by Gamble and Poggio [12], described later.

Functional arguments also suggest loose coupling, since the scene may present information only in one modality: such as shading, texture, motion. Each module should be able to feed information upward without the support of other modules, that is, the system should undergo "graceful degradation" when the input becomes noisy or impoverished.

7.1   Sharing Structure is Economical

As a practical matter, an implementation of a vision system will require a module to detect significant changes in the outputs of vision modules. Each module produces a derived scalar quantity or a map of orientation or depth (stereo – motion) or texture, for example. The Canny edge detection scheme can be applied to these scalar maps. It may be the case, for example, that in the human system, the mechanism for detecting rapid change in a modality is included in each module. However, it can be shared by all modules in the scheme presented here.

8   Integration

Integration offers a way to achieve robustness from incomplete input. A robust system is stable against noise in the image, and performs in a manner adaptable to image content. The system should be general; it should use no *a priori* information, and introduce no specific expectations. There are several attempts to integrate modules, for example, stereo and motion [42] [56]. Typically, these identify mutual constraints from the solution obtained by one module that simplify or make unambiguous the determination of depth values in the other. Here integration focuses on the means by which the modules interact to improve the processes of finding structural elements in the image and of identifying the physical causes of discontinuities.

8.1   Integration Using Image Formation Constraints

Specific constraints arise from the process of image formation [21] and the way modules selectively respond to various surface properties. At a boundary, the physical cause of the boundary can be determined from the modalities which change there. A set of rules can describe the relation between changes and physical causes. The theory of "intrinsic images" [2] describes such rules for a restricted world.

Texture directly provides cues for labeling boundaries [43]. The nature of texture change across a boundary constrains the interpretation of the boundaries, as implemented by Voorhees [55]. Similar observations suggest examining the correlation of image properties across edges, to determine their source [57]. The work of Voorhees extends these observations to determine the appropriate image features to measure in order to generate the location of boundaries. Texture [55] computations do not permit accurate localization of boundaries, since they are necessarily areal. Texture indicates the nature of boundaries [55] and suggests regions which identify coherent objects.

9   Integrating by Markov Random Fields

Markov Random Field [14] [39] is a method for integrating the output of vision modules. The Markov Random Field technique formulates the constraints among the values at sites in a lattice in terms of energy functions dependent only on local values. They have a direct interpretation in terms of Gibbs distributions [14]. Use of the Markov Random Field permits direct combination of discontinuity identification (via line processes) with the interpolation process. Multiple modules can be explicitly combined in the energy summation, which includes the formation of discontinuities, and the energy of bending, in the spatial sense, of the lines of discontinuity [39]. Some of the processes underlying image formation (under oversimplified assumptions) are surface depth, albedo, and *effective illumination*, which depends on the surface normal and on the illumination. Figure 8 shows several of the coupled Markov Random Fields, together with the associated line process layers, from [39]. This form of integration makes direct, explicit use of the image formation equation, and includes fields for each of the terms in the equation. Observable discontinuities, found by independent modules, play an important role. Gamble and Poggio [12] use the Markov Random Field to employ intensity edges to sharpen stereo interpolation and optical flow boundary recovery.

The Markov Random Field approach leads to algorithms either of the Metropolis type or stochastic algorithms specific for the problem [36]. All these algorithms may be implemented by parallel architectures of many processors with only local connections and by hybrid

FROM
EARLY
PROCESSING

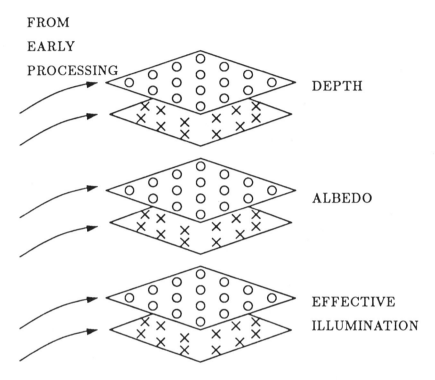

DEPTH

ALBEDO

EFFECTIVE
ILLUMINATION

Figure 8: Coupled Markov Random Fields (circles) and Line Processes (Crosses), from [38]

computer architectures [35] [23].

10 Adaptability

An important feature of a robust system is the ability to adjust dynamically to scene content. Robustness is sacrificed when a system is constructed with fixed or user-specified thresholds which are independent of scene content. A case in point is the Canny Edge Detector [7], which bases its thresholds on percentiles of the distribution of intensity gradient magnitudes. Because it is based on image properties, the Canny detector performs well on a large range of images;

nevertheless, more sophisticated analyses of image statistics have improved its performance. Fitting the Rayleigh distribution (gradient of Gaussian noise) to the gradient magnitude histogram yields better estimates of noise in images[54]. Further improvements may be achieved by basing its behavior on the structural properties of the output. Consider a measure of edge continuity in the image, say the number of connected curves. By varying the thresholds for *low* and *high* (see Section 6.1), and monitoring the continuity measure, a stable setting of the two parameters can be found.

These improvements require increased computation, as well as non-local communication. A mechanism for efficiently computing appropriate image statistics as well as distributing these statistics is an important component of a Vision Machine.

Alternatively, images can be scaled locally, to remove slow variations in illumination, making global thresholds less problematic. For example, Land's designator theory of lightness and color constancy [25] calculates a designator, $\delta(x, y)$ from the intensity, $i(x, y)$:

$$\delta(x, y) = \log \frac{i(x, y)}{\int_{-\sigma}^{\sigma} \int_{-\sigma}^{\sigma} \omega(p, q)i(x - p, y - q)dpdq}$$

where $\omega(p, q)$ is a weighting function, and σ is the radius of a large region at each point. Land does not specify the weighting function, but the form resembles a Gaussian distribution. Area summation is, of course, quite computationally intensive on a serial computer, and, in fact, on most parallel configurations. The region-summing operation on the Connection Machine, which takes time independent of the region size, allows that machine to implement this operation efficiently. Likewise, local histograms of intensity gradient magnitude can be computed for the Canny edge detector and analyzed to set local thresholds.

Many vision systems (for example, [15]) assume that several scales or resolutions of computation are pursued in parallel. The results from these multiple levels are combined. Usually, there is a dominance relationship among the levels, whereby the coarse level, for example, selects among the ambiguous results at finer levels. Collecting image statistics can guide cooperation among scales. An analysis of the signal-to-noise characteristics of the image selects the appropriate spatial scale. Geiger and Poggio [13] find the regularizing parameter λ from the signal-to-noise ratio, which is equivalent, in the case of edge detection, to determining the appropriate spatial scale. Computations such as these provide information to make a system adaptable and robust, and are only feasible with powerful, parallel computers.

11   Spatial relations and structure

Spatial computations, acting on full primal sketch tokens [32], such as edges, terminations and blobs, are important components of an integrated vision system. Middle vision processes *act* to form geometrically salient structures. Visual routines operate on the chunks of images, in a general fashion, to compute spatial properties and relations among image elements.

11.1   Spatial indexing and spatial structure

Visual routines [52] [31] describe a form of visual computation operating either to construct extended structures in the image, or to compute on these structures. An important component of the recognition process depends on the spatial relations computed by generic visual routines, such as left/right, above/below, and inside/out. These simple, qualitative properties are computed by a spatial visual module.

Chunking lines and regions, an approach to grouping presented by Mahoney [31], finds a decomposition of the spatial domain dependent on the arrangement of lines and regions. His procedures use a model of local computation, suggested by Ullman [51], where processors cannot communicate by passing their identifier, and are restricted to a given pattern of local communication. In this model, it is necessary to devise local communication patterns which facilitate solution of particular problems. Shafrir [45] and Edelman [11] have devised schemes for region coloring, inside/out computations, and boundary activation. These *activation* or *propagation* processes are useful in the general Vision Machine. Implementing them on the

Connection Machine, for example, can utilize *doubling* operations, for efficiency.

11.2   Continuity and Completion

Continuity is an important principle of vision systems. Many algorithms for binocular stereo [15] [1] use figural continuity [37] to disambiguate depths of edges. Information is propagated along contours in the stereo processing, as a specific example of constraints propagating along contours. Direct propagation along a contour, without propagation through non-contour areas is less likely than a scheme which combines both forms of propagation, perhaps with preference to information from adjoining contour points; in the optical flow algorithm described above, a smooth mixing between edge and intensity information is assumed.

Real images generate broken, partial edges. Completion is an important task, performed in combination of several modules. For completion, the principle of continuation is used: continue, unless there is positive evidence of termination [32]. The incomplete nature of most boundaries forces the visual system to fill gaps; such completion processes have a central role in the visual system. Local processes should operate on outputs of modules to fill gaps. Geometrically, a gap can be closed by observing whether a disc bridges the gap, and whether the center of the disc is contained in the region enclosed by the boundary. Subjective contours [50] are evidence that the visual system, as Marr [32] observes, must complete contours for which there is strong local evidence; it completes the contours even though the evidence for the contours may come from conflicting sources. Subjective contours are interesting from an architectural standpoint since they operate where there is no activity – they generate a percept where none is, rather than transform an existing stimulus. Whatever computation generates subjective contours has long-distance effects in the image coordinate system. The processes which jump gaps may take evidence from coarser scales, in the vision system, to complete boundaries.

Terminations play an important role by indicating that a boundary should not be closed. Treisman [47], in her work on "pop out" phenomena in preattentive vision has found that a broken circle in a field of closed circles will "pop out", whereas a closed circle in a broken field will not; this indicates that gaps, or line ends, are detected categorically. Also, she observes that an almost closed circle seems to activate the closure detector, but not as much as a completely closed circle. The asymmetry in the treatment of gaps and closures reflects the active nature of filling operations. Terminations at gaps are important signals telling the vision process *not* to continue. For a discussion of the role of terminations as textons, see [55]. In addition, terminations form tokens which can generate virtual lines[32]; in this role, they are good cues for occlusion.

The computational mechanisms for spatial structures can achieve some of the goals of "perceptual organization", to account for organizing processes in the perceptual system [58]. Lowe [30] describes criteria for grouping: similarity, proximity, closure, parallelism, symmetry, and continuation. In the system proposed here, similarity of image events can be computed immediately from activity in the layers, representing modules. Events with similar features show activity in the layer which is sensitive to their similarity. Proximity can be computed by the structuring mechanism, by activation and spatial subdivision. Closure, termination, and continuation have just been described. Parallelism is important for recognition; separating features into orientationally selective layers permit activation processes to bind nearby parallel elements together. The model of visual computation in the vision system described here should be able, in principle, to realize many grouping operations.

11.3   Regions

Since regions and edges are duals, in a formal sense, any process which determines regions must, implicitly, detect boundaries between regions. Region connect adjacent edges, across regions colored by activation processes. Regions, at a coarser scale, or from another mode, support edges. They are most important when the other modes fail. A region-forming process relies on underlying assumption of homogeneity, either in color, texture, intensity, or some other module; some property will hold for the entire region. In general, regions have homogeneous characteristics, without internal boundaries. Homogeneity can include uniformity (zeroth order homogeneity), planarity (first order). Regions are rarely homogeneous in intensity; they are, however, more uniform in color and texture and motion. Simple procedures for aggregating color, texture, and motion can be applied to find regions in an image; the resulting regions may have fuzzy boundaries, or, they may be numerous, but complementary boundary processes can refine their structure.

Blobs are small, compact regions, "doubly terminated bars" [32]. They can be constructed from isobrightness contours or level crossings of the output of some operator, such as the Laplacian of a Gaussian [33]. Blobs are tokens at fine scales, but at coarser scales are regions.

The principal role of regions are: first, to index large, connected regions, and, second, to connect boundaries along their perimeter, where cues to their physical origin are found.

12   Summary

Many different components of a Vision Machine have been examined; the communication requirements of each component have been analyzed. Early vision modules translate directly into separate layers in the memory of the fine-grained parallel machine. Most computations of early vision modules exhibit *spatial parallelism*, computations with homogeneous local communication. The location of boundaries are found on local evidence; they are linked into larger structures by non-local communication. Canny edge detection is a prototypical vision process: the first stages establish the location of boundaries through gradient calculation and non-maximum suppression; later stages compute appropriate thresholds, for adaptability, and then join boundary fragments, through linking with hysteresis. All early vision processes in the Vision Machine find discontinuities, which are then completed into connected pieces. The completion process, part of middle vision, combines spatial aspects, finding compact regions, and semantic aspects, where the rules identifying physical causes are applied at boundaries.

The Markov Random Field formulation of integration combines both early and middle levels, by computing interpolation and discontinuities simultaneously. Middle vision processes are important components of the Vision Machine; they find chunks, connect elements, complete boundaries and detect structural relations among simple features. Schemes have been presented for finding boundaries and computing image properties robustly which depend on concentrated local communication with a high degree of fan-in and fan-out. These can be easily implemented on fine-grained machines with powerful non-local communication. When extended image structures are constructed, non-local processing becomes critical. Later stages of vision must be able to access entire constructions, such as edges and regions, rapidly.

There are many open questions, even at the general level of this discussion, and further work to be done. Mahoney (personal communication) argues that segmentation is demand-driven. An incomplete, ambiguous pre-segmentation, mostly partial results, may be all that is necessary. A locally complete segmentation may only be generated on demand, from the partial results. Similarly, Voorhees [55] suggests an attentive scheme (similarly demand-driven) to localize and identify the physical causes of preattentively found texture boundaries. The rules describing inference of physical cause of boundaries may be implemented as simple finite state automata; the structure of these automata may be learned. The Vision Machine constructs a map of the structural image relations among discontinuities found by the cooperation and integration of many vision modules. This framework might be extended to a radical formulation of the structure of early vision which relaxes the requirement that a full, dense depth map of surfaces be computed. Instead only qualitative properties of surfaces between discontinuities such as convexity, or planarity are computed. The initial stages of a design for a Vision Machine are described here; an active system is the next stage, to identify interesting image structure, and to respond, by narrowing the field of view, zooming in and applying processing only to critical areas. This brings up the crucial question of control of attention in a vision system.

The opportunity to construct a full Vision Machine stems from the availability of parallel machines. The increase in computing power in these machines makes feasible systems which compute many component visual modules in near real-time. Integration is necessary for practical systems, and remains a complex issue. Fine-grained machines with flexible communication should provide a useful testbed for integrating vision modules.

13   Acknowledgements

The research described here originates from discussions with Tomaso Poggio, Guy Blelloch and other members of the Vision Machine Project. The work was performed at the Artificial Intelligence Laboratory at the Massachusetts Institute of Technology. Support for the A.I. Laboratory's artificial intelligence research is provided in part by the Advanced Research Projects Agency of the Department of Defense under Army contract number DACA76-85-C-0010, in part by DARPA under Office of Naval Research contract N00014-85-K-0214, and in part by a grant from Hughes Aircraft Company.

Bibliography

[1] H. H. Baker and T. O. Binford. *Depth from edge and intensity based stereo.* In Proceedings IJCAI, Vancouver, 1981, p. 631–636.

[2] H. G. Barrow and M. Tenenbaum. *Recovering intrinsic scene characteristics from images.* In A. R. Hanson and E. M. Riseman, editors, Computer Vision Systems, Academic Press, New York, 1978, p. 3–26.

[3] M. Bertero, T. Poggio, and V. Torre. *Ill-Posed Problems in Early Vision.* Technical Report AIM–924, Artificial Intelligence Laboratory, Massachusetts Institute of Technology, 1987.

[4] Guy E. Blelloch. *Scans as primitive parallel operations.* In Proceedings Int. Conf. on Parallel Processing, August 1987.

[5] Michael Brady. *Criteria for shape representations.* In E J. Beck and A. Rosenfeld, editors, Human and Machine Vision, Academic Press, New York, 1983.

[6] Heinrich H. Bulthoff and Hanspeter A. Mallot. *Interaction of different modules in depth perception.* In Proceedings of the International Conference on Computer Vision, June 1987, p. 295–305.

[7] John F. Canny. *A computational approach to edge detection.* IEEE Transactions on Pattern Analysis and Machine Intelligence, 8(6):679–698, 1986.

[8] Katherine H. Cornog. *Smooth Pursuit and Fixation for Robot Vision.* Master's thesis, Massachusetts Institute of Technology, 1985.

[9] M. Snir, C.P. Kruskal and L. Rudolph. *The power of parallel prefix.* Proceedings Int. Conf. on Parallel Processing, 180–185, August 1985.

[10] Michael Drumheller and Tomaso Poggio. *Parallel stereo.* In Proceedings of IEEE Conference on Robotics and Automation, San Francisco, CA, 1986.

[11] E. Edelman. *Fast Distributed Boundary Activation.* Master's thesis, Department of Applied Mathematics, Feinberg Graduate School, Weizmann Institute of Science, Rehovot, Israel, 1985.

[12] Edward Gamble and Tomaso Poggio. *Integration of Intensity Edges with Stereo and Motion.* Technical Report, Artificial Intelligence Laboratory, Massachusetts Institute of Technology, Cambridge, Ma., in progress.

[13] Davi Geiger and T. Poggio. *An optimal scale for edge detection.* In Proceedings IJCAI, August 1987.

[14] Stuart Geman and Don Geman. *Stochastic relaxation, Gibbs distributions, and the Bayesian restoration of images.* IEEE

Transactions on Pattern Analysis and Machine Intelligence, 6, 1984.

[15] W. E. L. Grimson. *From Images to Surfaces*. MIT Press, Cambridge, Mass., 1981.

[16] W. E..L. Grimson and T. Lozano-Perez. *Model-Based Recognition and Localization From Sparse Range or Tactile Data*. Technical Report A.I. Memo 738, MIT, August 1983.

[17] J. G. Harris and A. M. Flynn. *Object recognition using the connection machine's router*. In Proceedings IEEE Conf. on Computer Vision and Pattern Recognition, 1986, p. 134–139.

[18] Ellen C. Hildreth. *The Measurement of Visual Motion*. MIT Press, Cambridge, Mass., 1984.

[19] William D. Hillis. *The Connection Machine*. MIT Press, Cambridge, Mass., 1985.

[20] William D. Hillis and Guy L. Steele Jr. *Data parallel algorithms*. Communications of the ACM, December 1986.

[21] B. K. P. Horn. *Robot Vision*. MIT Press, Cambridge, Mass., 1985.

[22] Bela Julesz. *Textons: the elements of texture perception, and their interactions*. Nature, 290:91–97, March 1981.

[23] Christof Koch, Jose Marroquin, and Alan Yuille. *Analog 'neuronal' networks in early vision*. Technical Report AIM–751, Artificial Intelligence Laboratory, Massachusetts Institute of Technology, 1985.

[24] Christof Koch and Shimon Ullman. *Shifts in selective visual attention: towards the underlying neutral circuitry*. Human Neurobiology, 4:219–227, 1985.

[25] E. H. Land. *An alternative technique for the computation of the designator in the retinex theory of color vision*. Proceedings of the National Academy of Science, 83:3078–3080, 1986.

[26] Charles E. Leiserson and Bruce M. Maggs. *Fat-Trees: Universal networks for hardware-efficient supercomputing.* IEEE Transactions on Computers, c-34(10):892–901, October 1985.

[27] W. Lim, A. Agrawal, and L. Nekludova. *A Fast Parallel Algorithm for Labeling Connected Components in Image Arrays.* Technical Report NA86-2, Thinking Machines Corporation, December 1986.

[28] James J. Little, Guy E. Blelloch, and Todd Cass. *Parallel algorithms for computer vision on the connection machine.* In Proceedings of the International Conference on Computer Vision, June 1987, p. 587–591.

[29] James J. Little, Heinrich Bulthoff, and Tomaso Poggio. *Parallel optical flow computation.* In Proceedings Image Understanding Workshop, Los Angeles, CA, February 1987, p. 417–431.

[30] D. G. Lowe. *Perceptual Organization and Visual Recognition.* Kluwer Academic Publishers, Boston, 1986.

[31] James V. Mahoney. *Image chunking: defining spatial building blocks for scene analysis.* Master's thesis, Massachusetts Institute of Technology, 1986.

[32] David Marr. *Vision: A Computational Investigation into the Human Representation and Processing of Visual Information.* W.H. Freeman and Company, San Francisco, 1982.

[33] David Marr and Ellen Hildreth. *Theory of edge detection.* Proceedings of the Royal Society of London, B(207):187–217, 1980.

[34] David Marr and Shimon Ullman. *Directional selectivity and its use in early visual processing.* Proceedings of the Royal Society of London B, 211:151–180, 1981.

[35] J. Marroquin, S. Mitter, and T. Poggio. *Probabilistic solution of ill-posed problems in computational vision.* In Proceedings Image Understanding Workshop, Miami Beach, FL, December 1985, p. 293–309.

[36] Jose Marroquin. *Probabilistic solution of inverse problems.* PhD thesis, Massachusetts Institute of Technology, 1985.

[37] J. E. W. Mayhew and J. P. Frisby. *Psychophysical and computational studies towards a theory of human stereopsis.* Artificial Intelligence, 17:349–385, August 1981.

[38] Ken Nakayama and Gerald H. Silverman. *Conjunctive visual search for stereo-motion and stereo-color is parallel.* preprint, October 1985.

[39] Tomaso Poggio. *Integrating Vision Modules with Coupled MRF's.* Technical Report Working Paper 285, Artificial Intelligence Laboratory, Massachusetts Institute of Technology, 1985.

[40] Tomaso Poggio and the staff. *MIT progress in understanding images.* In Proceedings Image Understanding Workshop, Los Angeles, CA, February 1987, p. 41–54.

[41] W. Reichardt, T. Poggio, and K. Hausen. *Figure–ground discrimination by relative movement in the visual system of the fly. part ii: towards the neural circuitry.* Biological Cybernetics, 46:1–30, 1983.

[42] Whitman Richards. *Structure from Stereo and Motion.* Technical Report AIM–731, Artificial Intelligence Laboratory, Massachusetts Institute of Technology, 1983.

[43] Michael Dennis Riley. *The Representation of Image Texture.* Technical Report AI TR No. 649, Artificial Intelligence Laboratory, Massachusetts Institute of Technology, September 1981.

[44] Charles L. Seitz. *The cosmic cube.* Communications of the ACM, 28(1):22, 1985.

[45] A. Shafrir. *Fast region coloring and the computation of inside/outside relations.* Master's thesis, Department of Applied Mathematics, Feinberg Graduate School, Weizmann Institute of Science, Rehevot, Israel, 1985.

[46] Demetri Terzopoulos. *Integrating visual information from multiple sources.* In From Pixels to Predicates, Ablex Publishing Corporation, Norwood, NH, 1986, p. 111–142.

[47] Anne Treisman. *Preattentive processing in vision.* Computer Vision, Graphics, and Image Processing, 31(2):156–177, 1985.

[48] Anne Treisman and G. Gelade. *A feature integration theory of attention.* Cognitive Psychology, 12:97–136, 1980.

[49] Jeffrey Ullman. *Computational Aspects of VLSI.* Computer Science Press, Rockville, MD, 1984.

[50] Shimon Ullman. *Filling in the gaps: the shape of subjective contours and a model for their generation.* Biological Cybernetics, 25:1–6, 1976.

[51] Shimon Ullman. *Relaxation and constrained optimization by local processes.* Computer Graphics and Image Processing, 10:115–125, 1976.

[52] Shimon Ullman. *Visual routines.* Cognition, 18, 1984.

[53] A. Verri and T. Poggio. *Against quantitative optical flow.* In Proceedings of the International Conference on Computer Vision, June 1987, p. 171–180.

[54] Harry Voorhees and T. Poggio. *Detecting textons and texture boundaries in natural images.* In Proceedings of the International Conference on Computer Vision, London, England, June 1987, p. 250–258.

[55] Harry L. Voorhees. *Finding Texture Boundaries in Images.* Master's thesis, Massachusetts Institute of Technology, 1987.

[56] A. M. Waxman and J. H. Duncan. *Binocular Image Flows: Steps toward Stereo-Motion Fusion.* Technical Report Technical Report No. CAR-TR-119, University of Maryland, 1985.

[57] Andrew P. Witkin. *Intensity-based edge classification.* In Proceedings AAAI, 1982, p. 36–41.

[58] Andrew P. Witkin and M. Tenenbaum. *On perceptual organization*. In From Pixels to Predicates, Ablex Publishing Corporation, Norwood, New Jersey, 1986, p. 149–169.

[59] J. C. Wyllie. *The Complexity of Parallel Computations*. Technical Report 79–387, Department of Computer Science, Cornell University, Ithaca, New York, August 1979, p. 149–169.

Computer Architectures for Machine Vision

Azriel Rosenfeld
Center for Automation Research
University of Maryland

1 Introduction

It is well recognized that machine vision has many potential applications in industry, going far beyond the applications that are already developed or under development. The biggest constraint on practical advances in this area is the fact that useful machine vision systems must be time- and cost-effective—they must operate in real time and must not be too expensive.

Fortunately, computer power has been steadily getting cheaper, and it is clear that it will continue to do so for quite a few years to come. Many machine vision problems have already been solved in the laboratory, but these solutions require significant amounts of processing time on relatively large computers. However, as computer power continues to grow while its cost continues to drop, anything that we can do today in a research laboratory will sooner or later be doable in real time on low-cost hardware.

What types of computer architectures will be needed to make this possible? Vision potentially involves several types of data—pixel arrays, geometric representations, graphs, and knowledge bases. On each of these data types, various basic classes of operations may need to be performed. It is well understood how some of these operations can be greatly speeded up using various types of multiprocessor architectures; but for other types of operations, it is less clear how to achieve significant speedups. These issues will be briefly treated in the next three sections of this paper.

2   Types of Data

Machine vision tasks potentially involve several different types of
data:

Input images are usually numerical-valued pixel arrays, where
the pixel values are gray levels. Many other types of arrays, derived from the input images, may also be used in vision systems.
These include numerical (or even vector-valued) arrays such as filtered images, transforms, intrinsic images, Gaussian images, etc.;
as well as "symbolic images", in which the pixel values are labels
rather than numerical quantities—for example, binary images resulting from thresholding, feature maps, arrays resulting from connected
component labeling, etc.

Regions or features that have been extracted from an image in the
course of analyzing it can be represented by binary images, but they
can also be represented in more compact ways—for example, by sets
of coordinates, by run length codes, by boundary codes (e.g., chain
codes), by medial axis transformations, or by quadtrees. Similarly,
the three-dimensional objects that are to be recognized in an image
can be represented using various types of geometric data structures,
including surface models and solid models (e.g., Constructive Solid
Geometry).

Collections of image parts (or object parts), their properties, and
the relations among them can be represented by labeled graph structures in which the nodes represent the parts, the node labels represent property values, and the arc labels represent relation values.
More generally, declarative knowledge about images or objects (and
their parts) can be represented in various ways, for example using
semantic nets, relational databases, first-order logic, etc.

3   Types of Operations

Each of the data types described in Section 2 may need many different kinds of operations performed on it in a general vision system.
On array data, in particular, the following types of operations are
frequently performed:

1. Point and local operations—grayscale transformations, convolutions, "morphological" operations, etc.

2. Statistics computations—histogramming, texture analysis, etc.

3. Geometric operations—perspective projection, warping, etc.

4. Transforms—Fourier, Hough, etc.

5. Extraction of geometric entities (boundary curves or regions)—boundary following, region growing, etc.

It is less well understood what types of operations may need to be performed at the level of geometric representations, but an initial list might include the following:

- Boolean combinations

- Derived sets (convex hulls, Voronoi diagrams and skeletons, etc.)

- Visibility and mobility computations (path planning, etc.)

- Geometric property computations (connectivity, moments, etc.)

The operations that might be needed at the graph level are quite general, they include graph search and path finding, clique finding, subgraph isomorphism testing, and others. Finally, at the knowledge-base level, the operations are essentially those used in artificial intelligence applications, involving reasoning, learning, etc.

4 Types of Architectures

The next major advance in computer system speed will arise not from faster cycle times, but from massively parallel multiprocessing. Many classes of multiprocessor systems are being proposed and built; a few of them are

1. Pipelined systems, such as the various types of "cytocomputers" and "systolic" array processors. Such systems perform sequences of operations on a stream of input data; as soon as one operation has been performed on a given part of the data, the next operation can be initiated on that part. They are especially useful in "morphological" image processing, where long sequences of local operations are performed on a given image.

2. Mesh-connected systems, such as the Cellular Logic Image Processor (CLIP), the Massively Parallel Processor (MPP), and the Geometric Arithmetic Parallel Processor (GAPP). Such a system can perform local operations on an entire image simultaneously.

3. Trees and pyramids, such as Non-Von, the Ultracomputer, PAPIA, and numerous others. Such systems can perform global operations such as statistics computations, or large-kernel local operations, using divide-and-conquer techniques, in a number of processing steps that grows only logarithmically with the image or kernel size.

4. Hypercubes, such as the N-cube and the Connection Machine. Such systems combine the advantages of meshes and trees (or pyramids), and can also perform other types of global operations, such as transforms, in a logarithmic number of steps.

5. Shared-memory machines, such as the Butterfly. By using a suitable interconnection network for communication between the processors and the memory, such systems can simulate architectures in which the connections are hardwired, including those described in (a–d).

As these remarks indicate, it is well understood how to use most of these architectures to speed up processing at the array level. Much less is known, unfortunately, about how to use them to achieve speedups at the levels of geometric representations, graph structures, or knowledge representations.

It is commonly believed that speedup of array-level processing is all that is needed, since that level involves the largest amounts of data (images, transformed images, etc.), while the remaining levels involve only small numbers of entities (image parts, etc.). This belief may be dangerously misleading. Processing of image parts, for example, may lead to combinatorial explosions of derived parts and of relations among collections of parts. It should not be assumed that the computational bottleneck in machine vision systems is entirely, or even primarily, at the array level. We need to learn how to use the proposed architectures at the higher levels, or failing this, to design new architectures appropriate for these levels.

5 Conclusions

The design of computer architectures for real-time machine vision systems will be a major research theme over the coming years. Computer performance will need to be speeded up by many orders of magnitude before it can match human performance. Humans can carry out complex visual tasks, involving the recognition of unexpected objects, in a fraction of a second, which is enough time for only a few hundred "cycles" of the neural "hardware" in the visual pathway. The challenge that faces us is how to design computer architectures—and the algorithms to run on them—that can match, and eventually exceed, this level of performance.

Machine Vision Architectures and Systems — A Discussion

Chairman: T. J. Fountain
University College London

1 Introduction

The following notes are substantially a record of one of the evening discussion sessions which took place at the CAIP workshop on machine vision. However, because a number of relevant points were raised in informal meetings outside the regular programme, I have included them here.

One of the themes of the workshop was a meeting of minds between industrialists involved in the day-to-day application of machine vision, and academics involved in research on the frontiers of the subject. These two viewpoints were both strongly represented in the discussion session on architectures and systems, and produced one of the few real areas of conflict. The chairman began the session by proposing the following (deliberately provocative) points for discussion:

1. Only substantially parallel architectures are worth pursuing for machine vision.

2. The only type of massively-parallel system whose use is well understood is the SIMD mesh.

3. In order to advance the field, architectures which integrate various levels of the problem are needed.

4. Architectures have to go hand-in-hand with algorithms and software systems if worthwhile progress is to be made.

The responses to this (essentially academic) viewpoint fell into four categories.

2   An Alternative to Massive Parallelism

In his presentation earlier in the workshop programme, Peter Burt of RCA had described his pyramid smart sensor system. He proposed this pipeline machine as a valid alternative to massive parallelism, basing his argument particularly on its ability to retain all necessary information on defect areas whilst progressively reducing the resolution of the data images being processed. This substantial reduction in the amount of data to be processed, removed, supporters of this view suggested, the requirement for massive parallelism. There was a measure of agreement that this approach would be valid (and particularly cost-effective) for some types of industrial inspection, but some delegates felt that there were some areas where this approach would not work. Examples cited were those problems where the defect density approached the original pixel resolution, or where numerical measures at the original resolution were required.

It was apparent that the argument for the effectiveness of a pipeline system depended on the assumption that the total amount of data to be processed would reduce at later stages of the program. This led to a consideration of the first of the 'parallel' systems to be discussed as appropriate for machine vision, namely the pyramid.

3   Pyramids

There were present at the discussion at least two protagonists of the general notion of pyramid architectures, Professors Rosenfeld and Cantoni. It was suggested that two distinct views could be taken of the pyramid architecture, depending on the particular implementation. Professor Cantoni's PAPIA consortium, constructing pyramids of bit-serial processors, concentrates on the aspect of improved connectivity over that offered by the two-dimensional mesh. However, there was some support among delegates for the view that, rather than provide extra connectivity in the pyramid form, other methods not involving additional processors might be more worthwhile. In particular, the work of Li and others on the IBM YUPPIE system, involving reconfigurable direct connections between the inputs to processing elements, was proposed as an alternative. There was no serious disagreement with this view, and in fact Professor Cantoni's own preliminary thoughts on a successor to PAPIA involve a similar system. This consists of a planar array in which the connections between processors can be reconfigured so as to emulate all the higher levels of a notional quadtree pyramid. The proponents of such systems accept the inevitable limitations to data-passing bandwidth.

A second view of the pyramid architecture was put forward by those who envisage systems in which the processing element complexity increases in higher levels of the pyramid. Different levels of the pyramid are then assigned to different sections of the vision task. Professor Rosenfeld noted that the processing bottleneck in the vision task may not be at the low-level, pixel-based stage. A pyramid should therefore compensate for reduced numbers of processors in the higher levels by increasing their complexity and power. He also suggested that 'conventional' pyramids embodied poor feedback connectivity and that this might be a further bottleneck.

There was some discussion of the view of the human visual system as a pipeline of arrays of processors and whether this equated to the pipeline of layers in a pyramid. It was suggested, however, that the disparate natures of the 'processing' modules in the brain and their interconnection by apparent bottlenecks rendered the analogy tenuous at best. At this point the discussion moved on to consider alternative connection strategies and, in particular, the use of the Connection Machine.

4   Connection Strategies

Two of the participants in the discussion session described using the
Connection Machine marketed by Thinking Machines Corp. These
systems take the form of a two-dimensional mesh onto which is superimposed a hypercube network of message passing devices (16 mesh
elements to one hypercube node). Both users emphasised the fact
that pyramid connectivity could easily be emulated on such systems,
as indeed could a number of other connection schemes including the
perfect shuffle, and that this reconfigurability was of significant benefit in some applications. Some delegates commented, however, that
a 64k-element connection machine costs about $3M, and that such
costs are inappropriate for large classes of machine vision problems,
in particular for many industrial inspection tasks. In reply, the supporters pointed out that systems of this sort could be useful, because
of their flexibility, in developing specific, cost-effective solutions.

A final point which was discussed concerned systems which model
neural operations, variously known as connectionist, or quasi-neural,
networks. It was suggested that the most efficient multi-level vision
processing system known was the brain, and that this has a very
different structure to those under discussion so far, with a pseudo-
random network of simple nodes (neurons) having extremely rich
interconnections (about 1000 per node). The fault-tolerance of such
a network was suggested as one reason for its effectiveness, but it was
noted that there appeared to be no point of contact between methods
of operating these neural-based learning systems and conventionally-
programmed arrays. No-one was able to suggest a method of combining the advantages of both systems.

5   MIMD Processing

Dr. Segan, of AT&T Labs, pointed out that the discussion so far had
concentrated on SIMD systems, only the pyramids using different
operations in different layers departing significantly from this. He
questioned whether other methods of utilising MIMD processing were
known or were worth investigating. There was general agreement

that, as far as large arrays of processors were concerned, none of those present knew the answers to the problems involved, although the chairman's presentation on the following day would suggest one route towards such an understanding.

6   Conclusions

It was apparent from the general tenor of the discussions at the machine vision workshop that a strong dichotomy existed between those delegates whose main interest was to implement solutions to machine vision problems in situ, and those whose interest involved research into the theory and understanding of the field. This difference of view was reflected in the discussions on architectures by a fundamental difference in attitude to parallelism. The academic viewpoint was that parallelism was so fundamental and necessary as to be assumed, whereas the practical viewpoint was that parallelism was so costly and exotic as to be useless. There were certainly differences of detail within the 'parallel' view, but it seems to the author that the most important question which needs to be addressed by the machine vision community is how to make parallel processing available, both in terms of cost and comprehension, to those at the cutting edge of problem solving. Unless and until this is achieved, the field of application of machine vision will be unnecessarily limited.

7   Acknowledgements

I should like to thank all those who took part in the discussion session on architectures for machine vision for their contributions and for the forthright manner in which the discussions took place. I must also apologise to any delegates whose points I have distorted or omitted.

Industrial Machine Vision — Is It Practical?

Joseph L. Mundy
General Electric Corporate R&D Center

Abstract

It is not often that one has the occasion to produce an article which can take a broad perspective on a research area and comment on the issues likely to effect the emphasis of future research. I, therefore, express appreciation to Herb Freeman and the CAIP Center for organizing the workshop "Machine Vision - Where Are We and Where Are We Going?"

I came to this workshop with the goal of sharing what we have learned about the application of machine vision in industrial inspection. Our group has carried out a number of major projects in this area and we have gathered a rather broad understanding of the issues that are involved in a successful application of vision. This article will expand on my presentation at the workshop and hopefully contribute to the understanding of machine vision technology and its application characteristics.

1 Introduction

1.1 The Industrial Application of Vision

About fifteen years ago (1972), we began a research group on machine vision at GE's Corporate Research and Development Center. This group started by investigating the use of Hadamard spatial frequency encoding of image features. The idea was to use these features in a conventional statistical classifier for the purpose of recognizing patterns. This research effort also included the development of special purpose hardware to support the computation of the fast Hadamard transform.

After about two years, we felt that we had a sufficient background to attempt some application of this work to industrial problems within the manufacturing sector of GE. It was decided to organize a tour of a number of GE departments. The tour included many of the major GE product lines such as, appliances, consumer electronics, instrumentation and lighting. The format of the tour included a presentation by us on the technology of machine vision. We described our own work as well as the work of some major efforts underway at universities. In particular, we included a film on machine vision and robotics which was produced by the Stanford Artificial Intelligence Laboratory under the direction of Tom Binford.

After this presentation, the product and manufacturing engineers for each department would describe potential applications that they thought might be within the scope of the machine vision technology as we presented it. We also toured the factory area and observed the manufacturing processes so that we might discover applications not revealed in the survey by the department staff.

At the beginning we assumed that there would be two broad classes of applications; the visual control of robotic assembly, and automatic visual inspection. It was our intial hope that we could identify a robotic application because the interaction of vision and motion was an appealing research topic. However we were willing to take whatever path emerged as a project that would have good economic benefits and be within the scope of existing machine vision technology.

It was much to our surprise that we were able to uncover no applications for robotics and certainly none that involved visual feedback. On the other hand, many applications for the automation visual inspection were found and which covered the full range of technical difficulty. It may prove useful to describe these perceptions of the manufacturing requirements which were widespread a decade and a half ago, since the issues have changed little since.

1.2   Robot Vision

A major successful applications of robot manipulators in manufacturing has been the positioning of spot welding electrodes for car bodies. This application exposes many of the issues at are important for economic viability. A number of important aspects are:

- *The manufacturing operation is subject to frequent change due to rapid evolution in product design.* This situation certainly holds in the automobile industry.

- *The task is dangerous or extremely unpleasant for human labor.* Again, the welding operation is a good match to this requirement.

- *The expense of reprogramming is small enough to allow an attractive economic payback during the lifetime of the application.* The spot welding application seems to be a good example of the case where the use of a teaching pendant is effective. That is, the robot operator can manually guide the robot through the sequence of required welding locations.

- *The uncertainty of object position and orientation can be economically controlled by fixturing.* The assembly line transport system already requires fixtures for transporting and orienting the automobile components.

Our experience in the GE plants was that one or more of these basic requirements were violated in potential robotic applications. It seemed that either the tasks were too trivial, and thus did not present a very attractive investment payback compared to fixed automation methods, or the task was quite sophisticated and quite beyond the capabilities of even current technology. The introduction of vision technology, for guiding the robot position or eliminating some uncertainty in the environment, did not make these difficult tasks any more attractive; the cost of a vision system which can handle an unstructured environment would be considerably more expensive than the robot system itself.

There was some interest in using robots for flexible assembly in the early to middle 1970's but the basic economic justification of this task was not sufficient to support an additional application of vision to orient and locate parts for the assembly process. Perhaps the most significant issue in robotic assembly is the high cost of reprogramming the assembly system to deal with new products. It can take tens of man years of effort to set up one assembly sequence and even so, not all types of uncertainty or malfunction can be considered. As a consequence, the reliability of such assembly systems is quite low. These issues apply to fixed automation as well, however such systems are intended to provide the mechanization of a long term product manufacture and not to be frequently reprogrammed. Thus the large setup effort can be amortized over a long period of time.

The idea of robot part handling was also considered, but again the cost of overcoming the unstructured factory environment was too great to encourage any pervasive application of this type. In most cases, the obvious applications involved direct replacement of existing factory workers and it was difficult to project any significant cost savings in part handling, since the robot system would be generally slower than the human counterpart, and much less competent to deal with an unstructured environment.

In summary, the application of robotics in manufacturing faces a basic dilemma; it is difficult to program robots for flexible and changing tasks, but they are more expensive than fixed automation methods for stable, high volume manufacturing tasks.

1.3   Automatic Visual Inspection

The conclusions were quite different for the case of automating the process of visual inspection in manufacturing. The economics of quality is much different than that of fabrication. It is relatively easy to justify the automation of inspection if one or more of the following benefits can be identified:

- *Faulty components can be eliminated prior to assembly.* There can be considerable expense associated with building a faulty component into a complex assembly. In many case, the entire unit has to be discarded if it fails a final test. At the very least, repair is expensive and cannot be automated, as might be the case in the initial assembly process.

- *Field repairs can be reduced by catching errors prior to product shipment.* Here it is assumed that visual inspection with humans is prone to error for the case of a repetitive inspection, at high speeds over a long period of time. (We were to eventually learn that the human inspector is remarkably reliable and with accuracy difficult to match by machine.)

- *Quality reports can be automated as a consequence of automatic inspection.* It is often the case that the greatest expense associated with quality control is the generation of reports which provide quality statistics and initiate repairs.

The main factor that differentiates inspection from robotic assembly or parts handling is the process of decision making. It is possible to achieve the required mechanization of assembly or part transport using conventional and mature fixed automation techniques. Inspection, on the other hand, is a process of measurement and judgment which cannot be effectively automated without computer-based systems. Thus there is no competition for automatic visual inspection systems except for the human inspector.

There is also no need to restrict the application to custom or rapidly evolving manufacturing processes. In fact, the most attractive applications involve the stable, high-volume product lines where small improvements in efficiency and quality can pay large dividends in material and labor savings.

I present now a partial list of the inspection applications that were found on the tour which should give a good idea of the range of difficulty and pervasiveness of the visual inspection task.

- Detect uneven distribution of heating in elements for electric stoves. This application would probably involve the use of infra-red imaging.

- Discover flaws and non-uniformities in shadow masks for TV picture tubes.

- Measure the alignment of TV picture tube gun electrodes. This application borders on visual feedback, since the alignment measurements could be used to correct the electrode positions.

- Locate needle display locations on aircraft instruments so that calibration procedures can be automated.

- Detect small carbon inclusions in clear plastic extrusion.

- Inspect mylar layers of a multi-layer printed circuit board for defects in the copper runs. This application is a good example of cost buildup in assembly. If an early layer is defective, and the flaws go undetected,the whole board has to be discarded, wasting the material and labor involved.

- Measure the dimensions of compressor pistons and cylinders so that matching tolerances can be identified, leading to a smaller gap and greater efficiency.

- Detect flaws in painted surfaces including "orange-peel" and scratches.

- Identify flaws in incandescent coiled tungsten lamp filaments, including non-uniform pitch and other geometric defects.

We then began the process of narrowing down the list of potential applications. It was decided to consider only applications that could be handled with binary image data since the techniques for this mode were the best developed. In addition, most of the applications require relatively high thruput and special purpose hardware can be built to handle binary data in a relatively straightforward manner.

It was also clear that each application demanded a dedicated system which could incorporate the necessary part handling and disposition as well as special optical and imaging designs that would enhance the critical features involved in the inspection. The custom nature of such a development demanded that we chose a long term, high volume application so that the investment would be economically attractive.

We rather quickly settled on the lamp filament inspection application, since this seemed to combine technical feasibility with economic attractiveness. The filaments are produced in high volume and are manufactured in a highly automated and stable process.

2 The Automatic Inspection of Incandescent Lamp Filaments

2.1 Basic Requirements

A typical lamp filament is illustrated in Figure 1.

Figure 1: A Typical Tungsten Coil Filament with a Defective Turn.

A filament consists of coiled tungsten wire which is designed to provide efficient radiation of black body radiation. Any non-uniformity in the pitch of the winding will cause excessive local heating and result in a shorter life for the lamp. The end connection leads must also conform to geometric tolerances, since they are clamped to the lamp socket leads by automatic equipment which can tolerate only a small range in filament length and lead orientation.

The manual system of inspection involves observing the filaments in a small batch on a backlit table. A human inspector can quickly spot non-uniformities in pitch and other geometric defects. The filaments can also be quickly sorted for length by aligning them in groups against a scale.

After some study of the manual system, we concluded that the important defects could be detected in a binary silhouette of the filament with one view. In addition, the system would have to locate and report all significant defects as well as sort the filaments according to length and defect type.

2.2   The Feasibility Stage

Geometry Representation

We began the project by studying various alternatives for representing the geometry of the filament. It was quickly realized that we would have to forego our original Hadamard encoding schemes in favor of a more direct representation. This is a good example that there is no pervasive generic solution in machine vision; each application requires a careful study of alternatives and perhaps even the invention of a new technique.

It was soon realized that the median axis of the silhouette is a good representation of the filament geometry. In addition, the median can be reasonably approximated by a piecewise linear curve. For example, the median axis in the body of the filament is the average of two sinusoids which are 90 degrees out of phase. This curve is a sequence of nearly straight lines with alternating slopes. Thus the approximation with line segments quite appropriate in the body region. The leads are gently curving and can be represented with a few line segments.

Syntactic Analysis

In order to maintain accuracy, but at the same time reliably locate
the actual extrema of the body primary turns, we decided to employ
a syntactic analysis of the straight line sequence derived from the
medial axis. In this way, we could efficiently encode rules for ignoring
small secondary turns as well as identify gross defects which would
be grounds for immediate rejection of the filament.

As a brief background, the field of syntactic pattern recognition
was fashioned after the rather successful application of formal grammatical analysis to computer language compilers. The parsing of
these grammars can be achieved by various classes of formal machines such as a finite state automaton or a stack automaton. A
good review of these methods is found in the book by Fu [2]. The
basic idea is that some types of patterns can be thought of as sequences or strings of symbols. These strings can then be identified
as belonging to a language if the parsing process terminates successfully. As an additional byproduct, significant components of the
pattern can be identified during the analysis of the string.

In the case of the filament inspection task, the pattern or sequence components are as follows: $< lead > < body > < lead >$.
The $< body >$ component is defined as a subsequence; $[< peak >$
$< valley >]^*$. The symbol, $*$, indicates an indefinite repeat of the
subsequence in the square brackets. The geometric location of each
peak and valley is the essential information needed to inspect the
body and the geometry of the leads can be derived from the start
and stop locations of the initial and final lead symbol sequences. In
this context, the symbols in the sequence correspond to line segments
of various classes of slope and length. The symbols shown in Figure 2
were defined after some experiments with the segmentation of actual
filament median curves. Ultimately, the symbol classes can be derived by a statistical analysis of the distribution of segment lengths
and slopes which occur in a sample of filament images.

The class of regular or finite state grammars were selected to represent the line segment sequences. This class is easy to design and has
a fixed amount of computation for each symbol. From an implementation standpoint, the application of grammatical rules corresponds

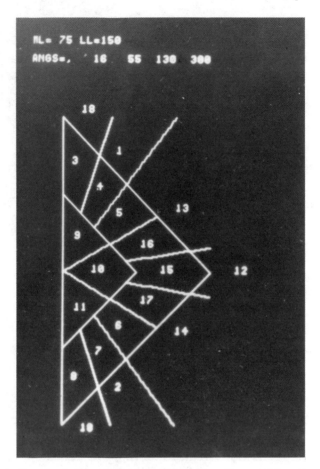

Figure 2: Symbol Classification of Median Curve Line Segments.

to looking up a state transition in a table. That is, the analysis can be characterized by a current state and current symbol. A two-dimensional table is designed which gives the next state for each combination of current state and symbol. If the string terminates in a state which belongs to a set of so-called accepting states then the sequence is taken to be grammatically correct. In our application, certain of the states in the language correspond to geometrically significant locations along the filament such as the transitions between $< lead >$ and $< body >$. The final grammar required about 80 states to represent all the significant events in the filament median curve.

The finite state grammar was efficient enough to allow the analysis of a filament in a standard minicomputer available in the early seventies, at the desired thruput. The median curve segmentation and syntactic analysis, followed by rather conventional tolerance checks on the geometry was able to identify the desired defect types. These algorithms were assembled into a successful feasibility demonstration by 1975.

2.3   Prototype System

The next phase in the project was to develop the ideas behind the feasibility demonstration into a prototype which would operate at the desired thruput and be able to carry out extensive statistical tests of the reliability of automatic inspection. Several significant developments were required:

- Optics and illumination to provide an accurate silhouette of the filament.

- An image sensor to provide a binary digital image with resolution of 1.5 million pixels.

- A hardware image processor to produce straight line segments from the binary image.

- A mechanical system to feed and orient the filaments as well as a sorting mechanism to dispose of the classified product.

It took until late 1976 to solve these problems. It proved quite difficult to find an illumination source that could provide enough intensity of well-collimated light to permit a read-out rate of 5Mhz. We eventually settled on a quartz halogen source with a high NA lens. The detector, a linear silicon diode array was combined with an automatic threshold selection circuit to provide a binary image slice of the filament image.

The other dimension of the image is swept out by the transport of the filament under the sensor. The filament transport is provided by a rotating glass disk which allows the transmission of back illumination. The filaments are placed on the glass disk by a complex feeding mechanism which uses a vibrating bowl feeder and buffer storage to produce a uniform stream of filaments. The classified filaments are sorted into jars by air jets placed after the sensor station at the periphery of the disk.

The image segmentation was implemented in special purpose digital hardware as well as a bit-slice microprocessor. This combination of special purpose and microprogrammable hardware proved very effective in overcoming unforeseen problems and expanding requirements. The final prototype configuration is shown in Figure 3.

Figure 3: Development Prototype of the Filament Inspection System.

2.4   Field Testing

The prototype took several months to debug and achieve an acceptable level of performance for testing. We then shipped the machine to the plant for further evaluation by the quality engineers. This test occupied about one year and included careful comparisons between the machine performance and the human inspector. Four-way tests between manual inspection and the prototype were carried out. The four combinations involve comparisons of the machine accepted and rejected samples with the samples accepted and rejected by the human inspector. The final statistical report concluded that the machine could achieve an inspection reliability comparable to the best human inspectors.

During the testing phase, hundreds of thousands of samples were evaluated, which points out that a prototype has to be able to support almost the same degree of reliability and thruput as the final factory system.

Eventually, it was decided to go ahead with the development of a number of production units. A number of rather major changes had to be made to make the system suitable for production:

- The production system involves a network of inspection stations which communicate with a central host. This architecture was not considered in the initial prototype.

- The user interface that we had developed for the system was suitable for experimentation and evaluation but was not ideal for the use of factory operators and quality personnel. The user interface was totally rewritten.

- The mechanisms for feeding and transport on the prototype were significantly altered to provide improved thruput and more robustness and reliability.

- Extensive documentation and maintenance procedures are needed to support regular production use of the system. We did not develop much of this material during the prototype phase.

3 Inspection of Turbine Castings

3.1 A More Diversified Application

Our research applications evolved through several stages in the late 1970's with grey level image analysis projects such as the measurement of small holes in castings[5]. We then decided to investigate the problem of inspecting the surface of castings (turbine blades) for jet engines. This application is quite challenging since there are many sizes and shapes for these castings with diverse inspection requirements. In fact, due to variation in stress concentration at different locations in the part, it is necessary to have variable inspection limits over the part surface.

These parts are also quite complex in shape . Figure 4 shows a typical example. Since these parts are used in a high temperature

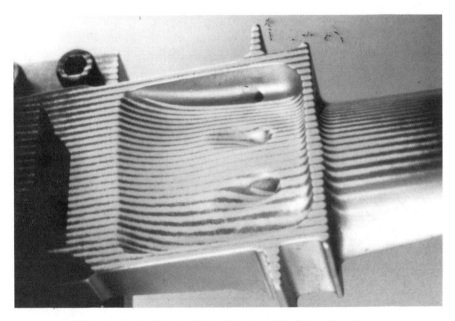

Figure 4: A Typical Jet Engine Turbine Casting.

and high stress environment, it is essential to inspect the surface and interior of the parts for flaws that could lead to fracture. The project, to be described here, was focussed on the problem of locating small cracks, dents and scratches on the surface of the part.

It is necessary to achieve inspection rates corresponding to several parts per minute in order to be economical, considering the expected complexity of such a machine. The surface defects can be as small as .003" and as shallow as .001". In the manual inspection procedures, these requirements are met with standard visual inspection and fluorescent penetrant inspection techniques.

For those not familiar with the fluorescent penetrant inspection (FPI) technique, a liquid dye is applied to the part surface which can penetrate small cracks. The part surface is then cleaned but the dye stays trapped in the crack. If a powder is then applied to the surface, the dye is drawn out of the crack by capillary action. The dye can be made visible by illuminating it with ultra-violet light, which causes the dye to fluoresce. The fluorescence is in the yellow-green wavelength band. With this method, even a very small crack can be visualized. In most applications, fluorescent indications down to about .010" are considered significant.

It is desirable to try to automate the visual and FPI methods so that the flaw detection rate can be improved and the generation of inspection reports can be made directly into the quality control system by maintaining an on-line quality data base. The automated method can provide a more quantitative description of the flaws which leads to a better analysis of their effect on performance.

3.2   The IBIS Concept

The approach to this inspection application is to try to support the two applications by designing an integrated system so that the development of part manipulation and flaw decision processing could be shared between visual inspection and FPI. The concept that was developed is illustrated in Figure 5. The system was denoted the Integrated Blade Inspection System, or IBIS.

In this concept, the surface of the part can be scanned by a visual or FPI sensor by fitting the appropriate sensor to a common part manipulation station. The visual inspection is accomplished by a 3D range sensor and the FPI inspection is carried out using a sensor based on laser illumination of the fluorescent dye. Each inspection module communicates with a central host which maintains a quality data base concerning the various inspection results at each stage of part manufacture. Also since there are many complex part types to be inspected, it was decided to use geometric part models to derive inspection scanning plans and inspection decision procedures. In this

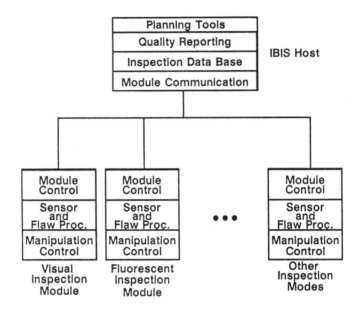

Figure 5: The Integrated Blade Inspection System concept.

way, the same mechanical and electronic system could handle a wide range of part types.

The central data base also maintains these scan and inspection plans which are down-loaded to the appropriate module as the parts reach each inspection stage. It is desirable that a module be able to be changed over to a new part type with a minimum of manual effort. This requirement implies very flexible manipulation and fixturing as well as the automatic calibration of sensors and manipulators.

A geometric model of the jet engine part provides the information needed to locate each point on the part surface and to determine the orientation of the surface normal at that point. This information is then used to position a six axis manipulator which directs the sensor to that point on the part surface. A full scan of the part involves continuous paths of manipulator position called swaths. The sensors take in a single line of surface data occupying up to an inch on the part surface. The scanning motion of the manipulator provides the other dimension of the sensor image. The model-derived swaths are also used to represent the location of detected flaws as well as the variable inspection tolerances.

3.3 The Geometric Model and Scanning Utilities

In order to support the type of requirements described above, we decided to use a bi-cubic surface model for the casting. A typical example is shown in Figure 6. The surface is divided into regions or

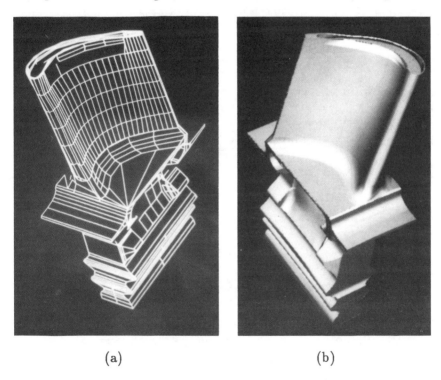

(a)   (b)

Figure 6: A Bi-cubic Surface Model.

    (a) The Surface Patches.
    (b) A Rendered Synthetic Image of the Part.

patches which can be accurately represented by cubic polynomials for the three dimensional variation of the surface. The intersections between patches are represented by cubic spline curves.

In the IBIS application it is necessary to maintain an accuracy of at least .005" in the surface position and within about 10 degrees of surface normal orientation. The representation should also be as smooth as possible so that discontinuities in surface position would not be translated into high accelerations in the part scanning motion.

The model is generated from part drawings by a standard CAD workstation. The scanning motions and swaths are developed from the model using a special utility developed for the project. The utility, called a scan plan generator, is used interactively with a display of the part model as shown in Figure 7. The operator defines a curve

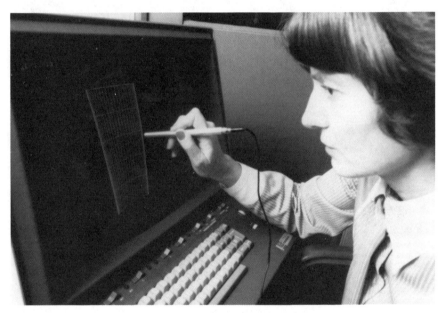

Figure 7: Scan Plan Generation.

on the part surface which is the intended path of the sensor. The scan plan generator (SPG) then computes the width of the swath which can produce valid sensor data. For example each sensor has an allowable depth of field for which the sensor data is valid. If the surface is highly curved in the region of the scan, then the swath must be kept narrow so that the sensor depth of is not exceeded as the scan moves away from the center of the swath. Other considerations can also limit the scan width, such as surface normal variations. For example,the range sensor can not obtain enough reflected light intensity if the surface normal varies more than 15 degrees with respect to the orientation of the sensor.

It is up to the operator to decide how to cover the part surface with swaths and to ensure that the swaths overlap slightly so that each portion of the surface is inspected. These decisions require a considerable amount of skill and the choices of swath placement greatly influence the subsequent inspection time. This process is carried out offline and once a suitable set of swaths is obtained, they become part of the data base for each part type.

Another utility, takes the position and orientation components along each swath and generates a set of commands for the part manipulator. The manipulator, to be described in the next section has six degrees of freedom, so that the sensor can be positioned along the swath and oriented along the surface normal at each point on the path. A swath is also considered to be a continuous dynamic entity so that the manipulator dynamics are controlled with respect to the desired performance along the entire swath. The utility generates the necessary positions and velocity commands for each point on the swath for each of the six manipulator axes. Static positioning is used to move from the end of one swath to the beginning of the next.

A final use of the model is to define inspection zones on the part surface. These zones are originally specified by the engine designer on the part drawing. The coordinates of the zones are used to determine which swaths lie in a given tolerance zone. In the present design, a swath is assumed to lie completely within one zone. This implies that a swath would be terminated if it crosses the boundary of a zone. Ideally, the tolerances should be considered position dependent along a swath, but this proved to be too difficult to implement.

3.4   The Part Manipulator

The geometry of the surface scanner is shown in Figure 8. The design splits the degrees of freedom between the sensor and the part. In this way, the inertial load associated with stacking axes on top of each other is reduced. The sensor axis configuration is designed to accommodate both the range and FPI sensor scanning heads. The part manipulator has a general gripping base so that adjustable fixtures can be quickly exchanged when the manipulator is switched to a new part type. The drives for the axes are conventional DC torque mo-

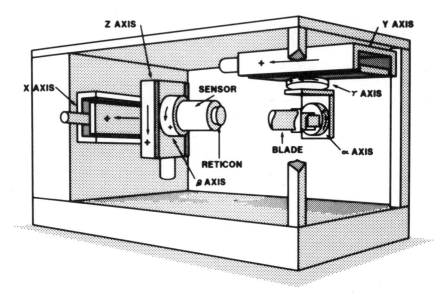

Figure 8: The Six Axis Sensor and Part Manipulator Configuration.

tors with digital/analog servos to control position and velocity. The manipulator was designed to allow the part surface to be scanned at up to 4 inches per second. This rate can lead to rather large acceleration requirements, particularly for the rotary axes. As an example, the inspection swath around the trailing edge of the airfoil section of a turbine blade can contain a change of surface orientation of 180 degrees in a path distance of less than .1 inches. These surface orientation changes, in turn, result in large translational motions. The translation is required to keep the swath at a fixed distance from the sensor as the orientation is varying at a large radius from the center of rotation.

It is also necessary to accommodate a wide variety of gripping configurations so that the castings can be held reliably and accurately. The intial design of this gripping mechanism is illustrated in Figure 9. A variety of primitive gripping surfaces were developed which could be mated to handle all gripping configurations. For example, a stable grasp of a cylinder is accomplished by mating a v-groove and a knife edge. A rectangle can be grasped by a three point contact and a knife edge. These various gripping surfaces are arranged on two turrets. The turrets can then be indexed to create a variety of part grippers. The gripper assembly is activated by compressed air which gives a fast and firm grasping action. The various

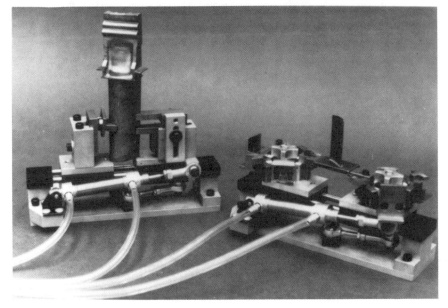

Figure 9: A Flexible Gripping Mechanism. The Turrets Allow Rapid Exchange of Multiple Gripping Elements.

primitives do have to be adjusted in position for a particular part type to allow for size and surface curvature variations. The initial turret design eventually evolved into a a simpler configuration of a pair of primitive grasp fixtures which can be quickly and accurately exchanged onto the gripper support base. This arrangement allows a mechanical library of pre-adjusted gripper fixtures to be stored near the manipulator and exchanged as the part type change over occurs.

It is essential that the part position and orientation be controlled accurately since the scan plan is executed as a sequence of open loop position and velocity commands. Any significant deviation from the nominal position for the part grasp would cause regions of the part surface to be missed during the scan. The mechanical design of the gripper base includes alignment pins so that the gripper assembly can be accurately relocated during change over. Calibration tables can be measured and stored for each fixture and thus further reduce the setup time for a new part type.

An additional sensor was included at the part loading station to insure the accuracy of the initial grasp. The sensor, based on two binary image sensors, can determine the position and orientation of the part in the load station. The load station consists of three axes, a translational axis to feed the part to the first scanner and an additional translation and a rotary axis for intial part setup adjustments.

The full part scanner/manipulator requires 15 axes since there are two scanning stations. One scanning station is used for each half of the part. The part gripper conceals some portion of the casting, so it is necessary to regrasp the casting and scan the portion which was not inspected in the first scanning station. For maximum efficiency, each station is assigned approximately one half of the part surface to inspect. Two parts are in the manipulator at one time so that the scans are carried out in parallel. The parts flow through the system in a pipeline fashion.

The axes are mounted vertically from a ceiling plate and a granite back face. The entire structure is supported on a granite base. The use of granite is essential for vibration damping and for thermal stability. These considerations are quite important in order to maintain a global position accuracy of .005" over a distance of about six feet. The structure is thus quite massive and rigid. A photograph of the complete manipulator is shown in Figure 10.

3.5   The Range Sensor

The inspection the surface for dents and pits is accomplished by the use of a structured light range sensor. This sensor is designed to resolve about .008" square surface elements with about .002" depth

Figure 10: The Part Manipulator. The Structure Is Granite, Steel and Aluminum.

resolution. The sensor is illustrated in Figure 11. This resolution is adequate to measure rejectable pits and dents. In order to achieve the necessary speed, the sensor uses mulitiple stripes of illumination and the parallax angle between the strip projector and the intensity sensor allows the surface depth to be determined by triangulation. The sensor also uses multiple wavelengths of illumination in order to normalize the data against surface reflectance variations. The principles of the sensor have been described in considerable detail in [4]. It is necessary to implement most of the signal processing that carries out signal normalization and triangulation in special purpose hardware. The intensity sensor is a linear diode array which is sampled at one million pixels per second. The final range data rate is 60,00ʳ range pixels per second since four intensity elements in each irᵣ dimension are used to compute a range value. The intensity elᵣ

Figure 11: The Range Sensor

are .002" at the part surface so that the final lateral dimension of the range element is .008".

The pixel rate can be reduced by low surface reflectance. In this case, the amount of light falling on the sensor must be integrated for a longer period of time to achieve an acceptable signal to noise ratio. Thus the scan rate of the manipulator is adjusted to permit adequate integration if low reflectance regions are encountered.

The standoff distance of the sensor is about six inches and the depth of field is about .05". The depth of field is limited almost simultaneously by aliasing of the multiple stripes in the projected light pattern and the optical depth of field of the image and projection lens systems. In this context, aliasing means that one stripe in a periodic pattern becomes confused with another when the stripe shift is large enough due to depth changes.

3.6 The Fluorescent Penetrant Inspection Sensor

As mentioned earlier, the presence of small and tight cracks in a casting surface can be detected by treating the surface with a fluorescent dye and then illuminating the surface with ultraviolet light. It is also the case that the dyes will fluoresce with illumination in the deep blue which can be produced by a HeCd laser at 4416 A^o.

The sensor geometry is illustrated in Figure 12. The fluorescent emission is collected by a number of lenses and collected into a single fiber-optic bundle. The multiple lenses are used to collect much of the light emitted by the dye by surrounding the defect with a hemisphere of sensing elements.

This fiber-optic link conducts the light to a single photomultiplier detector. The photomultiplier is used to provide sufficient sensitivity and dynamic range. The light reaching the photodetector is filtered to remove the wavelength corresponding to the laser illumination. The green-yellow fluorescent emissions are transmitted by the filter and reach the detector.

One line of the image of the part surface is swept out by scanning the laser beam with a galvanometer mirror in a direction across the direction of manipulator motion. The other direction of scan is provided by the manipulator, as in the case of the visual sensor. The scan of a defect is shown in Figure 13. The faint line is the laser scan and the bright spot is the fluorescence of the defect.

The data rate of the FPI sensor is about 500,000 samples per second. The depth of field is considerably more than the visual range sensor - on the order of .5 inches. The increased depth of field is due to the imaging method. A laser beam can be focussed with a good depth of field since the effective source diameter is on the order of a wavelength. In this design the surface resolution is provided by the laser illumination, rather than imaging in the detector.

3.7 Flaw Image Processing and Detection Analysis

The fundamental processing step used to isolate defect regions is based on differential operators. The local surface is represented by a

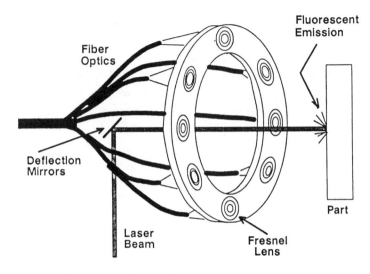

Figure 12: The FPI Sensor Configuration.

Taylor series expansion about image point, (x_0, y_0), as follows:

$$I(x, y) = I(x_0, y_0) + \frac{\partial I(x_0, y_0)}{\partial x}(x - x_0) + \frac{\partial I(x_0, y_0)}{\partial y}(y - y_0) +$$

$$.5\frac{\partial^2 I(x_0, y_0)}{\partial x^2}(x - x_0)^2 + .5\frac{\partial^2 I(x_0, y_0)}{\partial y^2}(y - y_0)^2 +$$

$$\frac{\partial^2 I(x_0, y_0)}{\partial x \partial y}(x - x_0)(y - y_0)$$

This form of defect description is applicable to both the visual and FPI flaw conditions. In the visual case, the intensity corresponds to surface depth, in the FPI case the intensity corresponds to the emission power of a quantity of trapped dye.

The coefficients of the expansion can be computed in an optimum least-mean-squares sense by convolving a set of masks against the sensor image data. These masks can be computed by assuming that the surface can be represented as a polynomial surface with relatively

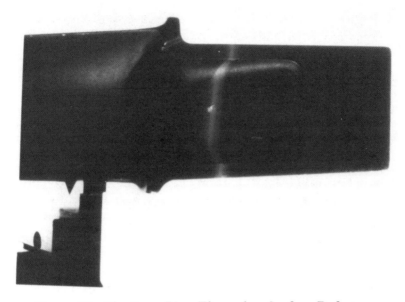

Figure 13: The Scan Line Through a Surface Defect.

low degree[1]. For example a 5×5 mask for $\frac{\partial I}{\partial x}$ is given by:

$$\begin{array}{rrrrr}
-1 & -2 & 0 & 2 & 1 \\
-4 & -10 & 0 & 10 & 4 \\
-8 & -16 & 0 & 16 & 8 \\
-4 & -10 & 0 & 10 & 4 \\
-1 & -2 & 0 & 2 & 1
\end{array}$$

Each term in the expansion is compared with a threshold and if that threshold is exceeded, then that particular image point is assigned to that class of defect topography. The thresholds are derived from specifications about flaw characteristics which are described in the drawings for each casting design.

In order to consider a wide range of surface curvatures and image sensor noise variation for range data, the data is smoothed by a programmable two-dimensional Gaussian kernel filter. The smoothed surface is subtracted from the actual surface position to give a residual depth corresponding to rapid local variations A slice through the kernel is an ellipse. The major and minor axes of this ellipse as well as its orientation can be changed under program control as the surface scan proceeds. This anisotropic filter kernel allows normal high surface curvatures to be passed by the detector while small variations in the direction of low curvature can be detected. An example of this case would be the detection of nicks along a knife edge, where the surface is highly curved in one direction but flat in the other. In this case, the filter ellipse would be long and thin and the major axis aligned along the knife edge.

The same capability is needed for estimating background fluorescence in the case of the FPI sensor. Again, the Gaussian filter output is subtracted from the image data to isolate sharp local variations.

The final design allows 5×5 differential operators and a Gaussian kernel up to 32×32. All of the processes are implemented in special purpose hardware and can be carried out at 60,000 points per second. For example, the full Gaussian convolution requires the weighted summation of 1024 image points in 16 microseconds.

As a final step in the sensor image processing, the image points which have been marked as potential flaw elements are collected into connected sets. The average geometric properties of the sets are computed and comprise the final representation of the image analysis. The representation consists of a list of regions with average differential surface parameters computed from the filters and with area and centroid specified for each region. This representation is used to make a final decision about the rejection of a surface condition.

The flaw analysis is represented as a decision tree which is based on the parameters just discussed. Each swath in the scan plan contains information determining the filtering parameters just discussed as well as a decision table which allows the consideration of the parameters in determining the flaw type and criticality of the flaw. The decision table is compiled from a special language developed which can be related to the flaw criteria usually discussed in the drawings. Typical criteria are maximum flaw diameter, area and aspect ratio. In the case of visual inspection, depth and radius of curvature of defect areas are also considered in the flaw description.

The flaw analysis is carried out in software based on the list of defect regions supplied by the hardware discussed earlier. If the analysis is bogged down by a large list of regions, the part scan can be reduced in speed to allow more time for the analysis. If an upper bound of defect regions are detected, the part is rejected as uninspectable and referred to manual analysis.

3.8 Project History and Status

The project began in 1977 with some feasibility studies on the various major aspects of sensor design. Several alternatives were considered for the visual sensor principle including coherent light diffraction and shape from the spatial variation of surface illumination. The FPI sensor principle was reasonably in hand right from the beginning, and the feasibility work in this area was directed at determining the sensitivity of the method. A prototype part manipulator was in use by 1978.

By 1979, the final system design was underway and the first visual module prototype was tested by the end of 1981. The FPI module was demonstrated about a year later. Development continued on thru 1982 when the systems were transferred to the Aircraft Engine Business Group (AEBG) for application within GE and military airfoil manufacturing and repair centers.

At this writing (1987), the FPI module , after considerable further development and testing by AEBG personnel, has demonstrated the ability to detect defects as small as .030" with 90% confidence. This performance exceeds that of the human inspector who can reliably detect FPI defects only as small as about .1". This performance is considered very sucessful and can provide a significant breakthrough in casting reliability.

The visual inspection module was not developed further than its state in 1983. There are many reasons for this but they are all related to the difficulties in detecting and describing visual defects. One major problem is that metallic surfaces exhibit a tremendous dynamic range in surface reflectance. It is common to experience local variations of 10^4 in reflectance with corresponding variations in sensed image intensity. The best dynamic range that might be achieved for a silicon diode array is on the order of 10^3.

Another difficulty is related to the stringent positioning requirements for the range sensor. The depth of field of .050" made it difficult to keep the sensor in range at high scan speeds, and even small
structural vibrations are manifested as ripples in surface depth due
to the relative motion of the sensor and part surface. This problem
does not occur in the FPI sensor, since its resolution and sensitivity is relatively insensitive to standoff distance and orientation. The
light emission from fluorescence is almost uniformly distributed over
observation angle. It is thus possible to scan at the full capability of
the manipulator.

A related difficulty is caused by the part modeling system itself. It proved impossible to eliminate small discontinuities at the
intersection between surface patches. These discontinuities manifest
themselves as rapid variation in surface normal orientation which
produce very high acceleration requirements when the manipulator
attempts to follow them. A partial solution to this problem was
achieved by smoothing the sequence of normal vectors and positions
along the scan path with a Gaussian kernel. It some cases it proved
satisfactory to fix the normal orientation along the entire swath. This
solution is not satisfactory if the surface actually has high curvature
since then the manipulator path does not keep the sensor in focus or
proper orientation to resolve the part surface.

Another major difficulty is the complexity of visual defect conditions. The relationship between defects and their manifestation
in range data is often complex. For example, the depth of a graz-
ing dent is not well defined against a curved background surface.
Another complicating factor is the dynamic range issue mentioned
above. For example, the reflectance at the bottom of a pit may be
too low to provide adequate image intensity to resolve range. In this
case, the defect is manifested as a region of undefined range.

In spite of these difficulties, it was demonstrated that the visual
inspection module could detect major flaws in part surfaces and re-
ject them on this basis. This capability would be useful in a casting
repair facility where used parts are inspected for reuse. A significant
percentage of the parts have large flaws and could be automatically
rejected prior to human inspection. However, the economic benefit

of this capability is not sufficient to justify the investment cost of the module.

In both applications, it was necessary to spend considerable time testing and modifying the scan plans so that collisions could be avoided. The scan plan generation utility positions the axes without regard for potential interference between the axes of the sensor manipulator. A detailed and accurate model of the manipulator itself would be required to detect these interferences offline; also the problem of planning a collision free path in the presence of complex obstacles is a major research issue, even at this writing. The expedient solution is to manually execute the scan plan in a step position mode and watch for collision conditions. In the case of interference, an alternative solution for the axis positions is manually chosen; multiple axis solutions are usually available. This testing and modification adds considerable expense to the creation of a scan plan.

4 The Future of Applied Machine Vision

4.1 Learning From Past Experience

The previous two application examples should provide a realistic background for the discussion of the future evolution of automatic visual inspection and perhaps for more general applications of machine vision itself. We have learned a number of significant facts about the problem of applying vision to industrial inspection and robotics which are summarized below:

- System cost is difficult to justify. A competent vision system will cost between 500K$ and 1M$ to replicate. This cost may be even higher if such hidden expenses as training, maintenance and integration are taken into account. On the other hand, skilled human labor is perhaps on the order of 30K$ per year; considering benefits and overhead expenses. These conditions imply that the inspection system must be much more competent than a human inspector, or significantly faster, or both.

- A large and risky development effort is usually required. As an example, the IBIS project described above involved perhaps 5 years of development with approximately 100 man years of effort. The problem of developing an inspection system is complicated by the fact that it is difficult to determine exact requirements without already having a system to quantitatively inspect and record a large number of sample flaw instances. Also over this time span the actual quality requirements may change, and invalidate initial system design choices.

- The factory environment is complex and relatively unstructured. The parts must be located and oriented before inspection can occur. Also the surface properties are variable with oil, scratches, and repair conditions that must be understood by the system. Finally, many applications involve a large number of part types and the sytem must accept considerable variation in scanning and handling.

- Variable inspection task programs are difficult to realize in practice. Part manipulation requires the solution of the collision avoidance problem which is still the subject of basic research. Even with the use of CAD part models the uncertainty of the environment and tolerance variations in part instances leads to difficulties in applying offline programming techniques. Finally, the generation of accurate and smooth surface models has still not been achieved; the problem is deeply rooted in the nature of polynomial representation of surfaces. Accuracy requires polynomials of high degree but the intersections of such polynomial surfaces are complex geometrically and topologically.

It is my opinion that these issues will not go away quickly. One way to get around the difficulties is to restrict the development of automatic inspection and robotic vision system to narrow applications that are high volume, stable in requirement, and relatively simple to achieve. The sophistication of such systems will gradually evolve, but the number of such applications will always be relatively small and the evolution will not represent a pervasive infusion of vision technology into industrial practice. However, as was noted in the introduction to this chapter, the application of vision research to such restricted inspection tasks was practical 15 years ago and is still an attractive way to demonstrate the utility of machine vision techniques.

The other possibility is to increase further the power of the system so that the factory environment and rapidly varying requirements can be accommodated. This approach is essentially along the lines that lead to the difficulties encountered in the IBIS system and for the application of robotics in general. However, if this goal could be achieved, then the widespread use of such systems would permit the economy of volume to support the development costs. This effect is seen in large operating system development for mainframe computers where the development is amortized over thousands of copies of the system. Another example is the development of complex integrated circuits for central processing units or memory. The system itself may require hundreds of manhours to develop but the unit cost is reduced to an attractive level by volume. In the next section we will consider the implications of this latter course of action on future research goals.

4.2   The Generations of the Visual Inspection System

We can illustrate the recent developments and potential future development of inspection and robotic vision by considering the evolution of these systems in terms of generations by analogy to the generations of computer architectures; e.g. the fifth generation under development in Japan. The first of such inspection architectures is shown in Figure 14. This generation illustrates the basic components of any visual inspection system where a sensing and illumination subsystem is used to scan the part in a fixed and unprogrammable fashion. That is, the camera and illumination sources are fixed onto the structure of the inspection station and the image field of view and illumination cannot be changed. The part is held in a fixture so that the field of view of a camera is directed at a given location on the part. The pattern matching and testing is a special purpose program that is developed within the fixed structure of the system and makes use of assumptions about the part geometry and image features to carry out the analysis. For example, the correct location of a hole may be determined by counting the number of pixels below a threshold in a fixed window of the image. There is no language for expressing this process in general; it is carried out in terms of the low-level primitives of the image hardware. The handling and disposition of parts is accomplished by fixed automation methods such as conveyer belts and special pallets and fixtures.

A ROBOTIC INSPECTION SYSTEM
(1st Generation)

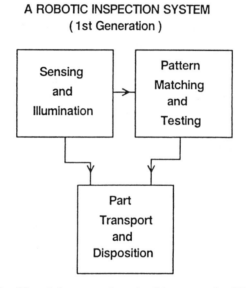

Figure 14: The Fixed Automation Architecture for Visual Inspection.

The 2nd generation is illustrated in Figure 15. The sensor is still fixed within the structure of the inspection station but the illumination and field of view can be changed by manually exchanging lenses and light sources. These adjustments allow a range of part sizes and shapes to be accommodated by the imaging system and the corresponding flexibility in inspection decisions are achieved by driving a fixed decision procedure but with a table of part dependent parameters. The part handling and disposition have fixed types of motion, but the actual speed and limit positions are also controlled from a part dependent table. The filament inspection system discussed earlier fits into this generation class.

The 3rd generation is shown in Figure 16. The major feature of this generation is the introduction of a central model of the geometry of the part to be inspected. This geometric model is used to derive the part scanning and handling motions. These motions are executed by a programmable manipulation system where the lighting, camera field of view and part position can all be controlled. The model is also used to represent the quality requirements for the part so that decision procedure can be specially derived for each part. The processing of image data is carried out in a general fashion with the extraction of image features that can be used in a wide range of flaw analysis procedures. The information generated about the part is also stored within the reference framework of the model. The IBIS system is an example of the 3rd generation.

PROGRAMABLE WITHIN A PART FAMILY
(2nd Generation)

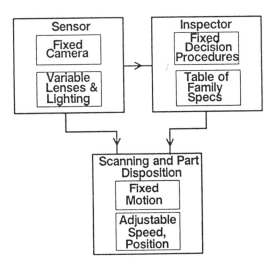

Figure 15: The 2nd Generation, Programmable within a Part Family.

As we have seen, even the model-based inspection system is limited in its ability to deal with the uncertainties that exist in manufacturing environments. The uncertainty is due not only to the normal

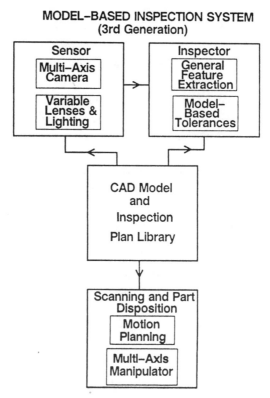

Figure 16: The 3rd Generation, the Model-based Inspection System.

variations in the location of objects but unforeseen situations that
require deviation from a plan developed for the typical case. An example of this case is when a part is so badly out of specification that
the predefined scan plan permits a collision between the part and the
camera.

It seems necessary that the system have command of an extensive
range of concepts that describe the environment and the nature of
part functionality. The system must then be able to "reason" from
these concepts to derive appropriate actions in the event of uncertainty, inaccuracy and changing quality requirements. It must be
possible to take functional requirements of part design and translate
them into analysis that can be carried out on the features extracted

from image sensors and to direct the appropriate scanning of the surface.

At the same time, the spatial relationships within the work environment must be acquired by sensing and model descriptions and these relationships used to determine safe and efficient part scanning motions. It is also likely that recent innovations in tactile and force sensing will be needed to reduce the consequences of collisions that cannot be avoided.

These components are shown in Figure 17 which describes the concept-based inspection system. Here the idea of the concept augments the model as a generic set of principles which can be used to determine appropriate and flexible behavior in new situations. Obviously this cannot be considered as a totally general capability, otherwise the problem of Artificial Intelligence would be solved. However, the main limitation of the 3rd generation is its lack of ability to respond to unforeseen events and take appropriate action. There is still a role for offline programming, but in this 4th generation the offline program represents only a nominal case and can easily be subverted by specific events occurring during the inspection process.

The additional information is provided by a set of concepts which embody the knowledge about the world specific to the system and its functions. For example, the concept of collision and its geometric implications should be available to the system so that it can determine an appropriate response when one occurs. In this case, it should be deduced that an initial movement normal to one surface at the point of contact between the two surfaces is a good strategy to remove the collision condition. Likewise if an unusual defect condition occur, say, for example, image occlusion by the part gripper, there should be a sufficient conceptual base to uncover the possible manipulator geometries that could interact with the sensor process to give the observed indication. In other words, there should be a sufficient conceptual basis to allow reasoning about the events that are likely to be encountered during the inspection process.

It seems that many of the situations will involve the geometric relationships of the manipulator axes or the illumination and sensor geometry. It follows that many of the concepts will relate to geomet-

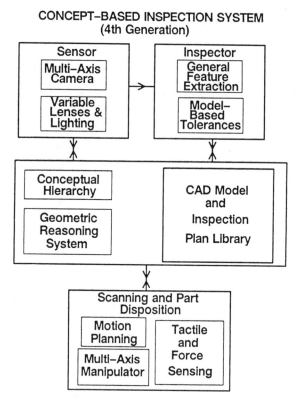

Figure 17: The 4th Generation, a Concept-based Inspection System.

ric relations and the deductions will involve geometric reasoning. The central process is thus to combine the general principles of geometry with the specific conditions imposed by the nominal part geometric model and the sensor observations of the environment. This emphasis creates a significant role for geometric reasoning methods; in particular, the ability to reason from general principles to specific cases is critically needed.

It is also clear that the general principles of illumination and optics must be available to continually refine the system's use of sensing to reveal the maximum amount of information about the surface of the part under inspection. For example, the system should observe a location from another viewpoint if the location is partially occluded and that viewpoint should be selected to give good sensor performance. In the case where multiple sensing modes are available, the information from multiple sensors should be combined to reveal as much as possible about the physical structure of a defect condition. In the casting inspection application context it should prove useful to combine the fluorescent indication evidence with surface topography as measured by range to determine the functional consequences of a defect. Thus it would seem that it may even be necessary to provide concepts about stress and fracture failure to the system.

At present there are only the beginnings of an understanding on how the 4th generation might be implemented[3]. There is much research to be done to understand how general formal concepts, such as geometry, can be used to derive specific behavior in a programmable system. It is even more difficult to see how this could be carried out in a time-effective manner within a high thruput production machine, since the known techniques are computationally prohibitive. The goal is worth striving for, however, since the successful application of vision on a widespread basis seems to be intimately coupled with the ability to represent and explain the world in detail.

Bibliography

[1] P. Beaudet, *Rotationally Invariant Image Operators*, Proc. 4th International Joint Conference on Pattern Recognition, 1978, p. 579.

[2] K. S. Fu, *Syntactic Methods in Pattern Recognition,* New York: Academic Press, 1974.

[3] J. L. Mundy, *Reasoning About 3-D Space With Algebraic Deduction*, Proc. 3rd International Symposium on Robotics Research, p. 117, 1986.

[4] J. L. Mundy and G. B. Porter, *A Three Dimensional Sensor Based on Structured Light*, in *Three-Dimensional Machine Vision*, Takeo Kanade, Editor, Kluwer Academic Pub., 1987.

[5] *Automatic Visual Inspection of Blind Holes in Metal Surfaces,* Proc. IEEE Conf. on Pattern Recognition and Image Processing, p. 83, 1979.

A Perspective on Machine Vision at General Motors

Wayne Wiitanen
Computer Science Department
General Motors Research Laboratories

1 Introduction

This survey of past work and present research must necessarily be restricted to a rather small part of GM (a rather large corporation): work flowing out of General Motors Research Laboratories' Machine Perception group. Involvement in machine vision is very widespread within the Corporation and in the vision companies in which GM has an interest. Within the corporation itself one finds at the Research Laboratories work in machine vision being conducted in the Computer Science, Mathematics, Engineering Mechanics, and Instrumentation Departments. At GM's Advanced Engineering Staff machine vision work is carried out by the Machine Intelligence group, and at GM-Hughes a vast amount of research is conducted in machine vision. Let me confine my remarks to work coming out of the Machine Perception group at the GM Research Laboratories.

2 GMR Systems

For nearly two decades General Motors Research Laboratories has been active in machine vision. In a memorandum issued in 1967, Joseph Olsztyn remarked that "progress continues to be slow ... in rapid processing by a computer" — and today the same lament is still heard! Early work was centered around using binary images, structured light, and two-dimensional gray-level images for industrial parts recognition. Several research projects have lead to successful applications, specifically, Sight-1, Consight, Keysight, etc., have been installed in GM factories. (References to the open literature describing these systems, and the corresponding GMR report numbers will be found at the end of this paper.)

One of the earliest successes of machine vision to come out of GM Research Laboratories was the Sight-1 system of Michael Baird. The purpose of this computer vision system was to locate and inspect integrated circuit chips for automatic alignment during various manufacturing processes at the GM Delco Electronics Division. This system was installed in 1977 and has led to many related applications that are in use today. Working with 50x50 digitized images the strategy was to determine the orientation of a Darlington chip by using gradient direction methods. Possible corners of the chip were located by means of corner template. Actual corners are found by exhaustively fitting an exact template, reflecting the geometrical constraints of the chip, to candidate corners. Only those corners in the correct geometric relationship would be selected as actual ones. Chip position and integrity can now be assessed [1].

Consight, a commercially available licensed product of GM, is a vision-based robot system that picks up parts randomly placed on a moving conveyor belt. The vision subsystem, operating in a visually noisy environment typical of manufacturing plants, determines the position and orientation of parts on the belt. A robot tracks the parts and transfers them to a predetermined location. Consight systems are easily retrainable for a wide class of complex curved parts and have been installed in several plants for production use. The function of the vision system is two-fold: object detection and position determination. A linear array camera and a structured light source are used to create a set of descriptive measures that can be used to identify the part and determine its position, described as (x,y,theta) values. The line-image of the part under the camera is sampled at belt-encoder determined intervals and the statistics for the part silhouette updated. Once this is done the line image is no longer required. Part location and orientation is then used to inform the part handling robot [4]. A typical system is running at a General Motors foundry in St. Catherines, Ontario, sorting bell housings for a truck differential.

Applications such as those just described are typical of today's installations. They share certain generic properties: first, application specific engineering. That is to say, each new application requires a unique engineering solution. This includes a suitable hardware configuration and usually custom-made software. Usually each new application requires systems integration: hardware acquired from several vendors, and software to link it together.

The second generic property is that time is required to learn about new technology. With the current rate of development for new algorithms, new cameras, new image-processing hardware, and new micro-computers, machine-vision engineers are hard pressed to keep abreast of appropriate technology. This is a generic problem in nearly every area of engineering.

Current research in General Motors Research Laboratories' Programmable Automation group is motivated by technical shortcomings of currently available technology. Several factors motivate research projects, and among these are issues of cost/performance. We seek hardware and software systems that provide the greatest flexibility and highest performance per dollar expended.

Another is a strong need for ease of programming and reprogramming applications. In this area we are interested in very high-level languages for problem specification, libraries of well-debugged generic operators that can be combined easily by a nonexpert into a functional machine-vision system. The prospect of using expert systems to aid in selection of hardware and software for specific machine-vision problems is quite exciting.

Systems that are easy to use by production engineers and factory personnel are needed. In this area we are interested in menu-driven sorts of systems. An example is an image-processing system developed at General Motors Research Laboratories for internal use.

New methods are needed that allow one to work with generic objects that may be easily-joined to simplify the task of systems engineering. Appropriate areas of interest here are object-oriented programming, especially languages that provide inheritance, message-passing, and real-time facilities.

Research in progress at GMR falls into several categories that are intended to address generic problems at GM. The entire flavor of the research work is system-oriented. Two areas of special interest may be singled out: sensor-based robot control, and machine vision. The first of these is supported in large measure by the second, and I will confine the bulk of my remarks to the machine vision research.

We are concerned with three major disciplines in machine vision at GMR: hardware, methodology, and software. In the area of hardware development two projects deserve mention: binary image correlation, and gray level edge-detection.

In one project a parallel/pipelined processor, called Multi-match, has been developed for visual object recognition. It detects the position and orientation of the top workpiece in case of overlapped workpieces. The processor consists of as real-time edge detector and a high-speed image correlator. The real-time edge detector detects contours of workpieces at the video rate of a solid-state TV camera. It is relatively insensitive to changes in ambient light through the use of a logarithmic Sobel operator instead of a standard one. The high-speed image correlator detects the position and orientation of the top workpiece having a complete contour without any hidden portion. This is done by correlating the edged binary image with a series of stored templates having known orientations. Correlation is done on binary images. Parallel and pipelined concepts are applied to make the image correlator carry out more than 100 million pixel-level operations per second [5,6].

Methodology is represented by four studies: Gaussian-based smoothing and edge detection, regression-based curve fitting based on edges in an image, surface reconstruction, and neural modeling.

Studies on surface reconstruction are being carried forward by Paul Besl [2], and a summary of his work with Prof. Jain appears in these proceedings.

A method for fitting linearly parameterizable curves without prior classification of edge data based on regression updating theory has been studied by David S. Chen [3]. A statistical test is applied to obtain a small subset of the total edge data belonging to a hypothesized model. The model is first trained with selected data. The remainder of the data is then iteratively tested for goodness of fit to the model. The model is updated with only the most qualified edge data. By repeatedly applying this procedure to the data excluded from the previous fitting, all of the underlying curves can be detected. The major feature that distinguishes this method from others is that classifying edge data prior to fitting is not required. Three advantages of this approach are: 1) the fitting error is minimized over the choice of both data and model; 2) the computational complexity increases only linearly with the size of the data set; and 3) the method can be extended readily to detecting 3-dimensional surfaces with range data.

Richard Young has long been interested in primate vision, and is pursuing studies involving Gaussian derivative models for biological and machine vision. Specifically, he has studied a new operator for early machine vision based on his study of the primate retina. A Laplacian of a Gaussian term plus an additional Gaussian term were required to describe the shapes of the receptive fields of ganglion cells in the foveal region of primate retina. He calls this new operator a "Helmholtzian of a Gaussian". In the major class of ganglion cells, this operator could be formed by a newly recognized neural mechanism called a difference of offset Gaussians (or DOOG) mechanism. The difference of Gaussians (or DOG) mechanism describes other classes of ganglion cells. A machine implementation of this new operator exhibits partial deblurring, noise suppression, excellent color segmentation and complete information transmission to higher processing levels [7,8].

Neural modeling is an area of research that is rapidly approaching epidemic proportions in the computer science community. Research in this area at GMR is concerned at the moment with providing a user-oriented modeling environment. This environment consists of several subsystems:

1. Continuous systems simulator

2. Neuromime design tool

3. Network design method and compiler

4. Network activity monitoring and display system

5. Signal analysis package

integrated into a top-level interactive control system.

Once models have been studied under simulation conditions, silicon compilers are available to implement models in analog hardware. It seems clear that neural models and subsequent hardware derived from such models are valuable for machine vision because we have excellent examples of the efficiency of low-level processing methods in both primates and insects. One finds, for example, center-surround (difference of Gaussians) in both the primate retina and the optic lobe of the honeybee. Finding identical mechanisms is such disparate phyla strongly suggests that center-surround mechanisms are appropriate and fundamental mechanisms for initial analysis of a general environment (as opposed to a highly controlled and rigidly specified artificial environment for which special low level processing may be more efficient).

Neural modeling has been of interest to to biologists and some mathematicians since the early 1940s. The following is a brief survey of the kinds of models found in the recent literature, classified into rather general areas. Papers included in this survey have not been restricted to those having explicit networks; any purporting to describe the behavior of some neural network in a formal and precise way have been included.

- Anuran visual system (2)
- Associative learning / memory (8)
- Attention (2)
- Brain theory (general) (4)
- Cat retina (4)
- Catfish retina (3)
- Cerebellum (4)
- Clustering / categorization (2)
- Cognition (1)

- Color vision (2)
- Encoding (1)
- Generalization (1)
- Hardware (3)
- Holographic memory model (4)
- Lateral inhibition (3)
- Learning nets (12)
- Memory (8)
- Movement/motion (5)
- Network analysis and dynamics (8)
- Network ontogenesis (4)
- Network identification (5)
- Networks, abstract and general (7)
- Neurolinguistics (1)
- Neuromimes (16)
- Oculomotor system (3)
- Operant conditioning / Conditioning (3)
- Optimization (1)
- Oscillators / pacemakers (2)
- Pattern recognition (11)
- Perception (2)
- Projections (mappings) (6)
- Punishment and avoidance (1)
- Retina, generally (10)
- Retina, modeling (3)

- Self-organization (1)

- Sensori-motor control (7)

- Small (simple) nets (2)

- Speech (1)

- Tectum (1)

- Thalamus (1)

- Turtle retina (1)

- Vertebrate retina (3)

- Vision models (general) (13)

- Visual cortex (14)

- Visual preception (1)

- Visual space (1)

The number of papers categorized is 198 in 46 subject areas! Clearly there is an enormous amount of work being done here and neural modeling represents a fertile area of research.

Research in software for machine vision is found in projects dealing with multi-computer coordination and networking, an image processing system for image research studies, and a graphical editor/interface for defining systems having parallel operations of robots and vision systems.

3   Future Directions for Machine Vision

It appears to me that a profitable future direction for machine vision would be one in which there is less dependency on the computational aspects vision and takes a deeper look the model provided by nature: animal vision. Several suggestions can be extracted from what is known about animal vision:

1. *Don't mimic the implementation of the optics*

   The reason for this is that as a precision optical instrument, the vertebrate eye leaves much to be desired. Most eyes do not focus properly, have irregularities that cause blurring, refract red and blue light differently. With modern materials for lens construction it would seem evident that we need not mimic nature here.

2. *An hexagonal packing of receptors is highly efficient*

   Hexagonal packing leads to certain computation conveniences; and a receptive field size that increases with eccentricity provides a convenience under the complex log mapping found from lateral geniculate body to visual cortex in primates.

3. *Difference of Gaussians (DOG) as principal receptive field output*

   This transform reduces blur, removes noise, and retains maximal information about the original scene. It should be done in parallel by a dedicated chip and the result converted to a raster image only at the last moment.

4. *Log-linear intensity reduction*

   This transformation, done at the retinal level in primates, compresses a large dynamic range into a smaller one, thereby minimizing the effects of changes in ambient lighting.

5. *Ego-centered coordinates*

   A convenient coordinate system is that centered about the fovea. This point of view has been adequately discussed by Jain and others. It provides a system that under the (approximate) complex log transformation translates a polar coordinate system into a rectangular one in which dilation in the visual field becomes translation along the ln(r) axis, and rotation about the center of the ego-centered polar coordinate system becomes translation along the i-theta axis.

6. *Make receptive field sizes larger as one moves towards the periphery*

   This suggests that not all regions of a visual field are equally

important. The central, high-resolution (foveal) region is good
for detail, the peripheral regions for movement into the visual
field. Having receptive field sizes increase exponentially with
eccentricity from the fovea means that under the complex log
transform what would be logarithmic compression of the radius
becomes a linear scale.

7. *Orientation classification (10 degrees)*
   Classification of orientation at this resolution is commonly seen
   in primate visual cortex. One might want to pursue the indications of biology in this respect.

8. *Binocular interactions*
   Left-eye and right-eye matching receptive fields map to adjacent structures (lamination). Here again is a suggestion from
   what we know about binocular interactions in primates as an
   area for research in machine vision.

Bibliography

[1] M. Baird. *SIGHT-1: A Computer Vision System for Automated
    IC Chip Manufacture.* IEEE Trans. Systems, Man, and Cyber-
    netics SMC-8, 1978, p. 133–139.

[2] P. J. Besl, and R. C. Jain. *Segmentation through symbolic sur-
    face primitives.* Proceedings of Computer Vision and Pattern
    Recognition Conference, (June 22–26, Miami, Fla.) IEEE-CS,
    NY, 1986.

[3] D. Chen. *A regression updating approach for detecting multi-
    ple curves.* Proceedings of 2nd World Conference on Robotics
    Research, (August 18–21, Scottsdale, Arizona) RI/SME, MS86–
    764, 1986.

[4] Holland, SW, L. Rossol and M. R. Ward. *CONSIGHT-1: A
    Vision-Controlled Robot System for Transferring Parts from
    Belt Conveyors.* In Computer Vision and Sensor-Based Robots
    edited by G. G. Dodd and L. Rossol. Plenum p 81–100, 1979.

[5] I. Masaki. *Parallel/Pipelined Processor Dedicated to Visual Recognition.* Proceedings, IEEE International Conf. on Robotics and Automation, St. Louis, Mo., 1985, p. 100–107.

[6] I. Masaki. *Modular Multi-resolution Vision Processor.* Proceedings, IEEE International Conf. on Robots and Automation, San Francisco, CA, 1986, p. 454–459.

[7] R. Young. *The Gaussian Derivative Model for Machine and Biological Image Processing.* In Electronic Imaging 85, Springfield Va: Society of Photographic Scientists and Engineers, 1985, p. 64–70.

[8] R. Young. *Simulation of Human Retina Function with the Gaussian Derivative Model.* In Proc. IEEE Computer Society Conf. on Computer Vision and Pattern Recognition, 1986, p. 564–569.

Industrial Machine Vision: Where Are We? What Do We Need? How Do We Get It?

Mark A. Lavin
Automation Research Department
IBM Research Division, Yorktown

Abstract

Over the past ten years, machine vision has evolved rapidly, with vision system prices falling while their performance and function increased. This has led to significant use of machine vision in Manufacturing, but that use is nowhere near the optimistic predictions of a few years ago. In order to realize its full potential, machine vision must enable qualitative changes in products and manufacturing processes. This paper will present several examples, and then discuss what advances in machine vision technology are needed.

1 Introduction

The modern age of Industrial machine vision started around ten years ago, marked by the development of the SRI Vision Module [1]. Since that time, machine vision has come to be used fairly widely in Manufacturing. Probably the major reason for this has been the decrease in machine vision system costs, at the same time that performance and function were increasing. These factors, in turn, are the result of the general evolution of computer hardware and software in the past decade.

However, the growth of Industrial machine vision has not kept pace with the rosy predictions of a few years ago (as those involved in

current, and late, machine vision start-up companies are well aware).
Why hasn't machine vision realized its full potential? In this paper,
I will explore this question, starting in the next section by trying
to describe the current use of machine vision. Then, I will describe
"what is needed" in terms of user requirements. Finally, I will suggest
a number of machine vision technology advances that are needed to
meet those user requirements.

Before I proceed, though, I want to make several disclaimers
about this paper:

1. It's "industry-centric:" I am discussing industrial machine vision, as opposed to image understanding, or automatic land
   vehicle guidance, or medical image processing. The "industrial" aspect presents some constraints, notably of cost, but
   also allows some simplification of the vision problems, because
   it's generally possible to control the visual environment to some
   extent.

2. It's "computer-centric:" I will be focussing on uses of machine vision in the computer and electronics industry (where I
   work), which will tend to emphasize some applications of machine vision (e.g., two-dimensional pattern inspection) while
   de-emphasizing others (e.g., three-dimensional assembly guidance).

3. It's "IBM-centric" and "Lavin-centric:" Consequences of who
   I am and where I work. This paper should not be viewed
   as a broad-based, objective survey of machine vision in the
   computer and electronics industries, but rather a distillation of
   my experiences in trying to develop and deploy machine vision
   in IBM.

2   Where Are We?

In this section, I will describe the current state of machine vision
in manufacturing industry, by listing a number of typical applications, and then categorizing current machine vision use along several
dimensions.

2.1 Applications

Here are some examples of where machine vision is being used in manufacturing today:

Part-number reading
> Bar-code and OCR character readers are used for reading part and serial numbers on parts and containers, for routing and for controlling test and assembly equipment.

Printed circuit pattern inspection
> A number of experimental and commercial systems have been developed to inspect printed circuit patterns on bare boards and substrates for "hard" and potential defects like shorts, line-width reductions, extraneous material, etc. [2].

Part acquisition
> A number of laboratory systems have been developed to determine the identity, position and orientation (2D and 3D) of parts so that they could be grasped by a robot, although only a few such systems (notably CONSIGHT [3]) have been put into practical use.

Electronic component placement guidance
> Some of the new generation of component insertion machines include machine vision capabilities for determining overall board registration. As I'll discuss below, there is a significant opportunity to use machine vision to precisely guide the placement of each individual component.

$2\frac{1}{2}$-D dimensional measurement (macro and micro)
> There are several commercial systems for performing dimensional measurement of mechanical parts, with some limitations on the ability to measure dimensions along arbitrary axes. Many of these systems use "vision" in only a limited sense, and are based on direct range sensors like "Yaser radar."

Surface finish inspection
> Machine vision is being used to check the uniformity of texture

and color of painted surfaces, optical components, and precisely
machined mechanical parts; an example of the latter is the
inspection of magnetic disks and recording heads [4].

Assembly step verification
machine vision is used in a number of ad hoc applications to
check for the presence and configuration of parts in an assembly. Perhaps the best known example is the GM KEYSIGHT
system [5], which checks for the presence of retaining clips on
automobile engine valve stems.

Electronic component verification
Closely related to assembly step verification, electronic component verification is used to check the presence, identity, and
position of electronic components on a circuit board. As I'll
discuss below, this may be an example of a machine vision
problem that is best solved by eliminating the need for it.

Integrated circuit critical-dimension measurement
Optical and machine vision techniques are used to check the
2D dimensions and thickness of IC masks and patterns for the
purpose of process control. Machine vision is also coming into
use for detecting qualitative defects in ICs, and its use will
likely grow as feature sizes shrink so that small defects become
more significant.

Print quality monitoring
IBM uses a number of internally-developed and commercial
machine vision systems to check the quality of printed output
from printers and typewriters to ensure conformance to certain
subjective standards for "contrast" and "legibility".

Part integrity checking
Machine vision is used in a number of applications to detect qualitative flaws (cracks, pits, voids, scuffs) in mechanical parts. Probably the most sophisticated example of this is
a model-driven system for inspecting turbine blades developed
and used by GE [6].

Guidance for welding, painting, gluing, machining

Machine vision can be used to "track" (usually in an offline training phase) the 3D trajectory of a weld seam to guide a robot carrying a welding torch or other continuous process tool.

Solder joint inspection

Machine vision systems have been developed to inspect solder joints on pin-through-hole component leads for voids, cracks, pinholes, etc., and commercial systems for inspecting surface-mount component solder joints (some employing X-ray imaging techniques) are starting to come into use.

2.2   Dimensions of Current Machine Vision Use

In addition to listing example applications, I can describe current machine vision use in terms of several dimensions. Some of these pertain to the machine vision systems:

Fixed application vs. general-purpose

Some systems are designed to handle a single application (e.g., the OTS system [7], for printed circuit inspection), while other systems, by analogy with general-purpose computers, attempt to provide a complete set of capabilities that would support a wide range of applications. The greater cost of fixed application systems – they have to be built "from the ground up" for each new application – is often justified by the economic impact of the application.

Software vs. hardware

In many early industrial machine vision systems (e.g., the SRI Vision Module [1]), only the image acquisition was performed in hardware; all subsequent processing was done with a general-purpose computer. This has changed, so that today most Industrial vision system perform at least some of their operations (e.g., contrast enhancement, frame subtraction, edge enhancement, thresholding, etc.) in special-purpose, video-rate hardware; the main reason for this has been the growth of IC technology, particularly the capability of designing custom VLSI quickly and (relatively) cheaply.

Cost-driven vs. performance-driven
Some machine vision systems are designed to minimize cost, in order to be usable for "low-end" applications. These are typically implemented as one or two cards that plug into a personal- or micro-computer bus, and rely heavily on the hardware and software of their host system. At the other end of the scale are systems designed to provide maximum performance (e.g., processing at a rate limited by the image sensor), irrespective of cost. The latter are typically hardware-intensive and handle a fixed application.

Perhaps more significant are the dimensions that categorize how machine vision applications are developed:

Programmed vs. taught vs. automatically generated
One of the great attractions of the SRI Vision Module [1] was that it could be "taught" to recognize parts by showing showing a series of samples. Even more attractive would be systems that do not even need to be taught, and which would automatically generate their application programs; for example, we defined (but did not implement) a system for generating dimensional measurement applications from CAD models of parts [8]. In practice, though, many of the current machine vision systems have to be explicitly programmed.

By "vision experts" vs. "application experts"
Today, most machine vision applications are developed by people whose major expertise lies in vision rather than the domain of the application (e.g., metallurgy and material science, for inspection of metal castings).

By technology developer vs. "end-user"
Similarly, most machine vision applications are developed by the same people who develop the systems they're implemented on. Unlike the computer industry, "system houses" for vision have not yet emerged.

There is an important message behind these latter dimensions: today, the set of vision practitioners is limited to the expert developers of vision systems. This, in turn, has limited the spread of machine vision in industry.

3   What Do We Need?

Having categorized the current state of machine vision use in industry, I now want to discuss what is needed to make it more useful. Industry needs machine vision technology

1. that lets us do what we have to do faster, better, cheaper, and sooner

2. that lets us do things we couldn't do (or didn't even know we wanted to)

3. that is subject to practical constraints (the HARD TRUTHS).

These are "motherhood" statements, so axiomatic that they need not (cannot) be defended logically. What I want to do instead is give some anecdotal evidence, starting with the "hard truths" and then presenting some examples of how machine vision could let us "do things we couldn't do...".

3.1   The Hard Truths

As a developer of machine vision technology, trying to "sell" that technology to manufacturing users, I find that my Truth ("programmable machine vision") is not their Truth ("we need to make product X quickly, at minimum cost"). In [9], I discussed a number of "hard truths," which I'll summarize here:

Flexible automation isn't
   Most programmable robots, lacking sensors, require hard tooling in the form of fixtures and feeders.

There are no "vision engineers"
   (Probably an overstatement) There are relatively few manufacturing engineers trained or experienced in machine vision.

Machine vision is "in" (beware!)

It's widely (and superficially) described in the trade and popular press, leading to unrealistic expectations.

Money talks

Surprise! The business of business is business.

Technology isn't the answer

We can't simply wait for 16Mbyte rams or 1 micron CMOS, because many of the problems we're attacking (e.g., IC inspection) scale with the technology itself.

Vision development time is getting squeezed

As computers join other electronic "commodities", market pressures require faster introduction of products.

We're reaching critical barriers

For example, when IC features shrink below one micron, we can no longer use light for photolithography or inspection; E-beams and X-rays may pose a whole new set of image processing problems.

Machine vision is a business (?)

There are a number of vendors today, so that certain problems can be regarded as "solved."

Zero defects is too many

As I'll discuss in greater detail below, being able to visually detect every defective part may not be cost effective if yields are too low.

"Real-time" systems aren't

I'll discuss this point below, as well.

The "90/10" problem: one of Murphy's laws

the last 10machine vision applications, this "10step of integrating vision with the rest of a manufacturing system.

The "Oh, by the way . . . " phenomenon

You know this one, too, if you've ever tried to do a real application: two days before the system is supposed to go into production use, the user comes up to you and says "Oh, by the way, we've changed the product slightly so that the leads are bent under the package, so you can't see them. Is that a problem?"

Politics

For example, an organization that fabricates a component may not support installation of a machine vision system, which can only reduce yield; furthermore, they get no credit if "downstream quality" improves.

3.2 Some Examples of How Machine Vision Can('t) Win

In this section, I present several examples of how machine vision does(n't) meet the needs of Industry.

Endpoint sensing for electronic assembly

The task of *electronic assembly* is ubiquitous in the computer and electronics Industry (for example, IBM has something like twenty plants throughout the world that have electronic assembly lines). Basically, that task consists of placing electronic components (e.g., dual-in-line, or DIP, packages) on printed circuit boards and attaching the electrical connection on the components (the "leads") to those on the boards (the "pads"). This is a four degree-of-freedom "pick and place" task that is within the functional capabilities of most industrial robots (although it is usually performed by specialized equipment for speed).

There is, however, a problem of accuracy, due to the relatively long chain of components (see Figure 1) through which tolerances can build up. In fact, Brennemann [10] has noted that, given the accuracy of most existing robots, the distortion of board dimensions, the variations of components, etc., it is impossible to have an electronic assembly system place components with leads on .020" (20 mil) centers within the accuracy (say q.008") that would guarantee that no lead accidentally shorts to an adjacent pad.

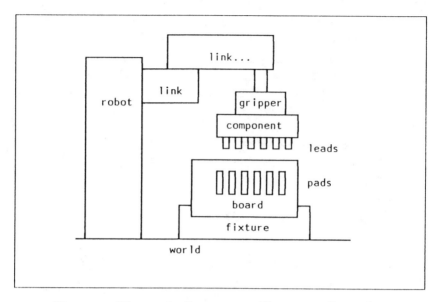

Figure 1: Electronic Component Placement Scenario.

There is a way to overcome this problem: endpoint sensing [11] can be used to directly measure the relation between leads and pads, from which we can compute the motion that the robot or other positioning mechanism would have to make to correct the position and orientation error. With this approach, lead/pad placement accuracy is limited by the local distortion of the board (at the "mount site"), the distortion of the component, the small scale accuracy (actually, linearity) of the placement mechanism, and the accuracy of the sensor itself. These are typically small enough that it's possible to assemble the 20 mil pitch components described above.

More significantly, the total error may be reduced to such an extent that it's possible to guarantee correct attachment for even smaller lead pitches. This is important because it raises the possibility of reducing lead spacing, thereby allowing both increased numbers of leads and/or decreased board area. That is, *the use of (visual) endpoint sensing enables an improvement in the product, namely, increased packaging density.* This is an example of where machine vision lets us do something we could not do before.

"But wait", you might object, "*why* machine vision? Couldn't I get the same benefit using people to align leads and pads?" Besides the cost factor, there is a speed factor: a person takes a few seconds to "land" a component using a microscope, and so cannot compete with special-purpose devices that can place up to five components per second. This raises the issue of "realtime" vision, discussed next.

Real-time vision for motion control

What is "real-time" vision, anyway? Some people's definition essentially boils down to "very fast." Many vendors of vision systems have a more specific (albeit parochial) definition: a "real-time" vision system is one capable of processing image data at TV camera rates (e.g., 10 Mpixels/second, for U.S. TV format). Probably a more useful definition of "real time vision" is: machine vision processing that's fast enough to meet the requirements of a particular application; note that "fast" may refer to *latency* (relevant for the visual servoing application described below) and/or to throughput, usually more relevant for high-volume applications like 100inspection.

Narrowing our focus to the application of vision for guidance in electronic assembly, there are still two kinds of "real time vision:"

"NEAR REAL-TIME" VISION FOR MOTION CONTROL. This case can be described by the following pseudo-code:

```
        visually determine X, Y, & theta of mount site;
        pick component, hold above mount site;
loop: visually determine X, Y, & theta of component;
        if alignment is OK, go to ok:;
        move component to correct misalignment;
        go to loop:;
ok:   done with component.
```

This kind of "real time vision" can improve the performance of the electronic assembly application under two assumptions:

- The time to acquire and process an image (including the time for the positioning mechanism to settle before a picture can be taken) is a relatively small fraction of the total component placement cycle time.

- The positioning mechanism is sufficiently repeatable and linear (and has been calibrated for scale, offset, etc.) so that the corrective motion can be reliably calculated from the "visual error" (otherwise the "hunting loop" will be executed many times).

REAL-TIME VISUAL SERVOING. In this case, the "view, compute, move" loop above is moved from the application program level down into the motion control system. If the "loop time" (the time to acquire and process an image, and compute a corrective move) can be made sufficiently small, it may be possible to compensate not only for variations in the component and board, and for "static inaccuracies" of the positioning mechanism, but also for "dynamic inaccuracies" (e.g., position errors due to the vibration of the mechanism's structure). Since typical placement mechanisms have natural frequencies of 10's of Hertz, and vision system capable of providing an X, Y, theta in 10 ms. may be sufficient to support this "visual servoing."

This rate (called "faster than real time" by some vendors) CAN be achieved, as demonstrated by Gary Bishop's 1-dimensional integrated linear array/correlator, which could deliver a delta-position value at 1000 Hz [12]. Although his work relied heavily on the use of a clever VLSI-based processor, it also exploited a key observation: if the "frame rate" is sufficiently high, the amount of change from image to image is greatly reduced, so that very simple (and hence efficient) "tracking" schemes can be used: i.e., "the faster you go, the faster you can go."

Of course, there is a limiting factor (one which drove Bishop to design his own sensor array): the speed with which image data can be taken out of the sensor. For machine vision systems based on the use of full fields of standard TV images, this factor limits the processing rate to be no more than 30 Hz.

This limitation notwithstanding, real-time vision, combined with endpoint sensing as described above, provides us with two qualitative breakthroughs in electronic assembly:

- We can place components very accurately, allowing us to reduce the dimensions of component leads and thus achieve higher i/o density.

- We can compensate for variations in the placement mechanism, allowing us to use very high speed, but not very high accuracy or rigidity, placement devices, which reduces cycle time and equipment cost.

Furthermore, with very accurate, very fast positioning mechanisms, we can start to imagine other applications besides electronic assembly, such as micro-welding and micro-cutting used for repair of high-density electronic packages and even chips. Thus, we have an example of how vision can let us do things we could not (or would not choose to) do before.

The component verification problem

OK, two winners so far. Now for a loser (or, at best, a non-finisher): Probably the majority of questions I hear from potential machine vision users in IBM concern the problem of *component verification*, which can include:

- Verifying that components are present

- Verifying that the RIGHT components are present

- Verifying that the gross orientation, position, and fine orientation of the component is within some specified bounds

- Verifying component integrity (e.g., checking for bent component leads)

Users would like to perform these kinds of verification after placement but before joining (e.g., wave soldering), so that placement errors can be detected and corrected(1)

There is an effective *ad hoc* solution to this problem for pin-in-hole components (e.g., DIPs): look for evidence of component leads on the back side of the board. The problem is considerably harder for surface-mounted (SMT) components, although a number of approaches have been investigated:

One might observe here that a successful vision-guided electronic assembly system as described above would eliminate a number of the types of errors defined here; however, even a well-placed component can be dislodged by subsequent placement or handling motion.

Image comparison

Subtract an image of a "golden" populated board from an image of the board to be verified; discrepancies indicate placement, etc., errors. *This method fails because many acceptable variations (e.g., package color, component id placement, etc.) result in significant image differences.*

Grayscale vision

Use edge operators to locate boundaries of components, compare with design specifications. *Again, variations among components of the same type (e.g., matte vs. glossy packages, with square vs. beveled edges) result in significant differences in the derived features; also, noise due to component markings and background confounds feature-linking.*

Pseudo 3D vision

Use multiple oblique illuminators to cast multiple shadows, which can be "unioned" to indicate component silhouettes. Densely packed components can hide or change the shape of shadows; entire boards, rather than components, must be "taught."

Hacks

- "Paint" the board to improve contrast with components.
- Mark components the "right way."

The trouble with the last two "hack" solutions (from a machine vision expert's point of view) is that they overly simplify the vision problem. In particular, we might expect that by using a suitable marking scheme, it would be possible to derive not only component identity but also position and orientation using a "vision system" not much more complicated than a bar-code reader. Of course, for this scheme to work, it is necessary for component suppliers and purchasers to agree on a marking standard. The Automated Vision Association (AVA), working with ANSI and with makers and users of electronic components and equipment, is in the process of developing such a standard.

The point here is that component verification is a questionable application to undertake because there are a number of obvious ways to eliminate the problem through "design for visibility."

The bin-picking problem

For many years, industrial machine vision research has pursued a "holy grail:" a solution to the *bin-picking* or *bin-of-parts* problem. We have attacked the problem in many variations:

- 2-D vs. $2\frac{1}{2}$-D vs. 3-D parts and arrangements

- Convex vs. general parts

- Separated vs. touching vs. overlapping parts

- Single vs. multiple part types

- Perfect vs. possibly-defective parts

- Ambient vs. structured illumination

The problem has continue to provoke interest, perhaps because it's so difficult for machines, or perhaps because it's so easy for people, or perhaps because it would seem to be such a useful addition to an intelligent robot. But, from the viewpoint of a hard-nosed manufacturing engineer, we need to ask "is this a real problem?" Consider:

- Many fabrication processes can produce oriented parts (e.g., Tape Automated Bonding (TAB) electronic packages).

- Expensive parts are usually shipped separated to prevent handling damage.

- Simple parts can be "singulated" (and even oriented) by mechanical feeders.

- Does anyone really mix multiple part types in one bin?

From these points, I draw the following conclusions:

- The "ecological niche" for vision-guided bin-picking is pretty narrow.

- Other domains (e.g., autonomous vehicle navigation) might be better drivers of science and technology development; this is because the visual world of such domains (unlike a manufacturing environment) cannot be controlled.

- This illustrates the more general problem for machine vision: users will always (correctly) prefer to make the problem go away rather than solving it.

When is inspection useful?

Probably the major use of machine vision in IBM today is for *inspection*, particularly of electronic components and packages. In spite of this, I have a sense that inspection is viewed in some areas as a "regrettable necessity." The reason for this might be explained by the overly-simplified model of inspection shown in Figure 2. In this model (often called a "screen"), every part is inspected, and parts that the inspection system classifies as defective are scrapped. In this regime, inspection can improve quality (by screening out bad parts) but only at the cost of reduced yield; other things being equal, no one wants to introduce a process that reduces yield. In addition, the costs of many kinds of inspection tend to scale as some power of the technological parameters.

$$\left(e.g., \frac{pixels}{chip} = \frac{die\ area}{line\ width^2}\right)$$

Figure 3 shows a more realistic model of Inspection. In this model, bad parts can be reworked and/or subjected to other inspection processes, in addition to being scrapped. More important, inspection information can be used in a number of ways in addition to screening or sorting parts:

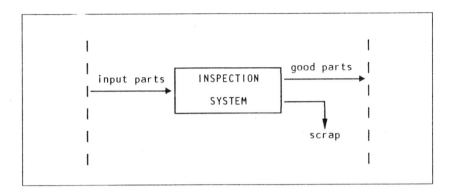

Figure 2: Inspection: Simple Model

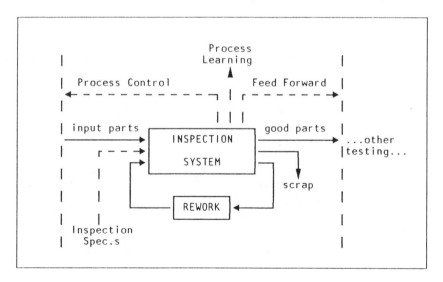

Figure 3: Inspection: Better Model

1. It can be fed forward to control subsequent processes (e.g., for rework).

2. It can be fed back "instantaneously" to adjust the processes whose products are being inspected (e.g., to control the temperature of a wave-solder system, or signal a tool change on a drilling machine).

3. It can be fed back "strategically" for the purpose of *process learning*; for example, historical data on defects might be used to develop material-handling regimes that introduce less contamination.

This model of inspection is far more palatable. Point 1 reduces yield loss, point 2 helps maintain yield, and point 3 helps accelerate the improvement of yield as new products and processes are being introduced. This latter aspect is particularly important as we try to decrease product development cycle time.

This preferred model of inspection, however, places several additional demands on a machine vision system used for inspection:

- It must be able to report parametric information, not just "go/no-go" results. Defects must be classified, measured, and localized.

- The kinds of inspection that are performed (and even the parts themselves) must be tailored to process control/learning. For example, a printed circuit inspection system must report not only defects but average line width; in addition, it may be desirable to introduce test sites, where process deviations produce more readily detectable changes.

The latter demand is significant because it implies that the development of a machine vision application for "smart" inspection must be integrated into the development of the manufacturing process as a whole and even into the design of the product. "Stand-alone" machine vision cannot be used nearly as effectively for inspection.

Summary

The examples above were intended to illustrate three aspects of "what we (manufacturing) need (and don't need) from machine vision:"

- Machine vision must enable qualitative (not just quantitative) improvement; it's particularly good to improve the product, rather than just the manufacturing process.

- Machine vision should not be applied to problems that can be solved (or obviated) by taking advantage of the constrained environment in manufacturing.

- Machine vision is most useful for manufacturing when it is integrated into the overall development of processes and products.

4 How Do We Get It?

What should the inventors and suppliers of machine vision technology be working on to meet the needs of industry?

4.1 An Integrated machine vision System

It's necessary to have a machine vision system integrated with other parts of manufacturing systems, in two senses:

- Integration with execution system(s): This will help address the "90/10" problem cited above by allowing the vision part of an application to be more easily connected with the non-vision parts like robot manipulation, database access, plant floor communication, etc. It will also be necessary to tightly couple a vision system with a robot control system in order to achieve the kinds of real-time visual servoing mentioned above.

- Integration with design system(s) This will be needed as a base for automatic (model-based) application generation. It will also provide a benefit in the opposite direction (manufacturing to Design) by providing designers with information to support "design-for-visibility"

To some extent, the hardware side of the integration problem is being eased by the emergence of *de facto* standards like VME-Bus, etc. The software side is partially addressed by a concurrent emergence of software standards like UNIX (r) and C. However, I believe there is some benefit in extending "standard" programming languages through the addition of abstract data types for vision, as described in [13], since these provide additional levels of portability and expressiveness.

4.2   Scalable Hardware

As noted above, vision systems can be (crudely) divided into the cost-sensitive, low-performance, software-based systems vs. the high-performance, hardware-intensive systems. While this division allows a wide range of cost/performance to be covered, it does so at the cost of *portability*, since often the specialized architectures of the high-performance systems imply algorithmic approaches not suitable for the "low-end" systems; thus, a pattern inspection algorithm developed for simple printed circuit boards may be difficult or impossible to apply to IC masks, even though the patterns and defect types may be similar.

What is needed is an implementation that spans a wide range of performance, whose cost is proportional to performance, and which presents a common programming model across the entire performance range. One way to achieve this may be through the use of *parallelism*, in which system performance is achieved through replication of system components (e.g., mesh elements, pipeline stages, bit slices, etc.). Parallelism also allows us to get out of the dilemma that the technology we want to manufacture scales as quickly as the technology out of which we build vision systems.

Currently, there is an expanding menagerie of parallel processors (hypercubes, SIMD arrays, pipelines, as well as the *Polymorphic-torus* architecture that we have developed [14]), many intended specifically for machine vision. The main technological limitation at this point is the programming technology, since we depend on the programming system to provide a common programming model across different configurations, and to hide some of the unpleasant details of the underlying hardware.

4.3 Fast Cameras

The performance of image acquisition devices represents a bottleneck for machine vision in several respects. The real-time visual servoing application mentioned above cannot achieve the desired 100+ Hz. rates using current TV-compatible cameras. What is needed is cameras that provide faster data transfer (either through higher rates and/or parallel access to image data) and also cameras that allow "random" (or at least controlled) access to portions of the entire imaging array. In the ideal case, processing would be done on the sensor itself (exemplified by Bishop's work [12]) so that the required data rate off-chip could be considerably reduced.

Image acquisition rates are also a limiting factor for high-end inspection applications (e.g., patterned wafer inspection) in which billions to trillions of pixels must be scanned on each part. Current Scanning Electron Microscope (SEM) technology is limited to data rates on the order of 10^7 pixels per second, resulting in enormous image acquisition times even when parallel processing could provide higher processing rates.

4.4 Well-Characterized Algorithms

A study we did of machine vision use in IBM and in the electronics industry indicated that the major impediment to machine vision use is the difficulty of developing applications (vs. cost or availability of underlying technology, etc.). The major underlying cause may be a lack of people trained in both machine vision and in particular aspects of manufacturing technology to which vision is being applied.

Brian Schunck [15] has suggested that what's needed is vision algorithms that are analogous to the $5\frac{1}{4}$" Winchester disk: well-understood, with a simple, well-defined interface, available in a variety of different implementations providing a range of performance. In other words, what we seem to need is another "magic bullet" like the SRI binary region analysis algorithm, which proved enormously useful in the "early days" of industrial machine vision. The problem may be that as the field has progressed, the range of problems we want to attach has widened, so that a crisply-defined (and implemented) process like binary connectivity analysis has no current analog (for example, it's not clear how a grayscale region analyzer or line finder should really behave).

Perhaps the best we can hope for is algorithms whose behavior can be characterized (crudely) by some criteria that can be formally stated (e.g., resolution, noise sensitivity, performance, etc.) so that application generators (see below) can manipulate these descriptions in the course of helping a user synthesize an application program.

4.5   Automatic Application Generation

Perhaps the ultimate "magic bullet" would be a program that automatically synthesizes a machine vision application given a *task level* description of that application (which may include a model or example of the object to be "seen"); this is analogous to the goal of task level robot programming systems like AUTOPASS [16]. It seems implausible to fully automate the generation of all machine vision applications at this point; however, some partial approaches along several lines may be both feasible and useful:

Teaching-by-showing

We've already cited the example of the trainable part-recognizer from SRI. Another example (available commercially today) is a system that can be taught to recognize characters or conventional symbols in different styles or fonts by showing examples (either literally or through a font-definition database). Much more speculative would be inspection systems that could be taught to recognize various kinds of defects by showing examples of those defects.

Model-based geometric vision for part acquisition

Given a complete description of an object in the form of a 3D model, it should be possible to generate a program capable of recognizing that object and determining its position and orientation. Some current vision systems, such as one from GM-Fanuc [17], provide a limited capability for model-based

2D image analysis, which already relieve much of the programming task for 2D applications.

Intelligent assistant program
This lies midway between the previous two approaches. In this
case, a program would lead an application developer through
a series of experiments to try different image processing and
analysis techniques in the course of synthesizing an application. This assistant could start with something as simple as
a structured set of menus with help messages. The end point
could be "intelligent" programs that reason about sample objects and about the user's responses to suggest the most plausible alternatives at each step.

4.6   User Education

So far, I've talked about a number of ways to help vision more usable for manufacturing, in many cases by trying to circumvent the
relative scarcity of vision practitioners. Perhaps a more straightforward approach would be to meet that scarcity head-on by training
more future manufacturing engineers in the use of machine vision.
While this might appear counter-strategic (from the point of view of
insuring job security for vision hackers), I would argue that it's to
everyone's benefit: as a local discount clothing chain in the New York
area says, "an educated consumer is our best customer." Ultimately,
this is the solution to the "oh, by the way" phenomenon that all of
us have encountered at one time or another.

5   Summary

I have described some of the current uses of machine vision in Manufacturing, and also tried to explain why it is not being used as
widely as many people had predicted a few years ago. I have argued
that machine vision will gain wider acceptance when users see the
possibility of improving not only manufacturing processes, but also
the products themselves. In order to do this, it is necessary to have

machine vision systems integrated with the overall design and manufacturing process. In addition, it's important to reduce the time
and cost of developing machine vision applications, and to focus our
efforts on problems that can't be readily solved by non-vision techniques. Finally, I have suggested a number of specific things that
machine vision scientists and technologists can do to meet the needs
of manufacturing.

Bibliography

[1] Charles Rosen, David Nitzan, et. al. *Machine Intelligence Re-
search applied to Industrial Automation Eighth Report* NSF
Grant APR75–13074, SRI International, Menlo Park, CA.
September 1986.

[2] J. R. Mandeville. *Novel method for analysis of printed circuit
images* IBM Journal of Research and Development 29(1):73–86,
January 1985.

[3] Steven W. Holland, Lothar Rossol, and Mitchell R. Ward.
*Consight-1: A Vision Controlled Robot System for Transfer-
ring Parts from Belt Conveyors* George F. Dodd and Lothar
Rossol, editor, Symposium on Computer Vision and Sensor-
based Robots, Plenum Press, New York, 1979.

[4] Jorge L. C. Sanz, Dragutin Petkovic, and Kwan Y. Wong. *Image Analysis Algorithms for digital Visual Inspection of Thin-
Film Recording Heads*, in V. Cappellini and R. Marconi, editor,
Advances in Image Processing and Pattern Recognition, pages
291–295, North-Holland, Amsterdam, 1986.

[5] Wayne A. Wiitanen *A Perspective on Machine Vision Research*,
(this volume), 1988.

[6] Joseph Mundy *Machine Vision in Manufacturing — Learning
from the Past*, (this volume), 1988

[7] Mark A. West, Stephen M. DeFoster, Edwin C. Baldwin, and
Richard A. Ziegler. *Computer-Controlled Optical Testing of*

High-Density Printed-Circuit Boards, IBM Journal of Research and Development, 27(1):50–58, January 1983

[8] Roger Y. Tsai and Mark A. Lavin. *Three-Dimensional Mechanical Part Measurement using a Vision/Robot System*, IBM Research, RC 10506, May 1984

[9] Mark A. Lavin. *Research Directions.* in V. Cappellini and R. Marconi, editor, *Advances in Image Processing and Pattern Recognition*, pages 247–252, North-Holland, Amsterdam, 1986.

[10] Andrew E. Brennemann, Mark A. Lavin, and Bela L. Musits. *Sensors for electronic Assembly.* Proceedings of 1986 European conference "Putting Vision to Work", Birmingham, UK, November 24–25, 1986

[11] Russell H. Taylor, Ralph L. Hollis, and Mark A. Lavin. *Precise Manipulation with Endpoint Sensing.* IBM Journal of Research and Development, 29(4):363–376, July 1985

[12] Gary Bishop *Self-Tracker: A Smart Optical Sensor on Silicon.* PhD thesis, University of North Carolina, Chapel Hill, NC 1984.

[13] Mark A. Lavin and Larry I. Lieberman. *AVLO: A Vision Language,* IBM Research, RC 8390, August 1980.

[14] Hungwen Li and Massimo Maresca. *Polymorphic-torus Architecture for Computer Vision*, IBM Research, RC 12492, February 1987.

[15] Brian Schunck.Personal Communication, 1985

[16] Larry I. Lieberman and Michael A. Wesley. *AUTOPASS: An Automatic Programming System for computer Controlled Mechanical Assembly.* IBM Journal of Research and Development, 21(4):321–333, July 1977.

[17] GMF Robotics, GMF V-210 Grayscale Vision System, number Manual VE-0440-000, Troy, Michigan, January 1986.

Bottlenecks to Effective Application of Machine Vision — A Discussion

Chairman: J. Sklansky
University of California Irvine

Abstract

The objective of this discussion was to identify characteristics of technologies and social processes that are inhibiting the development and/or evolution of machine vision. The discussers included Robert Haralick, Ramesh Jain, Goffredo Pieroni, Azriel Rosenfeld. Jakub Segen, Steve Tanimoto, and P.S.P. Wang. In addition comments were solicited from four people in absentia: a) Mr. Robert Thomason, President of Vartec Corporation, a machine vision company in Irvine, California; b) Dr. Behnam Bavarian, Assistant Professor of Electrical Engineering at the University of California, Irvine, specializing in robotics; c) Dr. Mark Lavin, Member of Technical Staff at the Manufacturing Research Department of the IBM Research Center, Yorktown Heights, New York, and d) Dr. Dragutin Petkovic, Manager of Machine Vision Group, Computer Science Department, IBM Almaden Research Center, San Jose, California.

The suggested bottlenecks fall into five categories: 1) education and training of personnel 2) technology (which includes software, hardware, algorithms, and theory); 3) design; 4) economics; and 5) dissemination of research results. Below we summarize the comments in each of these areas.

1 Education and Training of Personnel

In the machine vision business each new application presents special requirements. The range of applications is so broad that the range of knowledge among the available application engineers is often inadequate.(RT)[1] In some instances these "engineers" are actually programmers with no training in computer vision; their supervisors also may be without such training.(RH)

There are relatively few skilled practitioners of machine vision (other than developers of the technology). Knowledge about optics and illumination is particularly rare.(ML) Computer vision is heavily populated by "hackers" in machine vision companies and by mathematicians in academia.(RJ) In the education of computer vision specialists we need to place more emphasis on fundamentals.(RH,DP) These fundamentals include sensing, optics, statistics, architectures from algorithms, and techniques for realistic experiments.(DP)

Current machine vision systems are not designed to be "user-friendly" (for "real" applications). This demonstrates a need for better training in systems software.(ML)

2 The Technology (Software, Hardware, Algorithms, Theory)

The available technology of machine vision has in some applications too little resolution and too little speed. In some applications it may lack both.(RT) Thus there is a need for the development of a) higher resolution, b) faster electronic hardware than is currently available.(BB) Image acquisition is often a serious bottleneck: TV cameras run at only 10,000 pixels per second, scanning electron microscopes are even slower. For certain real-time applications, the 60 Hz frame rate of conventional TV cameras is the limiting factor ("randomly addressable" cameras may be required).(ML)

---

[1]The initials in each pair of parentheses are those of one of the discussion participants listed in the first paragraph or – in the case of "JSk" – the discussion Chairman.

Algorithms that are sufficiently robust for machine vision applications (i.e., algorithms that can operate under a variety of illuminations, sizes of objects, orientations of objects, positions of objects, and position of camera with respect to the object) tend to be computationally intensive, and hence require specialized electronic hardware in order to be sufficiently fast. As a result there is a need for many diverse image analysis functions or preprocessing functions which must be committed to hardware if practical speeds are to be achieved.(RT)

This need exists in spite of the fact that there are many commonly accepted image analysis functions included in several commercially available image processing systems, because many of those image analysis functions either are not adequately robust and/or do not carry out the required function. For example, the IRI machine has a wide range of image-analysis functions, but this range of functions is still not adequate for all applications. Often the applications determine the appropriate image-analysis function. Among such special functions are a) data-dependent masking, b) texture detection,c) heuristic-search segmenters.(RT,JSk)

Developed algorithms should have firmly established "track records" of performance – accuracy, efficiency and a list of cases of where they do or do not work. This is not the case today. They should also be well documented, so other people can use them.(DP)

In some applications the technology provides low performance at high cost while the customers want low cost and high performance. An example of low performance is insufficient robustness. Often the parameters of the system must be tweeked at the user site, in some cases requiring a level of specialized skills which may not be available to the user.(RT)

There is inadequacy in current theories. There is paucity of well defined problems that have well defined rewards associated with them.(ST, RH) Machine vision technology lacks a solidly established body of techniques for computing geometric measurements precisely and at high speeds.(JSk)

Another problem associated with current activities on the theory of machine vision is an underlying assumption that a theory of "general" machine vision is achievable. This assumption may be false.(ST)

To define a problem well and find its solution, one usually starts with a model, e.g. an underlying joint probability distribution. Such complete models are rarely available in machine vision, and are very difficult to obtain empirically. The current trend of experimenting with various operators can be thought of as an inductive process, focused on estimating selected properties (e.g. "roadness"), which is much easier than identifying the complete model.(JSe) Therefore, we must rely on realistic large-scale experiments to verify our theories and models.(DP)

It is conceivable — but not necessarily so – that if a general vision system is made sufficiently cheap and reliable, computer hobbyists would find in machine vision an extremely attractive class of gadgets with which to experiment. If this were true, the popularity of machine vision could stimulate the entire machine vision technology. It is not clear, however, what these hobbyists would do with cheap machine vision gadgets.(ST) It was suggested that if the sensors and display resolution were sufficiently increased and made sufficiently low in cost that computer photography could be revolutionized by these hobbyists.(JSk) Combining a low cost/high performance work station, such as a Sun, with a card-based image processor (e.g. Imaging Technology or Datacube) and adding an extensive library of image operations, would create a system that is useful to the researcher and still accessible to a casual user or a hobbyist. However, the currently available image processing libraries are embedded in the wrong hardware, and can't be easily ported to such an environment.(JSe)

In many applications there is a need for sensors that can fit in a small space, for example the gripper of a robot.(BB)

3   The Design Process

Machine vision applications take too long and cost too much to develop.(ML) Usually the number of disciplines required in the design of a practical machine vision system is large. These disciplines often include mechanical handling, optics/lighting, algorithm development, hardware design, software design, system integration, and installation.(RT) The integration of these disciplines is a tough engineering task.(ML)

Machine vision systems are not set up to be easily connected (at the application level) to other subsystems; there is a "tower of Babel" of different languages, operating systems, communication protocols, etc.(ML) In too many instances the testing of a machine vision algorithm is carried out on too small a set of images – the number of images in the test set is often five or less – sometimes just one.(RH) Hence we must create and make available to the machine vision profession a large number of images in a standard data base.(RK) The time is right to push this idea of a standard image data base.(ST)

Machine vision systems must be flexible, to facilitate application development by nonexperts. Toward that end some form of self-learning (based on models and examples) could be useful.(DP)

We must develop a set of building blocks (hardware/software) for particular classes of applications – such as pattern inspection, texture inspection etc. Then, the user can use an expert system advisor as an aid in manipulating these building blocks for solving the design process.(DP)

In addition to the standard data base, we need a benchmark - - i.e., a standard set of images for testing various vision algorithms – e.g., connectivity labeling, segmentation, boundary following.(AR)

4 Economics

Machine vision systems are too slow or too expensive to be justified economically. For very cost-sensitive applications, general purpose systems costing 20-40 thousand dollars may be unacceptable. For very "high-end" applications (i.e.,costly applications, such as IC wafer inspection) current technology cannot provide adequate throughput.(ML)

Current approaches for justifying capital equipment expenditure may not correctly capture the benefits of machine vision (and, more generally, of flexible automation technology).(ML)

People are very good at some visual inspection tasks and thus tough to replace. The leverage of machine vision is to find places where vision allows the use of new processes and even product technologies (e.g., real-time endpoint sensing for control of electronic component placement may allow substantial increases in the input/output density of circuit packages).(ML)

5   Dissemination of Research Results

We need more and closer cooperation between industry and academia.(DP) The referees for machine vision journals often accept manuscripts for publication that do not include reports of vigorous testing of the vision technique described in the paper. The standards should be raised so as to require thorough experiments and clear reporting of these experiments.(RJ) We need careful and thorough evaluations of methods for various applications, supported by large scale experimental results.(DP)

Published work should be well enough documented so that others may replicate the experiments, use the algorithms for their own work, and verify the claims. (DP)

6   Acknowledgement

The Chair of this session is grateful to the participants for nearly two hours of thoughtful discussion, and to the in absentia contributors for their oral and written comments. The above material for the most part is not verbatim – rather it is an attempt at an accurate paraphrase, and has been proofed and approved by the participants.

Inference of Object Surface Structure from Structured Lighting — An Overview

J. K. Aggarwal and Y. F. Wang
Computer and Vision Research Center
The University of Texas at Austin

Abstract

In this paper, we conduct a brief survey of a special class of 3D sensing and modeling techniques, which are generally referred to as grid coding or structured light projection. In this particular class of techniques, the scene is encoded using light cast through a slide marked with spatially variant patterns. The patterns may be either parallel sets of stripes or orthogonal grids. This spatially encoded scene is then observed from one or more camera positions. Two types of analysis are possible for relating the grid coded images to the 3D configuration of the scene. First, the correspondence of features (grid lines or grid junctions) in the grid plane and the image is established. 3D positions of the encoded surface points are then recovered via triangulation if the camera and the projector have been properly registered. Second, the orientation of the projected stripes in the image plane is measured and related to the visible surface orientation and structure without the correspondence of features being established. Implementation results are provided to demonstrate the validity of the algorithms.

1   Introduction

It has long been recognized that, in the real world, objects are fundamentally three-dimensional (except, of course, for limited cases such

193

as paintings and writings where objects of interest can be represented by two-dimensional shapes). Hence, in order to facilitate the computer analysis of the structure of 3D objects in vision, robotics and factory automation applications, a three dimensional modeling scheme is essential. It is, therefore, not surprising to note that the construction and analysis of the descriptions of 3D objects have been a topic of considerable interest and importance in computer vision research yielding fruitful results.

Depending on the applications, a modeling scheme may have either a synthesis or an analysis flavor. For instance in many geometric modeling applications, 3D objects are constructed by gluing together a number of simple primitive solids according to a certain parsing rule (a synthesis approach) [1][2], with the primitive solids being instantiations of models in a pre-established library. On the other hand, from the point of view of vision and automation applications where the descriptions of real physical objects are thought, the bases for modeling are usually images which depict the object of interest from possibly a number of different directions. Hence, an analysis algorithm needs to be developed in the first place for recovering the 3D structure of the object from the images before the application of modeling schemes on the reconstructed 3D data.

It goes without saying that the analysis aspect of the modeling applications is of a greater concern to the vision community in general. Here, the goal is to infer the 3D structure of the object from the images with a reasonable degree of accuracy (a reconstruction problem), and to represent the object in a way which is suitable for computer manipulation (a representation problem). In the first stage, i.e., the reconstruction of 3D structure from 2D images, techniques reported can be loosely classified based upon the sensing mechanism used (such as passive and active techniques) and the sensing configuration assumed (monocular and binocular approaches) according to the taxonomy proposed by Jarvis [3].

Passive monocular approaches in general rely on the change of image features with respect to different perspectives and illuminance conditions, or on some special assumptions about the class of objects being imaged. Various shape-from-shading techniques relate the perceived image illuminance to the characteristics of the light source, image geometry and surface properties such as reflectivity. Shape from texture or regular patterns exploits the change of the shape of known patterns to different perspectives. Surface structure can be reconstructed if enough knowledge about the properties of the object structure is available or if some constraints can be imposed on the surface reconstruction process. For example, scenes containing only polyhedral objects can be analyzed through junction dictionary and constraint satisfaction. Also, algorithms have been developed to reconstruct the 3D structure from 2D projections which maximize the regularity of the reconstructed surfaces.

Passive binocular methods, also referred to as stereopsis, use the shift of the projective positions of a point in two distinct images to infer the depth of that space point. The process involves first extracting features in both images, registering them by resolving the correspondence of features in the two images, and recovering the position of the features in three space. Features can be zero crossings (points of zero second derivatives), corners, edges or high-level semantic constructs.

Although a number of ingenious algorithms for shape reconstruction and analysis have been developed based upon passively sensed images, these types of techniques do suffer from some nontrivial difficulties. To name a few of them:

1. Images register the sensor response to the scene radiation. As mentioned before, a variety of factors affect this image formation process: the characteristics of the light source; medium attenuation, scattering and diffusion; surface reflectivity and orientation; and the imaging geometry. When the images are analyzed and the surface orientation in three-space is sought, the interaction of all these factors has to be separated and individual effects isolated. The analysis is not always possible with only a single image frame and without accurate modeling of the light source and the sensing configuration, as well as reliable knowledge about the surface reflectivity of the object being imaged.

2. Analyzing change due to perspectives exploits only the imaging geometry and the information about the shape of the surface patterns or masking. However, all objects do not have textural surfaces. Textures, natural ones in particular, are hard to characterize and use in the shape-from-shading techniques. Furthermore, the masking on the surfaces has to be relatively uniform and the spatial arrangement of primitives must be known *a priori*. Change in the shape of the textural elements across the image has to be due to the change of perspectives and not due to the change in spatial masking which is not totally unlikely.

3. Images from a single perspective in many situations simply do not convey enough information for an accurate quantitative description of the scene. In many junction labeling schemes, the qualitative descriptions - such as the concavity and convexity of the edges - can be deduced but not the precise numerical measurements such as lengthes and orientations. Generally speaking, quantitative descriptions demand assumptions (e.g. observed objects being in a special class or symmetry of the object surface structures) which may not hold true in all situations.

4. In stereopsis, although the process of recovering the position of registered features through triangulation is quite mechanical, registration of features is nevertheless nontrivial. Feature matching is further complicated by possible omission of features from one of the images due to the change of the viewing fields of the two cameras and by inclusion of extraneous features from other objects due to occlusion. The search space grows rapidly with the addition of features to be matched. Computation may become excessive and processing time may become too lengthy for real time applications.

Finally, accurate detection and extraction of features for image analysis are not always automatic and carefree in passive sensing where no control over the lighting is allowed. The performance of the algorithm and the accuracy of the results may degrade significantly due to the error in preprocessing and feature extraction.

More recently, trinocular vision has become quite popular. Although an extra image increases the complexity of processing and analysis, it also provides an additional degree of constraint against which the hypothesized correspondence can be checked. One does have to note other possibilities in constructing 3D description from 2D images using passive sensing principle. One such work has been described in detail by Martin and Aggarwal where occluding contours from multiple views are used. If the interframe transform is specified, the occluding contours observed from multiple viewpoints can be projected back into space, to intersect and create the bounding volume structure. This surface reconstruction process uses only silhouettes and is therefore less sensitive to noise. The technique of back projection with volume intersection is easy to implement and is general enough to produce a 3D scene description from various 2D representations. For example, this technique has been applied to generate octrees from quadtrees and to generate 3D rectangular parallelepiped coded structure from 2D rectangular coded images.

A large degree of the difficulties mentioned above stems from the way the images are sensed and acquired. In passive sensing techniques, one does not have the freedom to control the environments. Which is to say that the analysis is based upon the ambient light reflection off the object surfaces and whatever information contains therein. The perceived image intensity is determined by a variety of factors among which the effects due to surface orientation and structure have to be isolated and analyzed. Passive sensing is mandatory in natural scene analysis and some military applications where manipulation of the lighting and sensing configurations is not feasible. However, the ability to control the scene illuminance through the manipulation of the light source and the imaging geometry is highly preferable in other industrial and automation applications. Moreover, even though the passive sensing principles are widely adopted in the animal kingdom, using active mechanisms to sense the environments is not totally without precedence. For example, bats navigate by emitting ultrasound to probe the surroundings.

Active sensing generally refers to the class of imaging techniques which manipulate one, or a combination, of the following properties: characteristics of the light sources (for example, the coherency or color properties of the light source), the position and orientation of the light source, and the light patterns. Active monocular methods are usually time-of-fly techniques where the receivers are placed at the same position as the transmitters. The distance from the sensor to the object surfaces is recorded in the time required for sound or light to travel back and forth from the sensor, the shift of signal phase, or the amplitude modulation.

Applications of active sensing principle in binocular systems involve triangulation. The construction of an active binocular system is identical to that of a passive stereo system, except that one of the cameras is replaced by a controlled light source. The light source selectively illuminates the scene, and the illuminated portion can be readily detected in the image with triangulation principle applied for recovering its spatial position. The light patterns can be points, lines or complicated patterns such as orthogonal grids [4][18] or sets of parallel stripes [19][13].

Active sensing has a number of advantages over passive sensing: By controlling the positioning of the light source and the imaging configuration, the effect due to the surface geometry can be more readily deduced from the images. Furthermore, projected patterns in general create sharp contrasted features which can be reliably and automatically extracted from the images. However, the ease in feature selection and extraction does not always guarantee the ease in analyzing them. With simple patterns such as isolated points or lines, feature matching is relatively straight forward since only a small portion of the scene is illuminated at any given time instant. But a complete reconstruction of the visible surfaces requires data gathered by illuminating different portions of the scene through a scanning process over a lengthy period of time. Furthermore, precision engineered equipment is often needed to control the rotation of the scanning mirror and to register different stripe positions. The time required by the scanning operation can be drastically reduced by using more complicated patterns which encode a large portion of the scene at one time. However, the image analysis is complicated by the presence of a multitude of patterns of similar appearance.

We have just completed a quick overview of some of the popular geometric modeling techniques using a single or multiple images. Techniques can be loosely categorized as passive monocular, passive binocular, active monocular and active binocular according to [3]. In the following (Section 2), we are going to discuss a particular class of active binocular techniques - which are generally referring to as structured light projection or grid coding - in greater details. In this particular class of techniques, the scene is encoded using light cast through a slide marked with spatially variant patterns. This "spatial encoding" of the scene is then observed from the image plane with an analysis algorithm applied to recover the 3D information.

As mentioned before, the major obstacle in the analysis of grid coded images is the presence of a multitude of similar features - such as stripes and junctions of stripes - in the images, and hence, it is difficult to resolve the correspondence between features in the grid plane and images. Various techniques have been proposed to alleviate this problem of correspondence. Here, we are going to discuss some of the proposed techniques in detail. Furthermore, we are going to review techniques which, under proper assumption and simplification, were able to bypass the correspondence requirement in the analysis. Here, instead of matching grid junctions for recovering depth, the orientation of the projected patterns is analyzed and related to the visible surface orientation and structure in space. Implementation results will be provided to demonstrate the validity of the algorithms. Finally, Section 3 contains the concluding remarks.

2   Literature Survey

The idea of using spatially modulated light patterns projected onto a scene for analyzing the scene was first proposed by Will and Pennington [4][6]. In [4][6], an orthogonal grid pattern was projected to encode the planar surfaces in the scene. Distortion of the projected grid patterns on a planar surface is in general a function of the surface orientation and position in space with respect to the grid plane and the image plane. Moreover, distortion of the projected patterns manifests itself in angular and spatial frequency carrier shift in the Fourier domain. So the extraction of planar areas in the image becomes a matter of linear frequency domain filtering. Grid coding thus provides an alternative to other heuristic approaches for image segmentation. It makes use of the extra degree of freedom, viz the nature of scene illumination.

In more detail, consider a rectangular region, f, in the image plane with a black-and-white grating of a constant spatial frequency and modulation angle, θ, with respect to the x-axis. This region may result from, say, the observation of an encoded surface of a polyhedra in the field of view of the camera. If the grating is of a finite extent in the image, it may then be formulated mathematically as a grating (f_∞) of the same spatial frequency and modulation angle as f but of an infinite extent, superimposed by a rectangular window (f_{window}) the size of f.

$$f(\mathbf{x}) = f_\infty(\mathbf{x}) f_{window}(\mathbf{x}) \tag{1}$$

The well known theories of Fourier transform then give us

$$F(\omega) = F_\infty(\omega) * F_{window}(\omega) \tag{2}$$

Where $*$ denotes the convolution operator. If the size of the region is such that several grating periods appear in the window, then the Fourier spectrum of the grating consists of primarily a ($sinx/x$) envelop (from F_∞) modulated by a narrower ($sinx/x$) function (from F_{window}). Furthermore, the modulation pattern is constant along the direction of $\theta + 90^o$.

Hence, each planar encoded surface gives rise to a black-and-white grating of finite extent in the image plane, the Fourier transform of which consists of a crossed set of harmonically related functions. It is suggested that filters designed for separating the frequency contents of different encoded regions should be wedge-shaped, with narrow pass band in the angular direction and all pass in the radial direction. The inverse transform of the filtered image spectrum thus reconstructs images of isolated planar regions of a distinct modulation.

Will and Pennington have also suggested a stereo setup using grid coding for constructing 3-D information automatically [5]. The idea was later implemented in [7][19]. The system configurations in these investigations usually comprise a slide marked with the desired spatial pattern positioned in front of a controlled light source. The pattern may be either parallel stripes or orthogonal grids. The object of interest is illuminated with the selected patterns of light and the encoded scene is observed from one or more camera positions.

Techniques developed so far for inferring the 3D structures from the observered spatial encoding in general proceed in three steps: 1) the relative position of the controlled light source and the image plane is determined through a registration procedure, 2) the correspondence relations of features (for example the grid junctions) in the grid plane and the image plane are then established, and the spatial positions of features are recovered using triangulation and back projection, and 3) the surface structure in three space is determined by interpolating the sparse depth map of features.

The registration process can be carried out either manually or automatically. The displacement between the light source and the camera can be manually estimated. The orientation (the pan, tilt and zoom angles) of the camera and the projection device can be obtained by mounting the camera or the projection device on a calibration stand which automatically records the spatial orientation of the mounted object. If no special hardware is available, the position of the camera in the global reference system can be registered using a number of calibration marks of known position in three space. The projected positions of the calibration marks in the reference systems of the camera and the projection device can be measured locally. The transformation matrix (**M**) which relates different reference systems is given by

$$
\begin{bmatrix} Global\ coordinates\ of \\ the\ calibration\ marks \end{bmatrix} = \mathbf{M} \begin{bmatrix} Local\ coordinates\ of \\ the\ calibration\ marks \end{bmatrix} \quad (3)
$$

If enough registration marks are available, the transformation matrix can be solved for using linear system of equations [12].

2.1   Techniques with Correspondences

If the object of interest can be photographed under controlled environments and the object does not have transparent, highly reflective or totally black surfaces, the projected patterns usually create sharp contrasted features which can be easily detected in the images. However, matching features extracted from different image frames for the recovery of depth is still a nontrivial undertaking. The reason being that the evaluated features (the grid junctions and grid lines) are numerous and indistinguishable. Researchers have used heuristic search [7], time modulation [14], spatial labeling [16], relaxation technique [17], and color encoding [19] for alleviating this correspondence problem.

Heuristic Search

Potmesil and Freeman [7] have adopted a heuristic search algorithm for determining the correspondence between grid junctions in different images. A flow diagram of the analysis is depicted in Figure 1. The object, the surface of which is to be represented, is imaged from multiple stable positions. For each stable position, the object is placed on top of a rotating turntable to reveal different portions of the object surface to the cameras. Furthermore, multiple cameras may be used for each turntable position which gives a lot of freedom in image capturing. A calibration backdrop is carefully assembled for registering different camera positions automatically. Calibration marks are placed in known positions on the backdrop. The positions of the cameras with respect to the object are automatically calculated from the perceived configuration of the calibration marks.

Once the relative position of the cameras is obtained through the automatic calibration process, a heuristic search algorithm is applied to disambiguate the correspondence relationship of the grid junctions between image frames. The 3-D positions of the grid junctions are then recovered through triangulation, and the descriptions of the visible surfaces are obtained through a bi-cubic spline fitting. The angles of rotation of the turntable are obtained through marks on the turntable. Hence, surface descriptions gathered from multiple

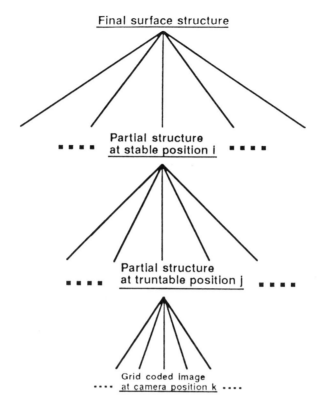

Figure 1: The Processing Hierarchy of the Heuristic Search Algorithm.

turntable positions are registered using the calibration marks on the turntable. The final structure is recorded in a multi-level quadtree representation with nodes at the lowest level representing the original surface patches. The higher level representations result from iteratively merging neighboring patches into coarser descriptions.

The surface elements generated from different stable positions are then coalesced to form a complete description of the object. It is required that the surface elements be imaged in such a way that their images partially overlap to allow merging by matching the common surface areas. A heuristic search algorithm is employed to find the spatial transformation between any two overlapped surface elements by maximizing the similarities in their position, orientation and curvature measurements. The initial transformation is obtained by aligning the surface orientation at the top level of the individual quadtrees. Control points are selected at various levels of the quadtree representations. A heuristic algorithm evaluates the differences in position, orientation and curvature measurements at the control points, and suggests the new transformation for the successor nodes in the search process.

Finally, a complete description of the object can be generated by reparameterizing two or more registered surface elements in a common parametric space. The authors reported that a complete description of the surface can be generated by the use of a relatively large number of grid-coded images.

Time Modulation

Posdamer and Altschuler [14] have presented a time modulation technique for assigning a unique "space code" or address to the grid junctions using a laser shutter / space encoding system. A single laser beam is converted into an array of projected rays by means of interference techniques. A high speed computer controlled shutter system is designed which can selectively block rays at particular positions. A reference image is created by shining all laser rays simultaneously. Images are generated with different rays deleted through proper shutter control. The effect of the presence or absence of the laser ray at a particular position is equivalent to the assignment of a binary space code to that position (Figure 2. The concatenation of the space codes of the intersecting horizontal and vertical stripes thus specifies the address of a grid junction - hence, the correspondence between the grid junctions in the image plane and those in the grid plane. The 3-D coordinates of the illuminated points can again be computed via triangulation after the space code of the laser beam is determined. A working model of the system has been implemented at the USAF School of Aerospace Medicine.

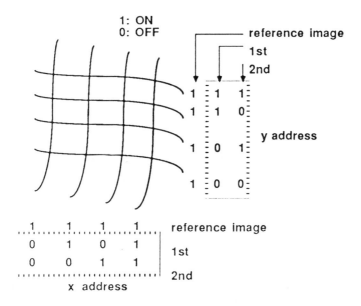

Figure 2: The Time Modulation Process.

Spatial Labeling

Another possibility in assigning a unique space coding to the grid junctions is through the use of a spatial labeling technique [16]. The grid patterns are augmented with a few black dots of known positions. The black dots are detected in the image and a counting procedure which measures the offset of a junction to the black dots 1s used to determine the space code of the junction (Figure 3).

In [16], the arrangement of the camera and the projection device is such that the baseline is vertical. In such a configuration, the projection of vertical stripes still perceives as vertical in the image. A Laplacian of a Gaussian operator is applied for the detection of the projected stripes. A vertical accumulator which sums up the intensity values of pixels along a vertical scan line in the image is applied. Peaks in the accumulator indicate the existence of vertical stripes. Hough transform is then used to find the accurate orientation of the vertical stripes. The positions of the grid junctions are located by running a horizontal accumulator around the neighborhoods of the

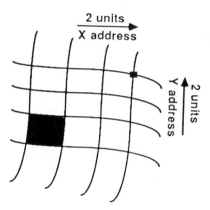

Figure 3: The Dpatial Labeling Process.

vertical stripes and detecting the positions of peaks in the accumulator. The labeling process then proceeds to locate the registration dots and measures the displacement of a junction to the dots. Note that the discontinuities of the grid lines and missing intersections will mislead the address labeling process. Hence, a global relaxation process is incorporated to resolve the inconsistency in labeling.

Relaxation

More recently, Stockman and Hu [17] have proposed yet another way to disambiguate the correspondence relationship of the grid junctions using a relaxation method (Figure 4). The goal is to use local and global constraints to find a consistent addressing of the projected junctions. A 16 * 14 grid pattern was used. The input grid coded images are processed via simple thresholding for detecting the grid junctions. A 2D connected component analysis is then applied to separate the input image into a number of disconnected 2D grid networks.

Geometric projective constraints are first imposed to find a small set of initial address assignments out of the 224 possibilities. The grid junctions in the image plane are projected back into space by connecting the grid junctions with the focal point of the camera. If the camera and the projection device have been properly registered,

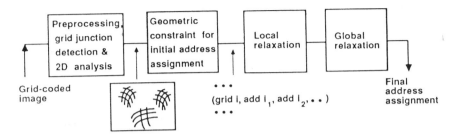

Figure 4: The Processing Flow of the Relaxation Technique.

then the distance between rays projected back from the image plane and the 224 projection rays from the projector can be measured. It is clear that, for a grid junction to be imaged at a particular image position, the projection ray from the projector has to be close enough to the particular back projected ray from that image position. A large number of possibilities can be eliminated in this way. The authors reported that, in general, only 3 to 16 possibilities left out of a total 224.

Then, a two-step relaxation process is applied to further disambiguate among the remaining assignments. Local constraints state that the addresses of the adjacent junctions can differ only by one, and also that the distance between the adjacent junctions in space should be relatively small. Global consistent checking extends the local one over a whole grid network. Barring anomaly resulting from a singular viewing configuration, a smooth 2D curve indicates a continuous 3D curve - thus the junctions along the curve should have either the same x or y coordinates. Furthermore, continuous 2D grid nets indicate continuous 3D surfaces - with consistent address assignments for grid junctions on the nets. The addresses across different grid networks should be unique since each grid junction can be imaged at one and only one position.

Color Encoding

The possibility of using patterns composed of stripes of different colors for disambiguating the correspondences has been addressed by

Boyer and Kak [19]. A diagram of the system construction is shown in Figure 5. A color video camera or a black-and-white camera with a set of suitable color filters is used to generate images in different visual spectrum bands. Preprocessing modules are incorporated to remove noises in the high and low frequency bands, and to equalize the signal strength in different color images. The high frequency noise $(> 2MHz)$ results from channel-to-channel cross talk while the low frequency noise $(< 500KHz)$ is attributed to the fluctuation of the average signal level. The gains in different color images are then adjusted to compensate the effects of uneven camera responses to different filters and poor color alignment.

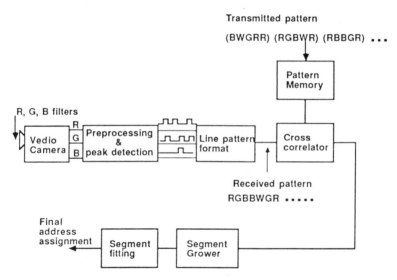

Figure 5: The Processing Flow of the Color Encoding Technique.

The stripe-indexing technique proceeds to assign a unique address to each observed color stripe. Corresponding scan lines in different color images are analyzed. A peak detection module is employed to detect the existence and location of stripes in different color images. A white stripe is identified by the simultaneous presence - at the same scan position - of stripes in all color images. The received pattern is then assembled in the *line pattern format* module. The received pattern is made of a list of positions of the detected stripes in current scan together with the colors of the stripes.

The transmitted pattern is composed of subpatterns of distinct arrangements of parallel color bars. The received pattern is matched against the transmitted subpatterns to find perfectly matched positions in the received pattern. These perfect match positions serve as 'seeds' to generate larger matched segments, or the matches are extended over the neighborhoods. Possible ambiguities in the assignments of correspondences are then resolved by a 'survival of the fittest' operation. The matched segments are hoarded into a remaining segment list. This list is sorted by the size of the segments in the list. The top of the list (or the longest matched segment) is removed and adds to the survival list which is sorted by the ordinal position of the segments and is initially empty. Any inconsistencies in the address assignment are revolved at this point in time. Notice that each transmitted stripe can be imaged at only one position, hence any segments in the remaining list which grew from the same subpattern as the segment under consideration should be removed. Furthermore, any received stripe results from the projection of one and only one transmitted stripe, so the segments in the remaining list should be trimmed so that no overlap exists with the union of segments in the survival list. This process is iteratively applied to append the largest remaining segment to the final survival list and at the same time, removes any incompatible assignments until all segments are accounted for.

As evident from the previous discussion, much effort in applying grid coding has been devoted to the determination of the correspondences between features. However, the degree of success is limited. Time required for the heuristic search usually grows exponentially as the number of grid junctions increases. A large number of images may be needed to uniquely determine the space codes of the grid junctions in time modulation techniques which adds to the complexity of the system. Furthermore, the object has to stay stationary and the images have to remain sufficiently registered over a long period of time. Spatial encoding fails when grid lines break over the jump boundaries and when junctions are missing due to improper lighting condition or imperfect edge detection routines. Relaxation cannot always guarantee that a unique assignment of the space codes be reached while color encoding technique may be affected by the color contents of the scene. The difficulties lie in that although sharp contrasted features can be created using controlled illumination, the ease in the detection of features does not imply the ease in matching them since their number is large and their appearances in the images are similar. In the process of integrating partial surface structures from multiple views, the major difficulty lies in determining the 3-D position of the partial surface structures. Previous research has relied on imaging the object in such a way that the extracted surface patches partially overlap so as to allow their eventual alignment by merging the common surface areas. A feature computation and matching scheme for registering partial structures from multiple views has been widely adopted. However, in a dynamic environment, the availability of overlapped surface patches cannot be guaranteed. Feature computation and matching are computationally intensive processes and are rendered useless if surface patches do not overlap.

2.2   Techniques without Correspondences

In this subsection, algorithms [20][23] based on the same structured light projection principle - but without the correspondence of features being established for analysis - are presented for 1) inferring the orientation and partial structure of surfaces visible from a set of single views, and for 2) integrating partial surface structures gathered from multiple viewpoints for completing the description of the imaged object.

The system configuration in the single view algorithm is shown in Figure 6. Here, the observed object rests on a supporting plane which is referred to as the base plane. For simplicity and without loss of generality, this base plane is assumed to be horizontal. The patterns marked on the grid plane are projected onto the scene and viewed by the camera. Two orthogonal patterns are used which are referred to as Δ_1 and Δ_2. Each pattern is a set of equally spaced parallel stripes marked on a glass pane.

In order to compute the relevant parameters of the geometric

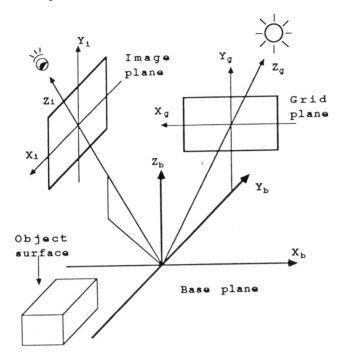

Figure 6: System Configuration in the Single View Algorithm.

configuration, the first step is to register the image plane with respect to the global coordinate system. The base plane appears as a uniform background in the image. Hence, the observed base plane encoding can be utilized to deduce the image plane orientation. Basically, we relate the orientations of the base plane stripe patterns observed in the image to the orientation of the image plane. The analysis asserts that, in order to observe the base plane patterns as those extracted from the images, the orientation of the image plane cannot be arbitrary - but has to lie on a curve in the Gaussian sphere. Each encoded image provides one set of constraints. Or the orientation of the candidate image plane must satisfy the following two constraints:

For the first stripe pattern Δ_1:

$$\nu_1 = -tan^{-1}(sin\Psi_i tan\Theta_i) \qquad (4)$$

For the second stripe pattern Δ_2:

$$\nu_2 = tan^{-1}(sin\Psi_i/tan\Theta_i) \qquad (5)$$

Where ν_1 and ν_2 are the observed orientations of the base plane stripes. 1 and 2 denote the first or second pattern. As mentioned before, each constraint equation gives rise to a curve. The orientation (Θ, Ψ) pairs along the curve satisfy the orientation constraint imposed by one set of the observed base plane encoding. Intersections of these two curves are the orientations that satisfy the constraints imposed by both sets of encoding. In general, there will be four possible image plane orientations given the observed base plane stripe orientations as constraints. This ambiguity can be discerned by using some easily distinguishable spatial masking.

Once the global coordinate system is defined and the image plane is registered in this global reference system, the orientation of visible object surfaces can be inferred. The algorithm proposed here is general enough to handle surfaces of arbitrary shape. Both planar and curved surfaces can be processed in a uniform manner. To determine the orientation of the object's visible surface, a geometric constraint satisfaction approach will again be adopted. Working backwards from the image plane to the grid plane, we see that the observed object surface stripes in the image can be back projected into space to intersect the object space. Then, the stripes thus obtained can again be back projected in the grid plane directions, and only those 3-D object surface orientations that give rise to the same stripe orientations as those marked on the grid plane are acceptable. Or the orientation pair, (Θ_o, Ψ_o), is valid if it satisfies the following conditions:

For the first stripe pattern Δ_1:

$$A\, sin\Psi_o + B\, sin\Theta_o cos\Psi_o = 0 \qquad (6)$$

For the second stripe pattern Δ_2:

$$C\, cos\Theta_o cos\Psi_o + D\, sin\Theta_o cos\Psi_o + E\, sin\Psi_o = 0 \qquad (7)$$

Where A, B, C, D and E are functions of (ρ_1, ρ_2), (Θ_i, Ψ_i), and (Θ_g, Ψ_g). Note that (ρ_1, ρ_2) are the orientations of the observed object surface stripes which can be measured from the image. (Θ_i, Ψ_i)

is the image plane orientation derived from the image registration process, and (Θ_g, Ψ_g) is the orientation of the grid plane which is assumed known.

Again, each equation represents a constraint curve on the Gaussian sphere. Intersections of the constraint curves produce the surface orientation that pass both orientation tests. It can be seen that if (Θ, Ψ) is a solution to the above equations, $(\Pi + \Theta, -\Psi)$ is also one. However, these two solutions are actually the two sides of the same surface, and we will only be able to see one of them at a time.

Finally, local surface structure can be computed by integrating a simple differential equation relating surface orientation to relative depth. Accuracy of computed relative depth is significantly better with a denser surface orientation map. But, in general, surface orientations at grid intersections, as just computed, form a sparse map. Therefore, the first step is to interpolate orientation between grid intersections to obtain a dense orientation map. Let (X_i, Y_i, Z_i) denote the coordinates of a particular point in space. Here 'i' denotes quantities measured in the local image plane coordinate system. A parameterization of (X_i, Y_i, Z_i) in terms of the stripe patterns Δ_1 and Δ_2 can be defined. A reference point is then chosen, and the depth at that reference point is arbitrarily fixed. The depth of any other point on the same surface patch relative to the reference one is then recovered by integrating along any path which lies on the object surface leading from the reference point to the surface point of interest. So we have

$$Z_i(s,t) =$$
$$\begin{aligned} &- \int [a(s',t')\partial X_i/\partial s' \quad + b(s',t')\partial Y_i/\partial s']ds'|_{t'=t_n} \\ &- \int [a(s',t')\partial X_i/\partial t' \quad + b(s',t')\partial Y_i/\partial t']dt'|_{s'=s} \\ &+ Z_{mn} \end{aligned} \quad (8)$$

where Z_{mn} is the depth at a particular image point
$$(X_i(s_m, t_n), Y_i(s_m, t_n))$$
which is arbitrarily chosen to fix the scale factor. The orientation interpolation makes available $a(s,t)$ and $b(s,t)$, hence Z_i is easy to compute at any parametric point (s,t).

The system configuration in the stage of integrating surface descriptions from multiple views is identical to that of single view,

Figure 7: The Soap Dispenser Used for the Experiment.

except that the object for which the surface structure is thought is placed in one of its stable positions on a turntable. The turntable is rotated through several known angles and the surface structure at each angular position is imaged. The intensity image is recorded at every angular position. However, the stripe-coded images may be missing from some of the angular positions which implies that the detailed surface structure cannot be recovered at those positions. Two sources of information extracted from the images are used in the new surface reconstruction process: the occluding contours and the inferred partial surface structures. Occluding contours present an estimate of the projective range of the invisible surface structures. The bounding volume description of the object can be established by intersecting the occluding contours in space. The local surface structures inferred from different imaging directions present pieces of strong constraint. This constraint dictates the structure of the object surface when viewed from some particular directions and should be incorporated into the final surface description.

Thus, the 3-D surface structure can be generated by exploiting two types of information embedded in the projections from different viewing directions. 3-D surface description is constructed first from

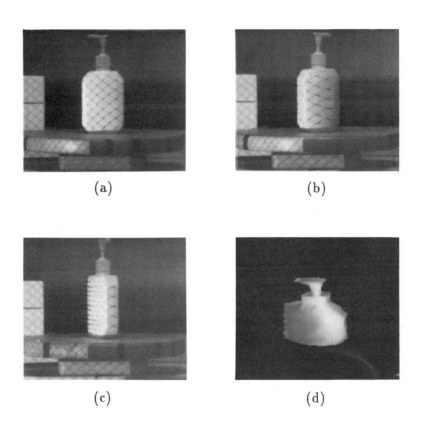

Figure 8: The Test Object Soap Dispenser.

(a) Spatially Encoded Scene: First Turntable Position.

(b) Spatially Encoded Scene: Second Turntable Position.

(c) Spatially Encoded Scene: Third Turntable Position.

(d) Final Surface Structure of the Soap Dispenser Constructed
Using Three Intensity Images and Three Sets of Stripe-coded Images.

a number of occluding contours; the description is then refined by the inferred partial surface structures. Whenever a partial surface structure is introduced, it overwrites the structure predicted by the occluding contours and is merged with other partial surface structures to refine the 3-D surface representation. If no detailed surface structure is inferred at certain portions of the viewing volume, the bounding surfaces constructed through the back projection of the occluding contours are used. If more images are acquired at a later time, a refinement process can be applied to refine the surface description of the object. First, the occluding contours from the new positions are used to refine the bounding volume description. Then, the partial surface structures (when available) are incorporated. The structure thus obtained is recorded in a data structure which delineates the object surfaces by a set of parallel planar slices. In this approach, the surface contours in each slice are recorded. The algorithms proposed thus make use of both passively sensed and actively sensed information and do not perform any time-consuming feature computation/matching operations.

The algorithms [20][23] reviewed here have been tested on camera-acquired images of real objects using a stripe projection setup. Here, a test object, a soap dispenser (Figure 7), is used. The test object is imaged at three turntable positions. At each turntable position, both the intensity image and the stripe coded images are acquired. The intensity images are thresholded to extract the occluding contours. The occluding contours are then rasterized and the initial bounding volume representation is generated using the back projection with volume intersection technique using the first two frames. The initial bounding volume is then modified when the third set of views is made available. Based on the striped coded images, the surface orientation of the visible surface patches at each turntable position is inferred. Results are displayed in Figures 8a, 8b and 8c.

After the bounding volume is constructed and the partial surface structures are inferred at each turntable position, the partial surface structures are incorporated to refine the bounding volume description. The final surface structures (using three intensity images and three sets of stripe coded images) are shown in Figure 8d.

3 Conclusions

In summary, we have made a survey of the existing structured light projection techniques for geometric modeling. And we have proposed a technique for modeling the structure of 3D object based on the same active sensing principle which we feel is adequate in tackling some of the difficulties encountered in using structured light projection.

The point to emphasize here is that there are pros and cons in adopting an active structured light projection technique. The advantages are that the extra degree of freedom in manipulating the light and the sensing configuration helps simplifying the image acquisition and the ensuing image processing. Image features are usually more conspicuous and can be reliably extracted through an automatic process. The disvantage is that the ease in feature extraction does not always guarantee the ease in the analysis. Furthermore, in some applications, it is not feasible to emit signals actively so as to expose one's own position. However, this type of techniques does find applications in factory and robotics applications, in which the manipulation of sensing environment is feasible. The reconstructed 3D configuration can then be used as basis in other vision applications such as object recognition and target tracking.

Bibliography

[1] A. A. G. Requicha, *Representations for Rigid Solids: Theory, Methods, and Systems*, Computing Surveys, Vol. 12, No. 4, p. 437–464, Dec. 1980.

[2] S. N. Srihari, *Representation of Three-Dimensional Digital Images*, Computing Surveys, Vol. 14, No. 4, p. 399–424, Dec. 1981.

[3] R. A. Jarvis, *A Perspective on Range Finding Techniques for Computer Vision*, IEEE Transactions on PAMI, Vol. PAMI-5, No. 2, p. 122–139, Mar. 1983.

[4] K. S. Pennington and P. M. Will, *A Grid-Coded Technique for Recording 3-Dimensional Scenes Illuminated with Ambient Light*, Optics Communications, Vol. 2, No. 4, p. 167–169, Sep. 1970.

[5] P. M. Will and K. S. Pennington, *Grid Coding: A Preprocessing Technique for Robot and Machine Vision*, Artificial Intelligence, Vol. 2, p. 319–329, 1971.

[6] P. M. Will and K. S. Pennington, *Grid Coding: A Novel Technique for Image Processing*, Proceedings of The IEEE, Vol. 60, No. 6, p. 669–680, Jun. 1972.

[7] M. Potmesil and H. Freeman, *Curved Surface Representation Utilizing Data Extracted from Multiple Photographic Images*, Workshop on the Representation of Three-Dimensional Objects, Philadelphia, PA, May 1–2, p. H1–H26, 1979.

[8] W. Frobin and E. Hierholzer, *Rasterstereography: A Photogrammetric Method for Measurement of Body Surfaces*, Photogrammetric Engineering and Remote Sensing, Vol. 47, No. 12, p. 1717–1724, Dec. 1981.

[9] W. Frobin and E. Hierholzer, *Calibration and Model Reconstruction in Analytical Close–Range Stereophotogrammetry Part I: Mathematical Fundamentals*, Photogrammetric Engineering and Remote Sensing, Vol. 48, No. 1, p. 67–72, Jan. 1982.

[10] W. Frobin and E. Hierholzer, *Calibration and Model Reconstruction in Analytical Close-Range Stereophotogrammetry Part II: Special Evaluation Procedures for Rasterstereography and Moire Topography*, Photogrammetric Engineering and Remote Sensing, Vol. 48, No. 2, p. 215–220, Feb. 1982.

[11] C. A. McPherson, J. B. K. Tio, F. A. Asdjadi, and E. L. Hall, *Curved Surface Representation for Image Recognition*, Conference on Pattern Recognition and Image Proceeding, Jun. 14–17, p. 363–369, 1982.

[12] J. B. K. Tio, C. A. McPherson and E. L. Hall, *Curved Surface Measurement for Robot Vision*, Conference on Pattern Recognition and Image Proceeding, Jun. 14–17, p. 370–378, 1982.

[13] E. L. Hall, et al., *Measuring Curved Surfaces for Robot Vision*, Computer, p. 42–54, Dec. 1982.

[14] J. L. Posdamer and M. D. Altschuler, *Surface Measurement by Space-Encoded Projected Beam Systems*, Computer Graphics and Image Processing, Vol. 18, p. 1–17, 1982.

[15] M. Potmesil, *Generating Models of Solid Objects by Matching 3D Surface Segments*, Proceedings of the 8th International Joint Conference on Artificial Intelligence, Karlsruhe, West Germany, Aug. 8–12, 1983.

[16] J. Le Moigne and A. M. Waxman, *Projected Light Grids for Short Range Navigation of Autonomous Robots*, Proceedings of the 7th International Conference on Pattern Recognition, Jul.30–Aug.2, p. 203–206, 1984.

[17] G. Stockman and G. Hu, *Sensing 3-D Surface Patches Using a Projected Grid*, IEEE Computer Society Conference on Computer Vision and Pattern Recognition, Miami Beach, FL, p. 602–607, 1986.

[18] K. Sugihara et al., *Regular Pattern Projection for Surface Measurement*, The Second International Symposium on Robotics Research, H. Hanafusa and H. Inoue eds., MIT Press, 1985.

[19] K. L. Boyer and A. C. Kak, *Color-Encoded Structure Light for Rapid Range Sensing*, IEEE Transactions on PAMI, Vol. PAMI-9, No. 1, p. 14–28, Jan. 1987.

[20] Y. F. Wang, A. Mitiche and J. K. Aggarwal, *Inferring Local Surface Orientation with the Aid of Grid Coding*, Proceedings of the Third Workshop on Computer Vision: Representation and Control, Bellaire, MI, Oct. 13–16, 1985.

[21] Y. F. Wang, A. Mitiche and J. K. Aggarwal, *Computation of Surface Orientation and Structure of Objects Using Grid Coding*, IEEE Transactions on PAMI, Vol. PAMI-9, No. 1, p. 129–137, Jan. 1987.

[22] Y. F. Wang and J. K. Aggarwal, *On Modeling 3-D Objects Using Multiple Sensory Data*, Proceedings of IEEE International Conference on Robotics and Automation, Raleigh, NC, Mar.31–Apr.3, p. 1098–1103, 1987.

[23] Y. F. Wang and J. K. Aggarwal, *Integration of Active and Passive Sensing Techniques for Representing 3-D Objects*, Accepted for publication in IEEE Journal on Robotics and Automation.

Range Image Segmentation

Paul J. Besl
Machine Perception Group
General Motors Research Laboratories

Ramesh C. Jain
Computer Vision Research Laboratory
The University of Michigan

Abstract

Since direct interpretation of large amounts of raw data by computer is difficult, it is often convenient to partition (segment) these image arrays into low-level entities (groups of pixels with similar properties) that can be compared with higher-level entities derived from representations of world knowledge. Using a piecewise-smooth surface model for image data, we have developed an algorithm that simultaneously segments a large class of images into regions of arbitrary shape and approximates image data with bivariate functions so that it is possible to compute a complete image reconstruction based on the extracted functions and regions. Surface curvature sign labeling provides an initial coarse image segmentation, which is refined by an iterative region growing method based on variable-order surface fitting. Experimental results show the performance of the algorithm on range and intensity images.

1 Introduction

Computer vision systems attempt to recover useful information about the three-dimensional (3-D) world from huge image arrays of sensed values. Since direct interpretation of large amounts of raw data by computer is difficult, it is often convenient to partition (segment) these image arrays into low-level entities (i.e. groups of pixels with particular properties) that can be compared with higher-level entities derived from representations of world knowledge. Solving the segmentation problem requires a mechanism for partitioning the image array into useful entities based on a model of the underlying image structure.

Most of the computer vision research has concentrated on using digitized gray-scale intensity images as sensor data. It has proven to be extraordinarily difficult to program computers to understand and describe these images in a *general purpose* way. One important problem is that digitized intensity images are rectangular arrays of numbers which indicate the *brightness* at individual points but contain no *explicit* information that is directly usable in *depth perception*. Human beings are able to correctly infer depth relationships quickly and easily among intensity image regions whereas automatic inference of such depth relationships has proven to be remarkably complex. Computer vision researchers recognized the importance of surfaces in the understanding of images. The popularity of various *shape from ...* approaches in the last decade is the result of this recognition.

In recent years digitized range data has become available from both active and passive sensors and the quality of this data has been steadily improving. Range data is usually produced in the form of a rectangular array of numbers, referred to as a *depth map or range image*, where the numbers quantify the distances from the sensor plane to the surfaces within the field of view along the rays emanating from a regularly spaced rectangular grid. Not only are depth relationships between depth map regions explicit, the three-dimensional *shape* of depth map regions approximates the three-dimensional shape of the corresponding object *surfaces* in the field of view. Therefore, the process of recognizing objects by their shape *should* be less difficult in depth maps than in intensity images due to the explicitness of the information. For example, since depth map information depends only on geometry and is independent of illumination and reflectivity, problems with shadows and surface markings do not occur.

In most easily interpretable images, almost all pixel values are statistically and geometrically correlated with neighboring pixel values. This pixel-to-pixel correlation, or *spatial coherence* , in images arises from the spatial coherence of the physical surfaces being imaged. In range images, where each sensed value measures the distance to physical surfaces from a known reference surface, the pixel values collectively exhibit the same spatial coherence properties as the actual physical surfaces they represent. This has motivated us to explore the possibilities of a surface-based image segmentation algorithm that uses the spatial coherence (*surface coherence*) of the data to organize pixels into meaningful groups for later visual processes.

Many computer vision algorithms are based on inflexible, unnecessarily restricting assumptions about the world and the underlying structure of the sensed image data. The following assumptions are common:

1. all physical objects of interest are polyhedral, quadric, swept (as in generalized cylinders), convex, or combinations thereof;

2. all physical surfaces are planar, quadric, swept, or convex;

3. all image regions are rectangular or regularly shaped and are approximately constant in brightness; and

4. all image edges are linear or circular.

The extensive research based on these assumptions solves many important application problems, but these assumptions are very limiting when analyzing scenes containing real-world objects with free-form, sculptured surfaces. Therefore, we have developed an image segmentation algorithm based only on the assumption that the image data exhibits surface coherence in the sense that the image data may be interpreted as noisy samples of a piecewise-smooth surface function. The algorithm not only segments images into regions of arbitrary shape, but also approximates image data defined over those regions with flexible bivariate functions so that it is possible to compute a complete image reconstruction based on the extracted functions and regions. We believe that an explicit image description based on flexibly shaped approximating functions defined over arbitrary connected image regions will be useful in many computer vision applications, but will be critically important to object reconstruction and object recognition algorithms based on range imaging sensors when object volumes are bounded by free-form smooth surfaces.

1.1   Literature Survey

Region growing based on function approximation ideas are used commonly in range image analysis (see survey [Besl and Jain 1985]). The uniformity predicate in the work listed below requires that region pixels are well approximated by planar or quadric surfaces. Shirai and Suwa [1971], Milgram and Bjorklund [1980], Bhanu [1984], Henderson and Bhanu [1982], and Boyter [1984] segment range images into fitted planar surfaces extracted via region growing. Other work has been geared toward detecting cylinders in range data [Agin and Binford 1973] [Nevatia and Binford 1973] [Popplestone et al. 1975] [Bolles and Fischler 1981] [Kuan and Drazovich 1984]. Hebert and Ponce [1982] segmented planes, cylinders, and cones from range data. Sethi and Jayaramamurthy [1984] handled spheres and ellipsoids in addition to planes, cylinders, and cones. Oshima and Shirai [1983] used planes, spheres, cylinders, and cones. Faugeras et al. [1983] at INRIA allow for region growing based on planar or general quadric surface primitives [Faugeras and Hebert 1986]. The above do not directly address other types of surfaces except that the INRIA and Henderson/Bhanu approaches have worked with arbitrary curved surfaces represented by many-faceted polyhedral approximations. Many of these methods obtain an initial segmentation of small primitive regions and then iteratively merge the small primitives until all merges (allowed by a smoothness or approximation error constraint) have taken place. The RANSAC method of Bolles and Fischler [1981] have used iterative model fitting directly on the data based on randomly selected initial points (seeds). Our approach also works directly on the data, but seed regions are extracted deterministically and the model may change as required by the data.

Concepts and techniques from differential geometry have been useful in describing the shape of arbitrary smooth surfaces arising in range images [Brady et al. 1985] [Medioni and Nevatia 1984] [Besl and Jain 1986] [Vemuri et al. 1986] [Ittner and Jain 1985] [Fan et al. 1986]. (This approach has also been applied to intensity image description [Peet and Sahota 1985] [Lin and Perry 1982] [Besl et al. 1985].) For segmentation based on differential geometric quantities, such as lines of curvature or surface curvature, the uniformity predicate requires region pixels to possess similar geometric properties. As the name implies, the *differential* geometry of surfaces analyzes the *local differences* of surface points. Although *global similarities* in surface structure are also analyzed, most theorems in differential geometry address only global topological similarities, such as the one-hole equivalence of a doughnut and a coffee cup with a handle. Global shape similarity theorems do exist for the surfaces of convex objects, and they have already been successfully utilized in Extended Gaussian Image (EGI) convex surface shape matching schemes [Horn 1984]. Difficulties arise when local descriptors are used to identify the shape and global similarities of arbitrary non-convex object surfaces from arbitrary-viewpoint range-image projections. The mathematics of differential geometry gives little guidance for an integrated global shape description or for computational matching methods in this general case. Brady et al. [1985] extract and analyze a dense set of integrated 3-D lines of curvature across entire surface patches to describe the global surface properties. This method can take hours to describe simple objects.

Many researchers have favored the extraction of lower-dimensional features, such as edges, to describe range images instead of surfaces [Sugihara 1979] [Inokuchi and Nevatia 1980] [Inokuchi et al. 1982] [Gil et al. 1983] [Mitiche and Aggarwal 1983] [Smith and Kanade 1984] [Herman 1985] [Tomita and Kanade 1985] [Hebert and Kanade 1985] [Bolles and Horaud 1986] [Bhanu et al. 1986]. The uniformity predicate in these approaches requires that range and the range gradient are continuous for all pixels in region interiors where only the region boundaries are computed explicitly. By detecting and linking range and range gradient discontinuities, the space curves that bound arbitrary smooth surfaces are isolated creating an image segmentation. However, most of the above edge-based work has focussed on straight and circular edges for matching with polyhedra and cylinders and their combinations. Although edge-based approaches offer important computational advantages for today's computer vision systems, we believe that such systems cannot provide the detailed surface information that will be required from future general-purpose range-image vision systems. Only more research experience will determine the advantages and disadvantages of these approaches for different applications, but the generality of an arbitrary surface segmentation and surface description approach is necessary today for automated free-form, sculptured surface reconstruction and shape acquisition tasks.

2   Mathematical Preliminaries

Rather than modeling the relevant underlying structure of an image as a random field, we view the relevant underlying structure of an image as a piecewise-smooth surface contaminated by noise as defined below. A 3-D *smooth graph surface* is a twice-differentiable function of two variables:

$$z = f(x, y)$$

A *piecewise-smooth graph surface* $g(x, y)$ can be partitioned into smooth surface primitives $f_k(x, y)$ over regions R_k:

$$z = g(x, y) = \sum_{k=1}^{N} f_k(x, y)\chi(x, y, R_k)$$

where $\chi(x, y, R_k)$ is the characteristic function of the region R_k which is unity if $(x, y) \in R_k$ and zero otherwise. A *digital surface* is a noisy, quantized, discretely sampled version of piecewise-smooth graph surface:

$$z_{ij} = \tilde{g}(i, j) = \lfloor g(x(i), y(j)) + n(x(i), y(j)) \rfloor$$

where the floor function indicates truncation (quantization) to an integer and the noise process $n(x, y)$ is nominally zero-mean with variance $\sigma^2(x, y)$ at each point. Hence, the noise process is assumed to be additive, but it needn't be Gaussian for the proposed segmentation algorithm. Also, the discrete image location (i, j) need not be linearly related to the Euclidean (x, y) location thus allowing the nonlinear relationships involved in many range sensors. A *range image* is a particular type of a digital surface where the z_{ij} values represent the distance to a physical surface from a reference surface. An *intensity image* is another type of digital surface where the z_{ij} values represent the number of visible photons incident at the (i, j) point of a camera. Other image types are defined based on the meaning of the sensed z_{ij} values. This underlying model is quite general and can be used to represent many types of images unless multiplicative noise or some other type of noise is present. Textured surfaces may be considered as an approximating smooth surface together with special types of structured noise which represents the given texture along with the usual sensor noise.

The *segmentation/reconstruction* problem that we are attempting to solve may be stated as follows: Given a only the digital surface specified by the z_{ij} values denoted $\tilde{g}$, find $\hat{N}$ approximation functions $\hat{f}_k(x, y)$ and $\hat{N}$ image regions R_k over which those functions are defined such that the total image representation error

$$\epsilon_{tot} = \|\tilde{g}(i, j) - \hat{g}(x(i), y(j))\|_I$$

between the reconstructed image function

$$\hat{g}(x, y) = \sum_{k=1}^{\hat{N}} \hat{f}_k(x, y)\chi(x, y, \hat{R}_k)$$

evaluated at the points $(x(i), y(j))$ and the data $\tilde{g}(i, j)$ is small and the total number of functions and regions $\hat{N}$ is small. The "one pixel per region" solution minimizes the approximation error (zero error), maximizes the number of regions, and requires no work, but is of course also useless. The "one function per image" solution minimizes the number of regions (one region), maximizes the approximation error, requires work, may be useful for some purposes, but does not solve the problem. We seek an algorithm that tends to segment images into regions that can be directly associated with meaningful high-level entities. In the case of range images, the surface functions defined over the image regions should mathematically represent the 3-D shape of visible physical surfaces in the scene.

The problem statement places no constraints on the functions except that they are smooth, no constraints on the image regions except that they are connected, no constraints on the form of the additive noise term except that it is zero-mean with some variance at each pixel. We want the total approximation error and the number of regions to be small, but we have not attempted to weight the relative importance of each. Without such weights, one cannot form an objective function and attempt to apply optimization methods.

It is not clear from our statement that such a problem can be solved. It is certainly straightforward to fit functions once the set of regions are known and also to determine the regions if the set of functions are known. But even the number of functions/regions present in the data is not known. We seek a signal-level, data-driven segmentation procedure based only on knowledge of surfaces.

3   Smooth Surface Decomposition

Arbitrary smooth surfaces can be subdivided into simpler regions of constant surface curvature sign based on the signs of the mean and Gaussian curvature at each point [Besl and Jain 1986]. As shall be discussed in more detail later, there are only eight possible surface types surrounding any point on a smooth surface based on surface curvature sign: peak, pit, ridge, valley, saddle ridge, saddle valley, flat (planar), and minimal. These fundamental surface shapes are very simple and do not contain inflection points. Our hypothesis is that these simple surface types are well approximated for image segmentation (i.e. perceptual organization) purposes by bivariate polynomials of order M or less where M is small. The experimental results included here and in [Besl 1986] attempt to show that this assumption is reasonable for a large class of images when $M = 4$ (biquartic surfaces). Even the range image surfaces of quadric primitives can be approximated well enough for segmentation purposes with such polynomial surfaces. This assumption is only limiting in the context of the segmentation algorithm when a large smooth surface bends much faster than x^4. If a particular application encounters a significant number of such surfaces, the limit of $M = 4$ can be raised. If a range imaging application can guarantee that only planar and quadric surfaces will appear, they can use only those types of functions for fitting purposes. In fact, any ordered set of bivariate approximating functions can be used if they satisfy the set of requirements defined below. In summary, arbitrary smooth surfaces may be decomposed into a union of simple surface-curvature-sign primitives that are well approximated by low-order bivariate polynomials.

The intermediate goal of a segmentation algorithm then is to isolate all underlying *simple surfaces* (surface-curvature-sign primitives) in the image data and fit those simple surfaces with simple bivariate approximating functions. This creates an image segmentation in terms of the support regions of the simple approximating functions and an image reconstruction in terms of those simple approximating functions evaluated over the support regions. If the boundaries of the *smooth surfaces* of the underlying piecewise-smooth surface model are desired, then smoothly-joining, adjacent simple surface regions can be merged to create the smooth surface support regions. This non-iterative post-processing step is covered in [Besl 1986] and is not discussed here. We currently leave the function description over the smooth surface regions in the form of a collection of simple polynomial surfaces. The final collection of smooth surfaces and their support regions is the underlying piecewise-smooth image description that we wished to recover in the problem definition. In applications, it may be desirable to go back and fit the segmented smooth surface with application surfaces, such as quadrics, composite Bezier patches, or rational B-splines, rather than leaving it as a set of polynomial surfaces.

3.1 Approximating Function Requirements

Arbitrarily complicated smooth surfaces can be decomposed into a disjoint union of surface-curvature-sign surface primitives. If these surface primitives can be approximated well by a small set of approximating functions, a composite surface description for arbitrary smooth surfaces can be obtained. There are several constraints that the set of approximating functions must satisfy. Of course, the approximating functions must be able to approximate the fundamental surface-curvature-sign surface-primitives well. For *dimensionality reduction* reasons, the approximating functions should be representable by a small amount of data. For *generality*, the approximating surfaces must be well-defined over any arbitrary connected region in the image plane. The approximating functions of the digital surface segmentation must be useful for *extrapolation* into neighboring areas of a surface in order for the region growing method to be successful. *Interpolation* capabilities are also useful for evaluating points between pixels if surface intersections are required. The approximating functions should also be easily *differentiable* so that differential geometric shape descriptors can be recomputed from them and so that other processes may compare surface normals and other differential quantities. Finally, the complete set of approximating functions should be *totally ordered* so that each approximant is capable of describing lower order approximants exactly, but cannot approximate higher order functions well. This provides the basis for a set of increasingly complicated hypotheses about the form of the underlying data. Note that general 3-D surface representation capability is not needed because digital surfaces are discrete representations of graph surface functions.

Low-order bivariate polynomials satisfy all of the above requirements, and the surface fitting procedure requires only a linear least-squares solver for the p x q $(p > q)$ equation $[A]\vec{x} = \vec{b}$. We have found that the set of planar, biquadratic, bicubic, and biquartic polynomials performed well in our experiments without significant computational requirements. However, any set of approximating functions that satisfy the above constraints may be used instead. To maintain generality in the algorithm description, it is only assumed that there is a set of approximating functions, denoted as F, that contains $|F|$ discrete types of functions that can be ordered in terms of the "shape potential" of each surface function relative to the set of fundamental surface-curvature-sign surface primitives.

In our case, $|F| = 4$ and the set of approximating functions F can be written in the form of a single equation:

$$\hat{f}(m, \vec{a}; x, y) = \sum_{i+j \leq m} a_{ij}x^iy^j \qquad (1)$$

$$
\begin{aligned}
= \quad & a_{00} + a_{10}x + a_{01}y + a_{11}xy + \\
& a_{20}x^2 + a_{02}y^2 + a_{21}x^2y + a_{12}xy^2 + \qquad (m = 4) \\
& a_{30}x^3 + a_{03}y^3 + a_{31}x^3y + a_{22}x^2y^2 + \\
& a_{13}xy^3 + a_{40}x^4 + a_{04}y^4 \qquad\qquad\qquad\qquad (2)
\end{aligned}
$$

Planar surfaces are obtained by restricting the parameter vector space $\Re^{15}$ to three-dimensional subspace where only a_{00}, a_{10}, a_{01} may be non-zero. Biquadratic surfaces are restricted to a six-dimensional subspace, and bicubic surfaces to a ten-dimensional subspace. A least-squares solver computes the parameter vector $\vec{a}$ and the RMS fit error ϵ from the digital surface data over a region quickly and efficiently. Moreover, a QR least-squares solution approach allows surface region fits to be updated recursively during the region growing process as new data points added [Golub and VanLoan 1983] [Chen 1986] for added computational efficiency.

3.2 Simple to Complex Hypothesis Testing

The key idea behind the algorithm, which is independent of the set of approximating functions actually chosen, is that one should start with the simplest hypotheses about the form of the data and then gradually increase the complexity of the hypothesized form as needed. This is the *variable-order* concept, which has not been used in previous segmentation algorithms. In our case, surface type labels at each pixel allow us to find large groups of identically labeled pixels. Then, a small subset of those pixels, known as a *seed region*, is chosen using a simple shrinking method that attempts to insure that every pixel in the seed region is correctly labeled. The simplest hypothesis for any surface fitting approach is that the data points represented in the seed region lie in a plane. The hypothesis is then tested to see if it is true. If true, the seed region is grown based on the planar surface fit. If the simple hypothesis is false, the algorithm responds by testing the next more complicated hypothesis (e.g. a biquadratic surface). If that hypothesis is true, the region is grown based on that form. If false, the next hypothesis is tested. This process continues until either (1) all pre-selected hypotheses have been shown to be false or (2) the region growing based on the surface fitting has converged in the sense that the same image region is obtained twice. Since all smooth surfaces can be partitioned into simple surfaces based on surface curvature sign, false hypotheses may occur only when the isolated seed region surface-type labels are incorrect (due to noise) or when the underlying surface bends faster than the highest order approximating surface. During execution of the algorithm, bad seed regions are usually rejected immediately when the surface fit error is poor and large quickly bending surfaces are broken into two or more surface regions.

4   Algorithm Description

The algorithm presented in this paper uses a general piecewise-smooth surface model to do pixel grouping assuming the image data exhibits *surface coherence* properties. If all pixel values are viewed as noisy samples of an underlying *piecewise-smooth surface* function defined over the entire image, the segmentation process should not only provide detailed definitions of the segmented regions, but should also provide the component surface functions of the underlying piecewise-smooth surface. Surface-based segmentation includes surface (image) reconstruction.

In the first stage of the segmentation algorithm described below, each pixel in an image is given a label based on its value and the values of its neighboring pixels. This label can only take on eight possible values based on two surface-curvature signs and indicates the qualitative shape of an approximating surface that best-fits the image data surrounding that point. This surface-type label image can be analyzed for connected regions using a standard connected component analysis algorithm. Any individual pixel label can be wrong, but it is likely to be correct if it lies in the interior of a large region of identically labeled pixels. Moreover, due to the constrained nature of the surface types represented by the eight labels, it is also likely that a simple surface function will approximate a group of correctly labeled pixels. The surface type label image is used to provide seed regions to the region-growing algorithm. A pixel's similarity with a group of other pixels is measured by comparing (1) the difference between the pixel's value and the other pixels' approximating surface value (at the given pixel location) and (2) a parameter that measures the goodness of the fit of the surface to the other pixels. This similarity measure allows for a pixel to enter and leave a group of pixels depending on the other pixels currently in that group. Hence, a mistake in grouping can be undone. Regions are grown until convergence criterion are met, and a concise, parametrically defined surface description is recorded along with a definition of the image region. It is common for images reconstructed from the segmentation description to be almost indistinguishable from the original image.

This algorithm can be viewed as a two-stage process. The first stage computes an "initial-guess" coarse segmentation in terms of regions of identical surface type labels. The second stage iteratively refines the coarse image segmentation and simultaneously reconstructs image surfaces. The entire algorithm is outlined below.

The first stage creates a surface type label image $T(i,j)$ from the original image $\tilde{g}(i,j)$ in the following manner:

- Compute partial derivative images $\tilde{g}_u(i,j)$, $\tilde{g}_v(i,j)$, $\tilde{g}_{uu}(i,j)$, $\tilde{g}_{vv}(i,j)$, $\tilde{g}_{uv}(i,j)$ from the original image $\tilde{g}(i,j)$ using local fixed-window surface fits that are accomplished via convolution operators.

- Using the partial derivative images, compute the mean curvature image $H(\tilde{g}_u, \tilde{g}_v, \tilde{g}_{uu}, \tilde{g}_{vv}, \tilde{g}_{uv})$ and the Gaussian Curvature image $K(\tilde{g}_u, \tilde{g}_v, \tilde{g}_{uu}, \tilde{g}_{vv}, \tilde{g}_{uv})$.

- Compute the sign $(+,-,0)$ of mean curvature, denoted $sgn(H)$, and the sign of Gaussian curvature, denoted $sgn(K)$. The signum function $sgn(x)$ maps negative numbers to -1, positive numbers to +1, and zero maps to zero.

- Use surface curvature sign to determine a surface type label $T(i,j)$ between one and nine for each pixel (i,j).

The second stage performs iterative region growing using variable-order surface fitting as described below. The input consists of the original image and the surface type label image. In order to determine the next (first) seed region to use, a connected component algorithm isolates the largest connected region of any surface type in the $T(i,j)$ image, and then a 3x3 binary image erosion operator shrinks the region until a small seed region of appropriate size is obtained. The output of the second stage consists of a region label image $\hat{l}_g(i,j)$, which contains all region definitions in one image, and a list of coefficient vectors $\{\ \vec{a}_l\ \}$, one for each region.

It is not necessary to maintain a separate version of the reconstructed image as this can always be recomputed from the surface fit list and the region label image. However, displaying this image during program execution is an excellent way to monitor the progress of the algorithm. The error image can also be recomputed from the surface fit list, the region label image, and the original image, but it must be maintained to avoid problems when surfaces grow slightly beyond their actual boundaries. The error image is updated at each pixel with the absolute error between the approximating surface and the original data when a surface/region is accepted. During the region growing procedure, the error image is consulted to see if the current approximating function represents a given pixel better than it has been represented before. If so, a pixel that was labeled as a member of a previously determined region is free to be labeled with a better fitting region as long as the pixel is connected to the better fitting region. Thus, *labeling decisions are reversible*. Later surfaces in the sequential algorithm can relabel a pixel even though it was already labeled as part of another surface.

The algorithm above terminates when the next seed region extracted from the surface type label image is too small (e.g. less than thirty pixels). However, some pixels may still be unlabeled at this point. These pixels are coalesced into a binary surface type image in which all pixels that have already been labeled are turned off (black) leaving all unlabeled pixels on (white). This new "left-overs" surface type image is then processed by extracting and fitting the next seed region as usual except that the region growing constraints are relaxed (e.g. the allowable RMS fit error limit is doubled). When the next seed region from the left-overs surface type image is too small, the algorithm finally terminates.

The outline above provides a high-level description of all the main elements of the segmentation algorithm. We have omitted the details that are covered in subsequent sections. The algorithm as stated here does not always yield clean high-quality edges between regions, and it is possible that some pixels may be left unlabeled. Hence, a local region refinement operator was needed to create the final segmentations shown in the experimental results section. Also, as mentioned above, surface curvature sign primitive regions must be merged at polynomial surface primitive boundaries that lie within the boundaries of a smooth surface. The details on the region refinement operation and region merging at smoothly joining surface primitive boundaries are available in [Besl 1986], and further enhancements are currently being developed. These fine points are not related to the performance of the segmentation algorithm as described here since the necessary procedures are performed after the termination of the iterative region growing.

5   Noise Estimation for Threshold Selection

Digital surfaces exhibit the property of surface coherence when sets of neighboring pixels are spatially consistent with each other in the sense that those pixels can be interpreted as noisy, quantized, sampled points of some relatively smooth surface. In order for the surface-based segmentation algorithm to group pixels based on underlying smooth surfaces, it needs to know how well the approximating functions should fit the image data. This information should be derived from the image data in a data-driven algorithm. If the noise in the image is approximately stationary, we can compute a single estimate of the noise variance (that should be applicable at almost all image pixels) by averaging estimates of the noise variance at each pixel. To compute an estimate of noise variance at each pixel, we perform a equally-weighted least-squares planar fit in the 3x3 neighborhood W_3 surrounding the pixel. If the pixel lies in the interior portion of a smooth surface region and if the radius of the mean surface curvature is larger than a few pixels, the error in the planar surface fit will be primarily due to noise. In contrast, steeply sloped image regions typically have large mean curvatures and bad planar

	$K > 0$	$K = 0$	$K < 0$
$H < 0$	Peak	Ridge	Saddle Ridge
	T=1	T=2	T=3
$H = 0$	*(none)*	Flat	Minimal Surface
	T=4	T=5	T=6
$H > 0$	Pit	Valley	Saddle Valley
	T=7	T=8	T=9

Figure 1: Surface Type Labels from Surface Curvature Sign.

fits. To get a good estimate of the magnitude of the additive noise and the quantization noise in the image, it is necessary to exclude these pixels where the gradient magnitude is large. Therefore, we only include pixels in the mean noise variance calculation if the gradient magnitude is below a preset threshold (8 levels/pixel was used in our experiments). A more detailed discussion of this idea is given in [Besl 1986].

6   Surface Type Labeling

Differential geometry states that local surface shape is *uniquely determined* by the first and second fundamental forms. Gaussian and mean curvature combine these first and second fundamental forms in two different ways to obtain scalar surface features that are *invariant to rotations, translations, and changes in parameterization* [Besl and Jain 1986]. Therefore, visible surfaces in range images have the same mean and Gaussian curvature from any viewpoint under orthographic projection. Also, *mean curvature uniquely determines the shape of graph surfaces* if a boundary curve is also specified while *Gaussian curvature uniquely determines the shape of convex surfaces and convex regions of non-convex surfaces*. There are eight fundamental viewpoint independent surface types that can be characterized using only the sign of the mean curvature (H) and Gaussian curvature (K) as shown in Figure 1. Gaussian and mean curvature can be computed directly from a range image using window operators that yield least squares estimates of first and second partial derivatives as in [Anderson and Houseman 1942] [Beaudet 1978] [Haralick and Watson 1981]. The key point is that every pixel in an image can be given a surface type label based on the values of the pixels in a small neighborhood about that pixel.

Surface curvature estimates are extremely sensitive to noise because they require the estimation of second derivatives. In fact, 8-bit quantization noise alone can seriously degrade the quality of surface curvature estimates unless large window sizes are used (at least 9x9). Yet reliable estimates of surface curvature sign can still be computed in the presence of additive noise and quantization noise [Besl and Jain 1986].

7 Seed Region Extraction

We adopted the following strategy that breaks the unwanted connections with other adjacent regions and attempts to provide small, maximally interior regions that are good for surface fitting. The largest connected region of any fundamental surface type in the surface type label image is isolated (denoted R_0) and then eroded (contracted) repetitively (using a 3x3 binary region erosion operator) until the region disappears. After the k-th contraction (erosion), there exists a largest four-connected sub-region R^k in the pixels remaining from the contractions of the original region. If we record $|R^k|$, the number of pixels in the largest connected sub-region, as a function of the number of contractions k, a *contraction profile* for the original region is created. Contraction profiles for several regions of a surface type label image (for the coffee cup range image) are shown in Figure 2. A seed region size threshold t_{seed} for the minimum number of pixels required to be in a seed region (e.g. 10) is a pre-selected parameter. If we examine the contraction profile, there will always be an contraction number k such that $|R^k| \geq t_{seed}$ and $|R^{k+1}| < t_{seed}$. The region R^k is selected as the *seed region* (or kernel region) for subsequent surface fitting and region growing. The circles in Figure 2 indicate the size of the selected seed region. The threshold t_{seed} must

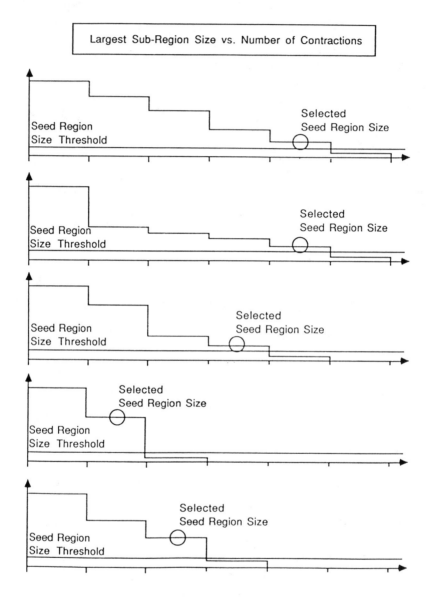

Figure 2: Contraction Profiles for Five Surface Type Regions.

always be greater than or equal to the minimum number of points required for the simplest surface fit (i.e. 3 points for a plane).

The fundamental purpose of the contraction profile computation for seed region extraction is to find a small enough isolated region that (1) is not inadvertently connected to any separate, but adjacent surface regions, and (2) is far enough inside the boundaries of the actual surface primitive to provide good surface fitting. The 3x3 erosion operation (i.e. zero out pixels that have zero-valued neighbors and leave other pixels alone) is a simple, common image processing operation that can be accomplished in less than a video frame time on existing image processing hardware. Other methods for obtaining seed regions are possible, but this method is simple and potentially very fast.

8   Iterative Variable Order Surface Fitting

A plane is always fitted first to the small seed region using equally-weighted least squares. If the seed region belongs to a surface that is not extremely curved, a plane will fit quite well to the digital surface defined by the original image data. If the plane fits the seed region within the maximum allowable RMS error threshold $\epsilon_{max} = 2.8\sigma_{img}$, then the seed is allowed to grow. If not, the seed is fitted with the next higher-order surface (e.g. biquadratic), and the algorithm proceeds similarly. When the seed is allowed to grow, the functional description of the surface over the seed region is tested over the entire image to determine what pixels are compatible with the seed region as described in the next section.

This surface fitting process may be stated more precisely as follows. Let I be the rectangular image region over which a hypothetical piecewise smooth function $z = g(x, y)$ is defined. Let $\hat{R}_l^{k=0}$ denote the seed region provided by the seed extraction algorithm that is assumed to be contained in the unknown actual region R_l in the image: $\hat{R}_l^{k=0} \subseteq R_l \subseteq I$. The seed region $\hat{R}_l^{k=0}$ must be converted to a full region description $\hat{R}_l$ that approximates the desired region description R_l.

Now, let $\vec{a}_l^k$ be the parameter vector associated with the functional fit to the pixel values in the given region $\hat{R}_l^k$ of the k-th iterative surface fit. Let $\Re^{15}$ denote the set of all parameter vectors for the set of approximating functions F, and let $|F| = 4$ be the number of different types of surface functions to be used. A particular function type (or fit order) is referred to as m where $1 \leq m \leq |F|$. The general fitting function of type m is denoted $z = \hat{f}(m, \vec{a}; x, y)$. The general surface fitting process, denoted $L_{\hat{f}}$, maps the original image data $\tilde{g}(x, y)$, a connected region definition $\hat{R}_l^k$, and the current fit order m^k into the range space $\Re^{15} \times \Re^+$ where $\Re^+$ is the set of possible errors (non-negative real numbers):

$$(\vec{a}_l^k, \epsilon_l^k) = \mathbf{L}_{\hat{f}}(m^k, \hat{R}_l^k, \tilde{g}) \tag{3}$$

that has the property that the error metric

$$\epsilon_l^k = \|\hat{f}(m^k, \vec{a}_l^k; x, y) - \tilde{g}(x, y)\|_{\hat{R}_l^k} \tag{4}$$

is the minimum value attainable for all functions of the form specified by m^k. Equally-weighted *least-squares* surface fitting minimizes the error metric

$$(\epsilon_l^k)^2 = \frac{1}{|\hat{R}_l^k|} \sum_{(x,y) \in \hat{R}_l^k} (\hat{f}(m^k, \vec{a}_l^k; x, y) - \tilde{g}(x, y))^2 \tag{5}$$

where $|\hat{R}_l^k|$ is the number of pixels in the region $\hat{R}_l^k$ (the area of the region). The parameter vector $\vec{a}_l^k$ and and the surface fit order m^k are passed onto the region growing procedure if the RMS fit error test and the regions test are passed. Otherwise, m^k is incremented and the higher order surface is fitted. If all four fit orders were tried and the error was never less than the threshold, the seed region is rejected by marking off the pixels in the surface type label image, and then continuing by looking for the next largest connected region of any surface type.

8.1 RMS Fit Error Test

The RMS fit error test tests the surface fit error, which measures the variance of the error of the fit due to the noise in the data, against the maximum allowable fit error as determined from the noise variance estimate for the image: $\epsilon_l^k < \epsilon_{max} = 2.8\sigma_{img}$. If the error is small enough, the surface fit passes the test; otherwise, it fails. The coefficient (2.8) is an empirically determined parameter.

8.2   Regions Test

The regions test is required because it is possible for a lower order function to fit a higher order function over a finite region within the maximum allowable fit error threshold even though the lower order fit is not appropriate. It is possible to detect the presence of a higher order function in the data (without letting the fit error increase all the way up to the error threshold) by analyzing the distribution of the sign of the fit errors (residual errors) at each individual pixel of the fit. We have generalized the runs test of nonparametric statistics to assist in the detection of higher order behavior. This test is discussed in detail in [Besl 1986].

9   Parallel Region Growing

After a surface of order m^k is fitted to the region $\hat{R}_l^k$ in the k-th iteration, the surface description is used to grow the region into a (hopefully) larger region where all pixels in the larger region are connected to the original region and compatible with the approximating surface function for the original region. The parallel region growing algorithm accepts as input the original digital surface $\tilde{g}(x, y)$, the approximating function $\hat{f}(m^k, \vec{a}_l^k; x, y)$ and the surface fit error ϵ_l^k from the surface fitting algorithm. It does not use the region definition until later. To determine the zeroth-order "surface continuity" compatibility of each pixel $p \in I$ with the approximating surface description, the polynomial based prediction for the pixel value and the actual pixel value

$$\hat{z}(p) \equiv \hat{f}(m^k, \vec{a}_l^k; x(p), y(p)) \quad and \quad z(p) \equiv \tilde{g}(x(p), y(p)) \qquad (6)$$

are compared to see if the pixel p is compatible with the approximating surface function. If the magnitude of the difference between the function value and the digital surface value is less than the allowed tolerance value, denoted $w_0 \epsilon_l^k$, then the pixel p is added to the set of compatible pixels, denoted $C(m^k, \vec{a}_l^k, \epsilon_l^k)$, which are compatible with the surface fit to the region $\hat{R}_l^k$. Otherwise, the pixel is incompatible and discarded. The result of this process is the compatible pixel list:

$$C(m^k, \vec{a}_l^k, \epsilon_l^k) = \{p \in I : |\hat{z}(p) - z(p)| \le w_0 \epsilon_l^k\}. \tag{7}$$

This set of compatible pixels $C(\cdot)$ is essentially a thresholded absolute value image of the difference between the original image data and the image created by evaluating the function $\hat{f}$ at each pixel. For our experimental results, the factor $w_0 = 2.8$ was used. This insures that approximately 99.5% of all samples of a smooth surface corrupted by normally-distributed measurement noise will lie within this error tolerance. This factor has been found to work well in the presence of other types of noise also.

The compatible pixel list is then post processed to remove any pixels that do not possess "surface normal continuity" compatibility with the approximating surface. Let $\tilde{g}_u(p)$ and $\tilde{g}_v(p)$ denote the first partial derivative estimates of the local surface as computed from the image data at the pixel p via convolutions as mentioned earlier. Let $\hat{g}_u(p)$ and $\hat{g}_v(p)$ denote the first partial derivatives of the approximating surface as computed from the polynomial coefficients at the pixel p. Let $\tilde{n}$ be the unit normal vector as determined by the data, and let $\hat{n}$ be the unit normal vector as determined by the approximating surface:

$$\tilde{n} = \frac{\left[\begin{array}{ccc} -\tilde{g}_u & -\tilde{g}_v & 1 \end{array}\right]^T}{\sqrt{1 + \tilde{g}_u^2 + \tilde{g}_v^2}} \qquad \hat{n} = \frac{\left[\begin{array}{ccc} -\hat{g}_u & -\hat{g}_v & 1 \end{array}\right]^T}{\sqrt{1 + \hat{g}_u^2 + \hat{g}_v^2}} \tag{8}$$

A pixel is compatible in the sense of surface normal continuity if the angle between the two unit normals is less than some threshold angle θ_t:

$$\cos^{-1}(\hat{n} \cdot \tilde{n}) \le \theta_t. \tag{9}$$

For our experimental results, the threshold angle is given by $\theta_t = 12 + 16\sigma_{img}$ degrees, where the coefficients were determined empirically.

The test may be rewritten in the following form to avoid square roots and to incorporate the derivative values directly:

$$\frac{(\tilde{g}_u - \hat{g}_u)^2 + (\tilde{g}_v - \hat{g}_v)^2 + (\tilde{g}_u\hat{g}_v - \tilde{g}_v\hat{g}_u)^2}{(1 + \tilde{g}_u^2 + \tilde{g}_v^2)(1 + \hat{g}_u^2 + \hat{g}_v^2)} \leq \sin^2(\theta_t). \qquad (10)$$

Since the compatibility test for surface normal continuity involves many computations per pixel, it is only applied to those pixels that have passed the compatibility test for surface continuity. Excellent segmentation results have been obtained without the surface normal continuity test on many images that lack small orientation discontinuities. However, a data-driven smooth-surface segmentation algorithm must always perform the test to insure that growing regions do not inadvertently grow over small or noisy orientation discontinuities.

9.1 Region Iteration

When the parallel region growing computation has operated on every pixel, the compatible pixel list $C(m^k, \vec{a}_l^k, \epsilon_l^k) \subseteq I$ is complete. The largest connected region in this set of pixels that overlaps the seed region $\hat{R}_l^k$ must then be extracted to create the next region $\hat{R}_l^{k+1}$. This process is denoted $\Lambda(\cdot)$. The output region $\hat{R}_l^{k+1}$ must have the property that it is the largest connected region in the list of compatible pixels satisfying

$$\hat{R}_l^k \cap \hat{R}_l^{k+1} \neq \phi = NullSet \qquad (11)$$

because it is possible to get larger connected regions in the compatible pixel list than the connected region corresponding to the seed region. The iterative process of region definition via largest, overlapping, connected region extraction may be expressed as follows:

$$\hat{R}_l^{(k+1)} = \Lambda(C(m^k, \vec{a}_l^k, \epsilon_l^k), \hat{R}_l^k) = \Phi(\hat{R}_l^k) \qquad (12)$$

where $\Phi(\cdot)$ represents all operations required to compute the region $\hat{R}_l^{k+1}$ from the region $\hat{R}_l^k$. It is interesting to note that since the regions of an image form a metric space [Besl 1986], the desired solution region is a fixed point $R = \Phi(R)$ of the mapping $\Phi(\cdot)$.

The new region is then considered as a seed region and processed by the surface fitting algorithm

$$(\vec{a}_l^{k+1}, \epsilon_l^{k+1}) = L_j(m^{k+1}, \hat{R}_l^{k+1}, \tilde{g}) \tag{13}$$

to obtain a new parameter vector and a new surface fit error. If this region is allowed to grow again $\epsilon_l^{k+1} < \epsilon_{max}$, then the compatible pixel list is recomputed

$$C(m^{k+1}, \vec{a}_l^{k+1}, \epsilon_l^{k+1}) \tag{14}$$

the largest connected overlapping region of $C(\cdot)$ is extracted and so on until the termination criteria are met.

9.2   Sequential vs. Parallel Region Growing

It must be noted that this parallel region growing approach is currently entirely equivalent to sequential, spiraling region growing approaches *until the last iteration*. At the last iteration, the processing of the compatible pixel list becomes an important feature of the segmentation algorithm. After the growing region has been accepted, any other sufficiently large (and reasonably shaped) regions in the compatible pixel list are also accepted as part of the same surface. For example, in the coffee cup image the flat background visible through the handle of the cup is correctly assigned to larger background surface without high-level knowledge, only the surface compatibility concepts. This is an good example of the data-driven pixel grouping capabilities of this segmentation approach. Non-adjacent compatible regions can be labeled as such without post-processing operations.

10   Termination Rules

The termination criteria are expressed as the following set of rules:

1. IF $|\hat{R}_l^k| \approx |\hat{R}_l^j|$ for any $j < k$, THEN Stop! Basically, this rule states the condition that we are looking for a fixed point of the mapping Φ in the metric space of image regions. Note that

only the size of the region is checked from iteration to iteration, not the detailed region description.

2. IF $\epsilon_l^k > \epsilon_{max}$ AND $m^k \geq |F|$, THEN Stop! The image data is varying in a way that the highest order function cannot approximate.

3. At Least Two (2) Iterations are required for a given surface fit order m^k before the algorithm is allowed to stop.

These rules state the essential concepts involved in terminating the surface fitting iteration. There is also a maximum limit on the number of possible iterations to prevent extremely long iterations. In all tests done to this point, the maximum limit of 30 iterations has never been reached and the average number of iterations is approximately eight.

11   Surface Acceptance and Rejection Decisions

After the surface growing iterations have terminated, we are left with the set of compatible pixels and the connected surface region itself along with the function parameters and the fit error. For growth surface regions that exceed the error threshold ϵ_{max}, but not by much, an acceptance zone is defined above the error threshold such that surface regions within the acceptance zone are accepted. The acceptance threshold used for our experiments is 50% greater than $\epsilon_{max} = 2.8\sigma_{img}$. Surface regions with fit errors beyond the acceptance zone are rejected.

When a surface region is rejected for any reason, the seed region responsible for the surface region is marked off in the surface type label image as having been processed, which prohibits the use of the same original seed region again. When a surface region is accepted, all pixels in that region are similarly marked off in the surface type label image so that they are not considered for future seed regions. In this respect, surface rejection and surface acceptance are similar. However, the surface acceptance process also updates the region label image, the reconstruction image, and the error image as described above. In addition, the acceptance process dilates the accepted region description and checks if there are any connected groups of pixels in that dilated region that are surface-continuity compatible with the accepted surface and connected with the accepted region. Surface-normal compatibility is not required when adding these pixels because of the difficulty in getting accurate normal estimates near surface region boundaries.

12 Experimental Results

The surface-based segmentation algorithm has been applied successfully to more than forty test images. In this section, the segmentation algorithm's performance on six range images and three intensity images is discussed. The following set of images is displayed for each input image:

1. Original Gray Scale Image (upper left)
2. Surface Type Label Image Segmentation Plot (lower left)
3. Region Label Image Segmentation Plot (lower right)
4. Reconstructed Gray Scale Image (upper right)

The surface type label image shows the coarse "initial guess" segmentation provided by labeling each pixel with one of eight labels according to the sign of the mean and Gaussian curvature. Each region in this image is an isolated set of connected pixels that all have the same surface type label. The region label image shows the final refined segmentation obtained from the iterative region-growing algorithm. Each region in this image is the support region over which a particular polynomial surface function is evaluated. The reconstructed image is computed from the region label image and the list of surface parameters, and it shows the visual quality of the approximate surface representation. For each image, we also list the noise variance estimate computed from the original image and the error statistics computed from the original-reconstruction difference image.

Figure 3: Segmentation Results for Coffee Cup Range Image.

When a user runs the program on an image, the name of the image is typically the only input required by the program. All internal parameters are either fixed or automatically varying based on the noise variance estimate. The user does have the option to change five of the fixed internal parameters and to override the three automatically set thresholds: (1) the maximum allowed RMS fit error, (2) the surface normal compatibility angle threshold, and (3) the regions test threshold. Eight of the nine images shown here were obtained without any adjustments whatsoever, but more interesting results were obtained by overriding the automatically set thresholds for the computer keyboard range image, which has nonstationary noise. This was necessary because of the stationarity assumption of the current noise variance estimation algorithm, which allows us to describe the image noise with a single number.

Figure 4: Segmentation Results for Cube with Three Holes Range Image.

12.1   Coffee Cup Range Image (ERIM)

The coffee cup range image is a 128 x 128 8-bit image from an ERIM phase-differencing range sensor [Zuk and Delleva 1983]. The segmentation results are shown in Figure 3. The measured noise variance is $\sigma_{img} = 1.02$, and the mean absolute deviation between the final reconstructed image and the original image is $E(|e(i,j)|) = 1.46$. The final segmentation clearly delineates the outside cylindrical surface of the cup, the foot of the cup, the inside cylindrical surface of the cup, the background table surface (which was recognized as a single surface with three sub-regions despite the non-adjacency of the region visible through the handle and the small hole in the side of the cup), and the cup handle surface (which is represented as two surfaces due to the twisting of the surface from this view). Although this image is easy to segment by many other methods, the subtle difference in surface variations between the foot and the main body of the cup is difficult to detect with an edge detector. Two meaningless small surfaces did arise on the steeply sloped sides of the cup because the laser range sensor has difficulty obtaining good results when most of the laser energy is reflected away from the sensor. Note that although this algorithm knows nothing about *cylinders*, the cylindrical surface of the cup is adequately segmented.

12.2   Cube with Three Holes

The cube with three holes drilled through it provides an interesting non-convex combination of flat and cylindrical surfaces. This range image was created by using a depth-buffer algorithm on a 3-D solid model created using SDRC/GEOMOD and then adding pseudo-Gaussian noise. The segmentation results are shown in Figure 4. The measured noise variance is $\sigma_{img} = 1.89$, and the mean absolute deviation between the final reconstructed image and the original image is $E(|e(i,j)|) = 2.94$. The three linear dihedral edges of the cube have been determined to subpixel precision by intersecting the planar descriptions for the three planes. The results here show the raw segmentation in the region label image.

12.3   Space Shuttle Intensity Image

The segmentation results for an image of a space shuttle launch are shown in Figure 5. The measured noise variance is $\sigma_{img} = 2.71$, and the mean absolute deviation between the final reconstructed image and the original image is $E(|e(i,j)|) = 4.32$. The reconstructed image lacks detail whenever the detail in the original image consists of only a few pixels (10 or less) or is only one pixel wide. For example, a small piece of the gantry tower is missing in the reconstructed image. The surface type label image segmentation appears completely incoherent when compared to the shuttle image. This is unlike most range images where some structure is usually perceivable. However, it still provided enough grouping information to the region growing algorithm to produce the final segmentation. The sky, the smoke

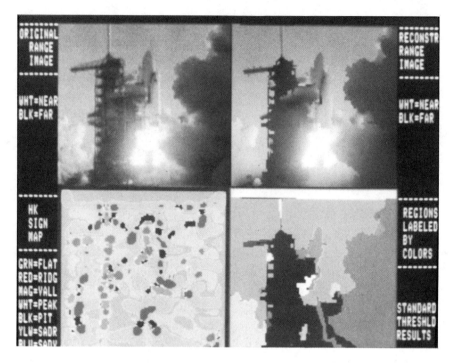

Figure 5: Segmentation Results for Space Shuttle Intensity Image.

clouds, the main tank, and the bright flames are isolated as intensity-image surface primitives.

13   Conclusions and Future Directions

The experimental results obtained by applying the surface-based segmentation algorithm with a fixed set of input parameters to a large test database of over forty images, including range and intensity images, indicates that segmentation of digital surfaces based on a piecewise-smooth surface model, surface curvature sign, and polynomial surface approximations is feasible.

This surface-based approach is very general in many respects. Flat surfaces are described explicitly as being flat, and arbitrary curved surfaces are described as being curved within the context of the same variable-order surface fitting algorithm. Most techniques in the literature need to handle flat and curved (quadric) surfaces as separate special cases. No *a priori* assumptions about surface convexity, surface symmetry, or object shape are used. The final segmentation/reconstruction description is driven by the content of the data, not by expected high-level models as is done in many other approaches. Moreover, the exact same algorithm with the exact same set of parameters is shown to be capable of segmenting range images and intensity images. We believe that any image that can be represented by a piecewise-smooth surface over sufficiently large regions (more than 10-30 pixels) can be segmented well by this algorithm.

The basic sign-of-curvature/iterative variable-order fitting approach is applicable to the segmentation of signals in any number of dimensions, not just scalar functions of two variables. The method is shown to be successful for edge interval segmentation in [Besl 1986]. If one-pixel wide edges can be obtained, x and y can be parameterized as a function of arc length yielding a vector function of a single variable. Only three sign-of-curvature labels are needed: concave up, concave down, and flat. In the future, we hope to be able to apply the algorithm to signals representing scalar functions of three variables, such as dynamic scenes and 3-D images from CAT scanners. In that case, 27 sign-of-curvature labels are needed, and approximating functions require many coefficients.

Bibliography

[1] G. J. Agin and T. O. Binford. *Computer description of curved objects.* In Proceedings of 3rd International Joint Conference on Artificial Intelligence, Stanford, CA, Aug. 20–23, 1973, p. 629–640.

[2] R. L. Anderson and E. E. Houseman. *Tables of Orthogonal Polynomial Values Extended to N=104.* Research Bulletin 297, Iowa State College of Agriculture and Mechanic Arts, Ames, Iowa, Apr. 1942.

[3] P. R. Beaudet. *Rotationally invariant image operators.* In Proceedings of 4th International Conference Pattern Recognition,

Kyoto, Japan, Nov. 7–10, 1978, p. 579–583.

[4] P. J. Besl. *Surfaces in Early Range Image Understanding,* Ph.D. Dissertation, Electr. Eng. Comp. Sci. Dept. (RSD-TR-10-86), University of Michigan, Ann Arbor, MI, March. 1986.

[5] P. J. Besl and R. C. Jain. *Invariant surface characteristics for three-dimensional object recognition in range images.* Computer Vision, Graphics, Image Processing, Jan. 1986, 33(1):33–80.

[6] P. J. Besl and R. C. Jain. *Three-dimensional object recognition.* ACM Computing Surveys, March. 1985, 17(1):75–145.

[7] P. J. Besl, E. J. Delp and R. C. Jain. *Automatic visual solder joint inspection.* IEEE J. Robotics and Automation, May 1985, 1(1):42–56.

[8] B. Bhanu. *Representation and shape matching of 3-D objects.* IEEE Trans. Pattern Anal. Machine Intell. PAMI-6, May 1984, 3:340–350.

[9] B. Bhanu, S. Lee, C. C. Ho and T. Henderson. *Range data processing: representation of surfaces by edges.* Proceedings of International Pattern Recognition Conference, IAPR-IEEE, 1986, p. 236–238.

[10] R. C. Bolles and M. A. Fischler. *A RANSAC-based approach to model fitting and its application to finding cylinders in range data.* In Proceedings of 7th International Joint Conference on Artificial Intelligence, Vancouver, B.C., Canada, Aug. 24–28, 1981, p. 637–643.

[11] R. C. Bolles and P. Horaud. *A Three-dimensional Part Orientation System,* Int. J. Robotic Res., Fall 1986, 5(3):3–26.

[12] B. A. Boyter. *Three-dimensional matching using range data.* In Proceedings of 1st Conference on Artificial Intelligence Applications, IEEE, 1984, p. 211–216.

[13] M. Brady, J. Ponce, A. Yuille and H. Asada. *Describing surfaces.* In Proceedings of 2nd International Symposium on Robotics

Research, (H. Hanafusa and H. Inoue Eds.), MIT Press, Cambridge, Mass, 1985.

[14] D. Chen. *A regression updating approach for detecting multiple curves.* Proceedings of 2nd World Conference on Robotics Research, Scottsdale, Arizona, August 18–21, 1986, RI/SME.

[15] H. Derin and H. Elliot. *Modeling and segmentation of noisy and textured images using Gibbs random fields.* IEEE Trans. Pattern Anal. Machine Intell., Jan. 1, 1986, PAMI-9, p. 39–55.

[16] T. G. Fan, G. Medioni and R. Nevatia. *Description of surfaces from range data using curvature properties.* Proceedings of Computer Vision and Pattern Recognition Conference, Miami, Fla., June 22–26, 1986, IEEE-CS, p. 86–91.

[17] O. D. Faugeras, M. Hebert and E. Pauchon. *Segmentation of range data into planar and quadric patches.* In Proceedings of 3rd Computer Vision and Pattern Recognition Conference, Arlington, Va., 1983, p. 8–13.

[18] O. D. Faugeras and M. Hebert. *The representation, recognition, and locating of 3-D objects.* Int. J. Robotic Res., Fall 1986. 5:(3)27–52.

[19] B. Gil, A. Mitiche and J. K. Aggarwal. *Experiments in combining intensity and range edge maps.* Comput. Vision, Graphics, and Image Processing, March. 1983, 21:395–411.

[20] G. H. Golub and C. F. VAN Loan. *Matrix Computations.* Johns Hopkins Univ. Press, Baltimore, Md, 1983.

[21] R. M. Haralick and L. Watson. *A facet model for image data.* Computer Graphics Image Processing, 1981, 15:113–129.

[22] M. Hebert and T. Kanade. *The 3-D profile method for object recognition.* In Proceedings of Computer Vision and Pattern Recognition Conference San Francisco, Calif., June 9–13, 1985, IEEE-CS, New York, p. 458–463.

[23] M. Hebert and J. Ponce. *A new method for segmenting 3-D scenes into primitives.* In Proceedings of 6th International Conference Pattern Recognition Munich, West Germany, Oct. 19–22, 1982. p. 836–838.

[24] T. C. Henderson and B. Bhanu. *Three-point seed method for the extraction of planar faces from range data.* In Proceedings of Workshop on Industrial Applications of Machine Vision Research Triangle Park, N.C., May. 1982 IEEE, New York, p. 181–186.

[25] M. Herman. *Generating detailed scene descriptions from range images.* In Proceedings of International Conference on Robotics and Automation St. Louis, Mo., March. 25–28, 1985. IEEE-CS, New York, p. 426–431.

[26] B. K. P. Horn. *Extended Gaussian images.* Proc. IEEE, Dec. 1984, 72:(12) 1656–1678.

[27] K. Ikeuchi and B. K. P. Horn. *Numerical shape from shading and occluding boundaries.* Artificial Intell. Aug. 1981. 17:141–184.

[28] S. Inokuchi and R. Nevatia. *Boundary detection in range pictures.* In Proceedings of 5th International Conference Pattern Recognition Miami, Fla., Dec. 1–4, 1980. p. 1031–1035.

[29] S. Inokuchi, T. Nita, F. Matsuday and Y. Sakurai. *A three-dimensional edge-region operator for range pictures.* In Proceedings of 6th International Conference Pattern Recognition Munich, West Germany, Oct. 19–22, 1982. p. 918–920.

[30] D. J. Ittner and A. K. Jain. *3-D surface discrimination from local curvature measures.* In Proceedings of Computer Vision and Pattern Recognition Conference San Francisco, Calif., June 9–13, 1985, IEEE-CS, New York, p. 119–123.

[31] D. T. Kuan and R. J. Drazovich. *Model-based interpretation of range imagery.* In Proceedings of the National Conference on Artificial Intelligence Austin, Tex., Aug. 6–10, 1984. American Association for Artificial Intelligence, p. 210–215.

[32] C. Lin and M. J. Perry. *Shape description using surface triangularization.* In Proceedings of Workshop on Computer Vision: Representation and Control Rindge, N.H., Aug. 23–25, 1982. IEEE-CS, New York, p. 38–43.

[33] G. Medioni and R. Nevatia. *Description of 3-D surfaces using curvature properties.* In Proceedings of the Image Understanding Workshop New Orleans, La., Oct. 3–4, 1984. DARPA, p. 291–299.

[34] D. L. Milgram and C. M. Bjorklund. *Range image processing: planar surface extraction.* In Proceedings of 5th International Conference Pattern Recognition Miami, Fla., Dec. 1–4, 1980. p. 912–919.

[35] A. Mitiche and J. K. Aggarwal. *Detection of edges using range information.* IEEE Trans. Pattern Anal. Machine Intell. PAMI-5, March. 2, 1983, p. 174–178.

[36] R. Nevatia and T. O. Binford. *Structured descriptions of complex objects.* In Proceedings of 3rd International Joint Conference on Artificial Intelligence Stanford, Calif. Aug. 20–23, 1973. p. 641–647.

[37] M. Oshima and Y. Shirai. *Object recognition using three-dimensional information.* IEEE Trans. Pattern Anal. Machine Intell. PAMI-5, July 4, 1983, p. 353–361.

[38] F. G. Peet and T. S. Sahota. *Surface curvature as a measure of image texture.* IEEE Trans. Pattern Anal. Machine Intell. PAMI-7, Nov. 6, 1985, p. 734–738.

[39] R. J. Popplestone, C. M. Brown, A. P. Ambler and G. F. Crawford. *Forming models of plane-and-cylinder faceted bodies from light stripes.* In Proceedings of 4th International Joint Conference on Artificial Intelligence Tbilisi, Georgia, USSR, Sept. 1975 p. 664–668.

[40] I. K. Sethi and S. N. Jayaramamurthy. *Surface classification using characteristic contours.* In Proceedings of 7th Interna-

tional Conference Pattern Recognition Montreal, Canada, July 30–Aug. 2, 1984. p. 438–440.

[41] Y. Shirai and M. Suwa. *Recognition of polyhedra with a range finder.* In Proceedings of 2nd International Joint Conference on Artificial Intelligence London, U.K., Aug. 1971, p. 80–87.

[42] D. R. Smith and T. Kanade. *Autonomous scene description with range imagery.* In Proceedings of the Image Understanding Workshop New Orleans, La., Oct. 3–4, 1984. DARPA, p. 282–290.

[43] K. Sugihara. *Range-data analysis guided by junction dictionary.* Artificial Intell., 1979, 12:41–69.

[44] D. Terzopoulos. *Computing visible surface representations.* AI Memo No. 800, MIT Artif. Intell. Laboratory, Cambridge, Mass, March. 1985.

[45] F. Tomita and T. Kanade. *A 3D vision system: generating and matching shape descriptions in range images.* In Proceedings of the International Conference Robotics. Atlanta, Ga., March. 13–15, 1984. IEEE-CS, New York, p. 186–191.

[46] B. C. Vemuri, A. Mitiche and J. K. Aggarwal. *Curvature-based representation of objects from range data.* Image and Vision Computing, May 1986. 4(2):107–114.

[47] D. M. Zuk and M. L. Delleva. *Three-Dimensional Vision System for the Adaptive Suspension Vehicle.* Final Report No. 170400-3-F, ERIM, DARPA 4468, Defense Supply Service-Washington, Jan. 1983.

Learning Structural
Descriptions of Shape

Jakub Segen
AT&T Bell Laboratories

Abstract

Descriptions specifying the structure of an object in terms of its parts
and their relationships are useful to model nonrigid shapes. An approach to automatic learning of such descriptions from examples is
discussed. Learning is applied not only to construct object descriptions, but also to identify the properties and relations to be used
as description primitives. These primitives are created by assigning
symbols to patterns discovered in shape geometry. The shape description primitives form a hierarchy, with simpler primitives being
used as elements of the more complex ones. The shape descriptions
are constructed from these primitives, using a statistical learning
technique that automatically limits description complexity.

1 Introduction

To recognize an object from its observed shape one needs a model of
shape suitable to viewing conditions. If objects undergo only rigid
transformations and are never occluded, then simple models describing shape as a vector of global features, such as area, perimeter,
or moment invariants, may suffice. Object recognition using such
models can be very fast, with time complexity as low as the loga-
rithm of the number of classes (using decision trees). However, such
simple models are not sufficient if object geometry is not rigid, in
particular if parts of an object are deformed in different ways. One
class of models which have been found useful in such cases is based
on structural properties of shape. Such models identify parts of an

257

object, and describe the shape in terms of these parts and their relationships. The most frequently used form of a structural model
is an attributed graph (or hypergraph) (Barrow et al. [1], Shapiro
[2], Wong and Lu [3]), or equivalent structure, such as semantic net
(Winston [4], Connel and Brady [5]). The vertices of a graph represent parts, and edges describe relations among parts. The vertices
have attributes describing properties of parts, for example "long",
"round", or "square" The edges also have attributes, that specify
geometric and topological relations, such as "parallel", "above", or
"touching".

While graphs provide a general and a very powerful representation of structure, there are two significant difficulties associated with
their use as shape models. The first one is well known: the task
of comparing two graphs is NP-complete under any useful definition
of match or similarity between two graphs. The second difficulty is
the choice of primitives of structural descriptions, in particular the
geometric properties and relations represented as graph attributes.
A symbolic attribute represents a range of some measured quantity,
for example "wide" may mean 10 to 15 inches, "above" may stand
for North with 10 degrees tolerance. Since there is no general rule
for selecting these primitives, in most applications they have to be
hand picked to make a graph model work.

The complexity of graph matching and the selection of structural
primitives are related problems. An upper bound on the match value
can be computed by comparing sets of attributes for two graphs. This
upper bound can be used to eliminate some potential matches. The
more diversified is a set of attributes, the tighter is the bound, and
more matches are eliminated. This relation suggests that investigating the issue of structural primitive selection might also provide
a partial answer to the problem of graph matching. Given a large
number of well-chosen structural primitives, it may be possible to
select the most informative ones to be used as features, just like the
global features mentioned earlier. Comparing shape representation
sed on these structural features would be very fast and could sub-
'ially reduce (possibly to zero) the number of graph matches
to identify an object. This leaves us with the question about

the origin of structural primitives. Clearly, selecting a large number of primitives by hand is not a right answer. Therefore, automated methods of their generation must be investigated.

One possible approach to automatic generation of structural primitives (Segen [6]), is based on unsupervised learning. The primitives are derived from shape data by discovering patterns in geometric relations. The structural primitives form a hierarchy: simpler primitives being used to express more complex ones, somewhat in the spirit of the representation proposed by Marr and Nishihara [7]. A supervised learning method is used to construct shape descriptions, using discovered primitives as features. These descriptions characterize some nonrigid shapes well enough to recognize them, without graph matching. The following sections describe the main elements of this approach and illustrate it with examples.

2 Overview of the Learning System

The input to the learning system i.e., the training set, is a set of shapes with a name of a class attached to each shape. The shapes in the training set are described by planar curves representing contours or edges extracted from image of an object. The first step towards a structural description is to extract from each curve a small set of localized measurements called *local features*. Local features describe the curve around points of extremum of curvature, and are represented by parameters giving position, orientation and curvature. Such local features are quite stable, and provide a good characterization of a curve (Marimont [8]).

The learning consists of two parts. In the first part, sets of local features extracted from training shapes are presented to the program that constructs structural primitives. This program generates a hierarchy of primitives, each describing a relation over a group of local features. Each of these primitives is associated with a binary attribute called a *structural feature*.

In the second part of learning, the training shapes are represented by sets of structural features and processed by a program which forms descriptions of classes of shapes. For each class of shapes this program finds an informative set of structural features, which together with their class-conditional probabilities form a class description.

3   Learning Structural Primitives

The process learning the structural primitives seeks patterns in configurations of local features, observed in training shapes. The form of a configuration of local features used in this process is a binary tree. The local features are the terminal nodes of this tree, while each higher node represents a geometric relation between the two local feature configurations represented by its children. We call this structure a *relational tree* or R-TREE. R-TREEs are constructed bottom-up, one level at the time, by a recursive application of three operations: clustering, labeling and composition. The simplest, or 0-order R-TREE is a local feature. A first order R-TREE is a pair of local features, a second order R-TREE corresponds to a pair of pairs of local features, and so forth. Examples of R-TREEs up to order 3 are shown schematically in Figures 1 − 3, overimposed on a contour of a toy (Gumby). These examples are discussed in detail at the end of this section.

The representation of R-TREEs is the same for every order. This makes it easy to generate them recursively. R-TREE is represented by a structure consisting of 5 components: *order, orientation, position, characteristic and label.* The key part of this description is the characteristic. It consists of parameters that are invariant under rotation, translation and reflection. For a 0-order R-TREE the characteristic is a scalar equal to the curvature of the associated local feature. For a higher order R-TREE the characteristic is a vector of 4 elements: label-1, label-2, distance, and angle. They represent the labels of the two component R-TREEs, as well as the distance, and the angle between these R-TREEs. The label is a symbol representing a group of R-TREEs. The orientation and position (X and Y coordinates) localize R-TREE on a plane. These parameters are needed to construct next higher order R-TREEs.

A **composition** of two R-TREEs of order m is R-TREE of order m+1. If O1, O2 are the orientations of these two R-TREEs,

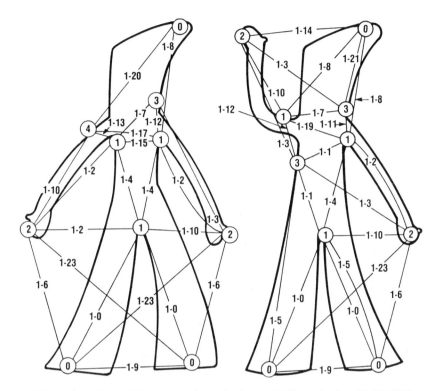

Figure 1: Local Features (Circles), and First Order R-TREEs.

the points (X1,Y1) and (X2,Y2) are their positions, and the symbols L1, L2 are their labels, then the elements of the characteristic of the new R-TREE are computed taking *label-1* and *label-2* to be, respectively, the minimum and the maximum of (L1,L2), *angle* to be the smaller angle between two lines with directions O1 and O2, and *distance* to be the distance between the points (X1,Y1) and (X2,Y2). The *orientation* of the new R-TREE is the direction of a line passing through the points (X1,Y1) and (X2,Y2). The *position* is the midpoint between the points (X1,Y1) and (X2,Y2). The *label* is initially NIL.

A set of R-TREEs of the same order can be partitioned into groups by **clustering** their characteristics. The clusters detected in a set of R-TREEs correspond to patterns of local feature configura-

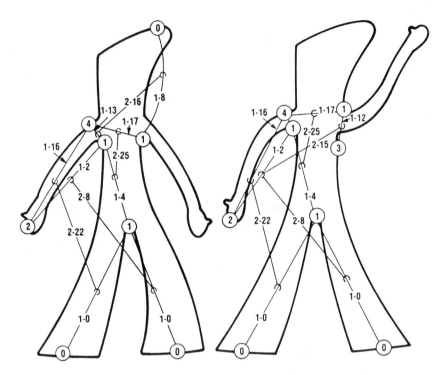

Figure 2: Second Order R-TREEs.

tions. A 0-order cluster represents a group of local features having similar curvatures, and is characterized by the mean and the variance of the curvature. A higher order cluster is a group of R-TREEs whose characteristics have identical symbolic parts: *label-1* and *label-2*, and similar numerical parts i.e., *angle* and *distance*. Such cluster is described by the same parameters as a characteristic, plus variance values given for the numerical parameters.

A **labeling** operation applied to an R-TREE and a set of clusters finds the nearest cluster, and if the distance between this cluster and the R-TREE is less than a fixed threshold, sets the label of the R-TREE to that of the cluster.

With each cluster of R-TREEs we associate a predicate, which is true for a shape if at least one of its R-TREEs is given the label of the cluster, and false otherwise. We call this predicate a *structural*

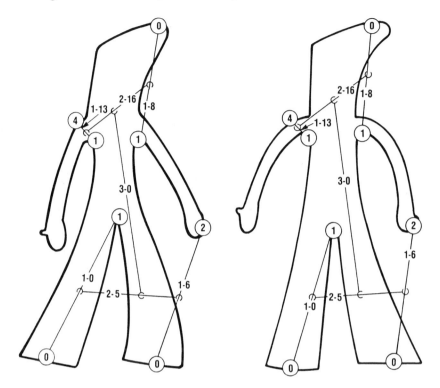

Figure 3: A Third Order R-TREE.

feature.

The following program generates a hierarchy of R-TREEs.

1. For each shape in the training set represent the local features as 0-order R-TREEs. Set the current order m = 0. The cluster library is initially empty.

2. Cluster the set of m-th order R-TREEs collected from all training shapes and add the clusters to the cluster library. Label the m-th order R-TREEs in each shape, and delete all the R-TREEs whose label remains NIL.

3. In every shape, pair each m-th order R-TREE P with its k nearest neighbors which do not share local features with P.

Eliminate duplicate pairs. Exit, if the list of pairs is empty for every shape.

4. Apply composition to the pairs of R-TREEs, and save all resulting m+1 order R-TREEs for each shape.

5. Increase current order to m+1, and go to step 2.

Examples of R-TREEs discovered by the above program are shown in Figures 1 – 3. Circles show positions of 0-order R-TREEs (local features). The numbers in circles are their labels. A line joining two circles represents a first order R-TREE, its label is printed along the line. A labeled line joining two first order R-TREEs shows a second order R-TREE, and similarly a line joining two second order R-TREEs represents a third order R-TREE. Figure 1 shows all R-TREEs of orders 0 and 1 identified in the displayed shapes. Figure reff5.2 shows several second order R-TREEs found in two different shapes. Figure 3 displays a single third order R-TREE. Since smaller R-TREEs span only a part of a shape, the same R-TREE can be found in two, quite different shapes, if they have a similar part. Several such examples are present in Figures 1 and 2. One can notice, that R-TREEs are somewhat flexible, and each accommodates a range of configurations. The flexibility of an R-TREE is the result of clustering used in its construction. The range of configurations is specific to each R-TREE and is determined by the variances of the cluster parameters.

4 Learning Shape Descriptions

The combinatorial nature of the program generating structural features causes the number of features to be very large, with many interdependencies. Treating such set of features as one long feature vector and using a standard statistical classifier, as it is done with global features, may lead to a well known problem (Kanal [9]) of low classifier performance caused by too many features. Therefore, the description learning program selects a relatively small set of "relevant" features for each class, using the method proposed by Segen

[10]. The objective is to find for a class C a set of structural features $f_1, f_2 \ldots f_k$ and their conditional probabilities, $P(f \mid C)$, to obtain a low value of the merit function:

$$Q(C, f_1, f_2, \ldots f_k) = D(C \mid f_1, f_2, \ldots f_k) + \sum_{i=1}^{k} S(f_i)$$

The function D above is a negative log likelihood, and it represents a discrepancy between a class description and the training set. The value S(f) is the number of bits needed to specify the feature f, or its *complexity*. The feature complexity here plays a role analogous to a prior probability, and its role has been discussed in [9].

Descriptions are constructed independently for each class using a simple, incremental search. The program begins with an empty list of features, and adds features one by one, each time selecting the feature that causes the largest decrement of Q. In some steps the decrement may be negative i.e., Q may increase. The program keeps track of the minimal value of Q achieved so far. The search stops when the sum of the feature complexities reaches the minimum of Q.

Descriptions constructed by this program, can be used to compute the posterior probability of each class, given an unknown shape. A shape classifier assigns a shape to the class with the highest posterior probability, if it is greater than a significance threshold.

5 Example

The learning program has been applied to a training set consisting of 56 examples and 3 shape classes. The shape classes in this example represent 3 different Gumby's poses, identified as "Help", "Hi", and "Draw". Figures 4 – 6 show some instances of each of these classes. The description constructed for the class "Help" consists of one structural feature "1–18", with $P(f \mid C) = 1$. The corresponding R-TREE is shown in Figure 4.

The description of the class "Hi" (Figure 5) consists of two structural features: "1–31" with $P(f \mid C) = 17/20$, and "1–46" with $P(f \mid C) = 15/20$. While neither feature is present in all the training shapes in this class, each of the training shapes contains at least

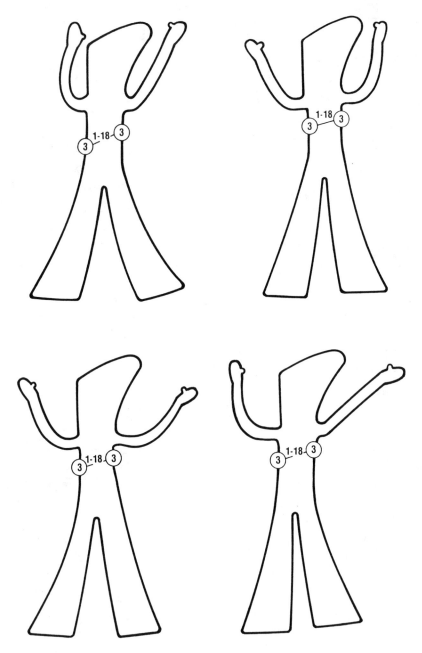

Figure 4: Examples of Class "Help".

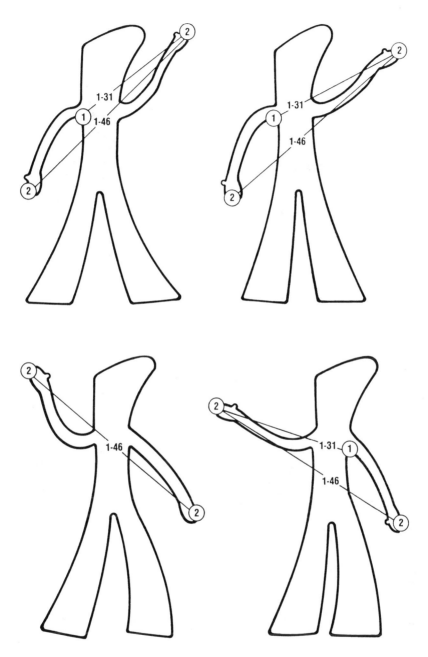

Figure 5: Examples of Class "Hi".

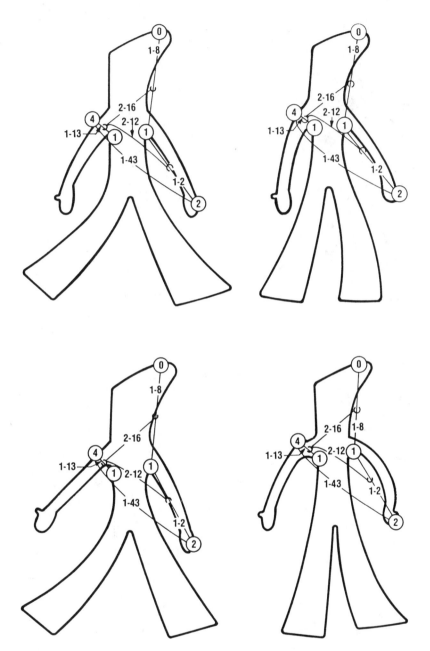

Figure 6: Examples of Class "Draw".

one of these features. The description of the class "Draw" has again only one feature "1-43" with $P(f \mid C) = 1$. The first order R-TREE "1-43", corresponding to this feature, is present in all the shapes shown in Figure 6. A formal evaluation of recognition rates achieved by these descriptions would require a significant effort, and it has not been attempted. However, an informal judgement places these rates very close to 100 percent.

All the features selected by the learning program in this example were of order 1. This simplicity might be surprising, but it is explained by the fact that the program seeks only features that discriminate among the classes in the training set, and these were found sufficient. To see if there are any informative higher order features, the program has been forced to seek them, by restricting the number of neighbors used in R-TREE composition, which prevented it from generating some of the useful first order features. This changes the description of class "Draw" to two second order features: "2-12" with $P(f \mid C) = 14/16$, and "2-16" with $P(f \mid C) = 15/16$. Both R-TREEs are shown in Figure 6.

6 Conclusion

Learning can be used not only to form structural descriptions of objects, from a given set of primitives, but also to construct the primitives used by these descriptions. These primitives can be created automatically, by assigning symbols to patterns discovered in data. Such data-derived primitives should characterize objects better than a fixed set of primitives, obtained by an arbitrary quantization of measured variables, and do not require manual fitting to each application.

One case of such learning is the R-TREE generation method described in Section 3. The main power of this method comes from a simple parametric representation of R-TREEs, which allows their recursive formation, fast matching, and their clustering in a vector space. The R-TREEs are quite robust, and in spite of their simple form they characterize well the structural properties of shape. While the R-TREE learning method still contains several parameters, which have to be set by the user, the final results are not very sensitive to their values. The selection of these parameters can be automated at some computational expense.

The method described in Section 4 constructs parsimonious descriptions, that recognize nonrigid objects, if they are completely visible. However, the lack of redundancy makes these descriptions unsuitable for occluded objects. Learning redundant descriptions, appropriate for occluded objects, is the subject of ongoing work, that explores redundancy present in the set of R-TREEs.

The discussed approach to learning is an attempt to bridge the gap between the classical, statistical learning and the learning methods based on combinatorial exploration, investigated in artificial intelligence (Michalski [11]). This approach combines the power of statistical inference for handling noise, with the potential of combinatorial construction of models, that are sufficiently complex to represent real objects.

Bibliography

[1] H. G. Barrow, A. P. Ambler and R. M. Burstall, *Some Techniques for Recognizing Structure in Pictures*, in Frontiers of Pattern Recognition, S. Watanabe (ed.), Academic Press, New York, 1972, p. 1–29.

[2] L. G. Shapiro, *A Structural Model of Shape*, IEEE Trans. on Pattern Analysis and Machine Intelligence, Vol. PAMI-2, March 1980, p. 111–126.

[3] A. K. C. Wong and S. W. Lu, *Recognition and Knowledge Synthesis of 3-D Object Models*, Proc. IEEE Conf. on Computer Vision and Pattern Recogn., CVPR'85, San Francisco, June 1985, p. 162–166.

[4] P. H. Winston, *Learning Structural Descriptions from Examples*, The Psychology of Computer Vision, Winston, P. H. (Ed.), McGraw Hill, New York, ch. 5, 1975.

[5] J. H. Connel and M. Brady. *Learning Shape Descriptions*, Proc. 9th Int'l. Conf. on Artificial Intelligence, IJCAI'85, Los Angeles, August 1985, p. 922–925.

[6] J. Segen, *Learning Structural Descriptions of Shape*, Proc. IEEE Conf. on Computer Vision and Pattern Recogn., CVPR'85, San Francisco, June 1985, p. 96–98.

[7] D. Marr and H. D. Nishihara, *Representation and Recognition of Spatial Organization of Three-Dimensional Structure*, Proc. Royal Soc. B200, p, 1978. 269–294

[8] D. H. Marimont, *A Representation for Image Curves*, Proc. National Conf. on Artificial Intelligence, AAAI, Austin, Texas, August 1984, p. 237–242.

[9] L. Kanal, *Patterns in Pattern Recognition*, IEEE Trans. on Inform. Theory, vol. IT-20, November 1974, p. 697–722.

[10] J. Segen, *Feature Selection and Constructive Inference*, 7th Intern. Conf. on Pattern Recogn., Montreal, Canada, July 1984, p. 1344–1346.

[11] R. S. Michalski, *A Theory and Methodology of Inductive Learning*, Machine Learning, R. S. Michalski, J. G. Carbonell, and T. M. Mitchel (Eds.), Tioga, Palo Alto, 1983.

Machine Vision as State-Space Search

Steven L. Tanimoto
University of Washington

Abstract

While machine vision and artificial intelligence have been closely associated for many years, there remain many ways to improve their symbiosis. Ideas in two areas of artificial intelligence appear to be in a dominant position to influence this relationship in the future: state-space search and machine learning. A formal model of vision as path finding is presented here, and some of the problems that may arise in applying the model are discussed.

1 Introduction

1.1 Motivation

The technology and practice of machine vision at the pixel level is relatively mature. Low-level image processing operations are well understood, and numerous systems have been designed and built which efficiently support these computations. On the other hand, there is little consensus either among vision researchers or practitioners as to how to best use symbol processing. Some promote the use of rule-based approaches, while others opt for graph matching, constraint satisfaction or schema instantiation.

Two kinds of information processing which have been extensively studied in artificial intelligence seem to have a particularly strong potential to advance the capabilities of machine vision systems: state-space search and learning. Some of these techniques have been applied to vision in the past; however, there is much yet to be done.

By bringing state-space search and learning into machine vision systems, we hope to improve two critical aspects of these systems: (1) generality, and (2) ease of developing algorithms for new applications.

1.2   History of Heuristic Search

The Logic Theorist: One of the early experiments in artificial intelligence used a program called the Logic Theorist to explore an approach to automatic theorem proving [6]. This program systematically applied operators to its various states of knowledge in order to derive new states. Beginning with the five axioms for the propositional calculus from *Principia Mathematica* of Whitehead and Russell, the program was able to construct proofs for a substantial number of theorems. In addition to showing how proof-finding can be formulated as state-space search, Newell, Shaw and Simon demonstrated with the Logic Theorist how the strategies of forward chaining and backward chaining can be applied.

The Combinatorial Explosion: While state-space search developed into an almost universal framework for automatic problem solving [7], it was obvious as early as 1957 in the work on the Logic Theorist that formalization of a problem in terms of state-space search is not sufficient to insure the computational feasibility of solving the problem. It is possible and in fact very common to construct a description of a state space in very simple terms and end up with a huge number of states. In the system of *Principia Mathematica*, the number of one-step proofs is five; there are 42 four-step proofs, 115 six-step proofs and 246 eight-step proofs, etc. Such rapid growth is usually termed the *combinatorial explosion*.

A Combinatorial Puzzle: Another example of a simply described state space of large size is that consisting of all arrangements of a set of k "painted squares" [10]. A sample set of four painted squares is shown in Figure 1.

By permuting, rotating, flipping and shaping the set of squares into any of the 15 quadramino shapes, we can create any of over

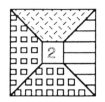 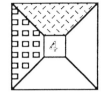

Figure 1: Four Painted Squares Used in a Puzzle Illustrating the Combinatorial Explosion.

a million different arrangements. In order to tame wild combinatorics such as these, one can apply ordering strategies and pruning heuristics. Before investigating such methods, we will mention some previous applications of state-space search in vision and present more formal descriptions of the kinds of problems we wish to solve.

1.3   State Space Search in Vision

The state-space search approach has been used in the past for particular aspects of computer vision. These include region growing and consistent scene labelling [2] and contour tracing [4,5]. Related approaches include planning [3,1], (in which the utilities of applying alternative subprograms are computed before one of the subprograms is selected), and tree search for inexact matching of models of geometric objects [9].

2   Search Problems

2.1   Simple Search Problems

A *simple search problem* S is a system with four components, i.e., $S = \langle K, T, s, G \rangle$ where K is a set of states, T is a set of transformations or "operators," s is the "start state," a designated member of K, and G is a subset of K—the "goal states."

Each operator $t \in T$ is a partial function from K to K. For a state $k \in K$, $t(k)$ may be either undefined, or may be a member of K.

A *solution* to S is a sequence $t_1, t_2, \ldots, t_n$ such that

$t_n(t_{n-1}(\ldots t_1(s)\ldots)) \in G$.

If K and T are both finite then S is a *finite simple search problem*. If K is either finite or countably infinite, and T is finite, then S is an *ordinary simple search problem*. We note that while usually finite, T may be a countably infinite set or even an uncountably infinite set. If T is uncountably infinite, we generally assume that K is also uncountably infinite; in this case we call S a *simple search problem with an uncountably infinite state space*.

2.2   Reachability and Solvability

For a simple search problem S, we can partition K into two subsets: (1) those states k for which there exists some sequence $t_1, t_2, \ldots, t_n$ such that $t_n(t_{n-1}(\ldots t_1(s)\ldots)) = k$, and (2) those states for which no such sequence exists. The first subset is called the set of *reachable states* and the second subset is the set of *unreachable states*.

If at least one goal state is reachable, then S is *solvable*. Otherwise, S is *unsolvable*.

This model of a search problem incorporates the key notions of states and operators; however, it does not admit all of the criteria that permit us to describe solutions in a way that is really useful. We generally desire a solution that is not merely a sequence of operators (path) taking us from the start state to a goal state, but a particular kind of sequence or path. We desire that such a path have a high degree of merit, or equivalently, a low "cost."

2.3   Cost Functions

It is convenient to define cost functions in terms of state-space graphs; therefore, we define state-space graphs. The *state-space graph* for a search problem S consists of the set K of states now considered as nodes, together with a set A of arcs, where (k_1, k_2) is an arc provided there is an operator $t \in T$ such that $t(k_1) = k_2$.

A *cost function* $C : K \times K \to \mathbf{R}^+$ is a non-negative function on the arcs of the state-space graph.

2.4 Minimum-Cost Path Problems:

A *minimum-cost path problem* $\mathcal{M} = \langle K, T, s, G, C \rangle$ consists of five components, the first four of which constitute a simple search problem and the fifth of which is a cost function. A solution to a minimum-cost path problem is a sequence of operators that corresponds to a path from the start node to a goal node for which the sum of the costs along the path is less than or equal to the sums for all other paths from the start node to a goal node.

2.5 The Uniform-Cost Algorithm

The *uniform-cost* algorithm for the minimum-cost path problem computes a solution as follows: A list of currently "open" nodes is initialized to contain only the start node. Its distance from the start node is recorded as 0, and a backpointer associated with it is recorded as null. A list of currently "closed" nodes is initialized as empty. The following steps are repeated until a goal node is removed from the list of open nodes. The first element on the list of open nodes (call it n) is removed from the open list. Then n is put onto the list of closed nodes. Its successors are generated by applying all the applicable operators to it. For each successor m of n, the arc cost is computed for the arc (n, m); then m is given a distance value which is the sum of the distance for n and the arc cost just generated. If m does not already occur on the open list, then a pointer to n is recorded as the backpointer for m and m is put into the list of open nodes, such that the list is maintained in order of ascending distance values. However, if m is already on the open list, then the distance for m is set to be the smaller of the distance just computed and the distance stored previously; if the distance for m is changed in this way, then the backpointer for m is changed to point to n, and m is repositioned on the open list to take its new place in the ascending order. At the point when a goal node g is removed from the open list, the searching terminates. The minimum-cost path is obtained in reverse order by following the chain of backpointers from g to s.

3   Heuristic Search Methods

3.1   Evaluation Functions

In order to avoid the combinatorial explosion, we must somehow limit
the portion of the large state space which must actually be searched.
This may be accomplished either by "pruning" (cutting off the search
along certain branches) or by ordering (visiting those states first
which are deemed likely to lead to a solution). In implementing either
of these approaches, it is useful to have some way of evaluating states
(or equivalently, nodes) in order to distinguish the more promising
ones from the less promising ones.

The standard mechanism for comparing states is based upon the
application of an *evaluation function*. Such a function assigns to
each state a real number which summarizes the relative merit (or
alternatively, the relative lack of merit) of the state. We follow the
conventions that for a heuristic evaluation function f, the lower the
value $f(n)$, the more likely node n is to be close to a goal node, and
the closer we expect it to be.

3.2   Best-First Search

The *best-first* algorithm solves simple search problems when some
heuristic evaluation function f on states is available. Like the
uniform-cost algorithm, it maintains a list of open nodes which is
sorted in ascending order by the values associated with the nodes.
Unlike the uniform-cost method, however, the value $f(n)$ depends
only on n and not on the path taken to reach n, and so there is no
need to adjust the values of nodes on the open list once they have
been put on that list. As for the uniform-cost method, the best-first
method begins with only the starting state on the open list; a list
of closed nodes is initially empty. Then a loop is executed until a
goal node is generated as a successor to the current node. The loop
begins by removing the first node on the open list and making this
node the current node. The successors of this node are generated
and their f values are computed. Each of these successors which is
not already on the open list or the closed list is put onto the open

list in its proper position. This loop is executed as many times as necessary to reach a goal node or until the open list becomes empty.

3.3 The A* Algorithm

Description of the A* Algorithm When we can compute the exact distances from the start node as each node is reached, it is possible to apply the uniform-cost search algorithm. If we also have heuristic information estimating the distance between each node reached and the closest goal node, we may take advantage of this information by using the A* algorithm. This algorithm is detailed in Figure 2.

In order to give priority during the search to nodes deemed likely to lie on the shortest path between the start node and a goal node, the A* algorithm adds g, the cost of the best path found so far from the start node to the current node, to h, the estimated distance between the current node and the closest goal node. In effect, the A* algorithm is a best-first method with an evaluation function

$$f(n) = g(n) + h(n).$$

If we know that the estimate h never exceeds the actual distance between the current node and the goal node, we are assured that the A* algorithm will always find a shortest path between the start node and the goal node.

3.4 Martelli's Edge-Tracing Method

One way to apply the heuristic search approach in computer vision is in finding paths through the grid of pixel boundaries in an image [5]. By designing a cost function which takes curvature along the path and contrast across the path into account, a minimum-cost path may be made to correspond to what a human would consider to be a good contour separating a region from its background in the image. The cost increases as the integrated local curvature increases, and the cost decreases as the integrated contrast across the path increases. Since a proper contour is a closed path, ending up where it starts, there is a potential problem in prematurely terminating the search for the

---

ALGORITHM A*

begin
    input the start node s and the set GOALS of goal nodes;
    OPEN $\leftarrow \{s\}$; CLOSED $\leftarrow \phi$;
    $G[s] \leftarrow 0$; PRED$[s] \leftarrow$ NULL; *found* $\leftarrow$ **false**;
    while OPEN is not empty and *found* is **false do**
      begin
        L $\leftarrow$ the set of nodes on OPEN for which F is the least;
        if L is a singleton **then** let X be its sole element
            else if there are any goal nodes in L
                then let X be one of them
                else let X be any element of L;
        remove X from OPEN and put X into CLOSED;
        if X is a goal node **then** *found* $\leftarrow$ **true**
            else begin
            generate the set SUCCESSORS of successors of X;
                for each Y in SUCCESSORS **do**
                    if Y is not already on OPEN or on CLOSED **then**
                      begin
                        $G[Y] \leftarrow G[X] + distance(X,Y)$;
                        $F[Y] \leftarrow G[Y] + h(Y)$; PRED$[Y] \leftarrow X$;
                        insert Y on OPEN;
                      end
                    else /* Y is on OPEN or on CLOSED */
                      begin
                        $Z \leftarrow$ PRED$[Y]$;
                        temp $\leftarrow$ F$[Y]-$ G$[Z] - distance(Z,Y)+$
                                $+ G[X] + distance(X,Y)$;
                        if *temp* $<$ F$[Y]$ **then**
                          begin
                            $G[Y] \leftarrow$ G$[Y]-$ F$[Y]+temp$;
                            $F[Y] \leftarrow temp$; PRED$[Y] \leftarrow X$;
                            if Y is on CLOSED **then**
                            insert Y on OPEN and remove Y from CLOSED;
                        end;
                    end;
            end;
      end;
    if *found* is **false then** output "Failure"
    else trace the pointers in the PRED fields from X back to s, "CONSing"
      each node onto the growing list of nodes to get the path from s to X;
end.

Figure 2: The A* Algorithm. It Combines the Use of Actual Distances and an Estimation Function h.

best contour if the starting point is reached. The cost of a path can be made independent of length, so as to avoid the tendency of the system to find "short circuits." Such a cost function does not obey the triangle inequality and cannot be computed with the incremental method embodied in the A* algorithm as detailed in Figure 2.

However, we may apply a variation of the A* procedure in which the method for updating costs has been modified. A cost scheme that takes these criteria into consideration is $f(n) = g(n) + h(n)$, here $g(n)$ is the cost of the path from s to n given by $C(\gamma)$ below and $h(n)$ is an estimate of the cost of the path from n back to s. The cost of path γ is

$$C(\gamma) = \frac{w_1}{n} \sum_{i=1}^{n} \frac{1}{1 + |\alpha_i|} + \frac{w_2}{n - d + 1} \sum_{i=1}^{n-d+1} |\kappa_i|.$$

where n is the length of the path; w_1 and w_2 are weighting factors; the local contrast α_i is given by $V(P_{i_1}) - V(P_{i_2})$ where P_{i_1} and P_{i_2} are the pixels to the left and right, respectively, of the ith edge element in the path, and V gives the value of a pixel; and κ_i is the local curvature at the ith edge element.

The local curvature may be defined using a table-lookup scheme where a small number d of edge elements are examined, and the pattern of their relative directions determines what the local curvature value is. For $d = 3$ there are five possible relative configurations, after symmetry has been taken into account. These five patterns and their curvature values by one (albeit an arbitrary) assignment is shown in Figure 3.

Thus κ_i, the local curvature at the ith edge element, may be computed by examining the ith, $i + 1^{th}$, and $i + 2^{th}$ edge elements. The table of curvature values here takes only two angles into account at a time. If larger tables are used, considering three or more angles at a time, a greater degree of control can be attained.

The weighting factors w_1 and w_2 can be adjusted to regulate the relative influence of the contrast and the curvature. As with any edge-detection method, the success of this approach depends upon the quality of the edges present in the image. However, the method

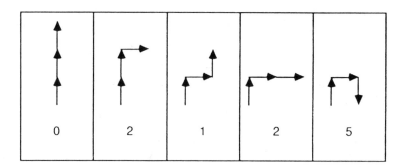

Figure 3: An Assignment of Curvature Values to Sequences of Length 3.

constructs contours that are connected, and it gets around the edge-linking necessary with other methods.

This search method requires that some point on the contour be given as a starting state. Such a point may be found by scanning the image with a simple edge detector such as a horizontal difference of two adjacent pixels, until a pair of pixels is found that is very likely to lie on an edge. The edge between these two pixels is vertically situated, and the initial direction for search may be chosen arbitrarily as upward (north). From that location on, the contour is extended by one edge element at a time by heuristically searching for the completion of the contour. Figure 4 illustrates the choices for the second edge element in tracing a contour by such a means. The starting ele-

P_1	P_2	P_3
P_4	P_5	P_6
P_7	P_8	P_9

Figure 4: Contour Tracing Between Pixels with Heuristic Search.

ment is the segment between pixels P_4 and P_5, written (P_4, P_5). The contour may be extended taking either (P_4, P_1), (P_1, P_2), or (P_2, P_5) as the next segment.

The use of heuristic search in this context has several benefits. First, it allows a separation of the criteria for judging contour quality from the mechanism that executes the search. This makes it easy to modify the criteria, and to separate their effects from those due to the search algorithm. Second, the method has built-in recovery from dead ends; this means that it can tolerate the presence of noise, degrading gracefully in performance as the amount of noise increases. Third, it offers efficiency of search.

4 Vision as Path Finding

Let us now consider the problem of incorporating heuristic search in a more general model of the vision process.

Vision can be viewed as problem solving. The job of a vision system is to find an appropriate interpretation of an image that has been input. The appropriateness of an interpretation can be computed with a criterion function not unlike that used to evaluate contours in Martelli's method. By viewing the space of possible partial interpretations as a state space, the problem becomes one of finding a path that both leads to an interpretation and "proves" that the interpretation is justified by the image data.

In order to understand machine vision from this perspective, we first must show the meaning of each component of a minimum-cost path problem $\mathcal{M} = \langle K, T, s, G, C \rangle$ in the context of vision. The states may be representations of the pictorial information in the input image, or they may be states of knowledge or some combination of the two. The transformations include image processing operations as well as more general data-processing operations. The start state corresponds in some direct way to the input image. The goal states may correspond to object prototypes or other acceptable final forms for an interpretation. The cost function measures the distortion, information loss, or introduction of questionable aspects to the interpretation. We call such a minimum-cost path problem an *image-interpretation problem.*

4.1   Representation of States

The representation of these partial interpretations is the first design issue that we address. In order to allow the same state-space search mechanism that finds the interpretation to perform any necessary preprocessing of the image, the state representation must be flexible enough to incorporate the results of such preprocessing.

Data Objects as States: One approach is to consider as a state a data object representing information about the image either in image form or in some more abstract form such as a list of regions and their shapes and colors. In this scheme, a state would not include any assertions or hypotheses unless these are regarded as direct representations of the image data.

In this method where we regard a data object as a state, any operator which produces a smaller data structure as output than it takes as input leads to a state whose representation is smaller than the one before. If the goal states are represented as very small data objects, then a solution path through the state space corresponds to a sequence of operators that reduces the image data until a data structure is produced which matches a goal state. For this sort of search problem, a best-first or a heuristically ordered depth-first strategy would be appropriate.

States of Knowledge: A second approach treats a state as a state of knowledge, the sum total of all results of image processing operators applied so far. With this approach, evidence of all forms may be gradually accumulated through the application of different operators. Normally, there would be no backtracking, since to do so would be to throw away information that could potentially lead to the solution. However, backtracking would seem to be appropriate from a state of knowledge containing a logical inconsistency or from a state of knowledge so voluminous that storage space must be reclaimed in order to proceed.

A goal state is a state of knowledge containing a confident assertion about the interpretation of the image; e.g., that the scene contains certain objects. A search method for this sort of system is "hill climbing," in which the successor state selected at each step is the best successor of the current state.

Selected Knowledge as States: These two approaches are not completely antithetical. It is possible to make a compromise. A state can be a representation of selected aspects of the image: more than just one simple data structure, but not necessarily containing everything that has been computed about the input image so far. Operators do not necessarily have to reduce the volume of data in the current description of the image, and yet some of them may do so. Backtracking can then be made to serve a useful purpose, and some useful work may be obtained from a search mechanism of an A* sort.

We assume in the following discussion that such a compromise is taken; a state can represent one or more (potential) aspects of the input image, and an operator may have the effect of reducing, augmenting, or otherwise modifying the information in the current state.

4.2   Distortion Cost

We must design the distance or cost function for paths so as to indicate appropriateness of interpretations. A path is to represent a chain of operators which, when applied successively to the input image, transforms it into the abstract representation of a known object or other final form. However, the transformation should be "natural" and should not involve arbitrary mappings that have nothing to do with likeness or any reasonable view of the perception process.

Therefore, the cost of a path should reflect the level of distortion of the image information under the corresponding sequence of operators. Some amount of distortion must be tolerated in order to permit interpretations under noisy or unforeseen conditions. However, the appropriateness of an interpretation depends in large part on the reasonableness of these distortions. (These costs should be context-dependent; we discuss this matter further after we describe the other principal concepts of our model.)

4.3   Goal Nodes

The way goal nodes are described will depend upon the application. One idea is to represent goal nodes with geometric models. Another is to use symbolic descriptions to represent the goal models. Another approach is to use a predicate that can be applied to any state to determine whether that state is a goal state. A compromise approach is to define a predicate in terms of some stored prototype models, without calling the models themselves "states."

4.4   Seeing and Hallucinating

With a given image, *seeing* some object is identifying a path from the start state s (which corresponds to the given image) to a goal state that is associated with that object. Such a path is a "solution path." Seeing *properly* is identifying the solution path of lowest cost.

"Hallucinating" is seeing, but with a high cost on the path, or with a path which is obviously *not* the lowest-cost path. If there are no low-cost paths to goal nodes, one might reasonably conclude that there is nothing of significance in the image; this is probably preferable to hallucination in most applications.

4.5   Vision Problems and Vision Algorithms

Vision Problems: A collection of minimum-cost path problems that differ only in their start states may be thought of as comprising a more general problem. When the minimum-cost problems are image-interpretation problems, we call this more general problem a *vision problem*. Each image-interpretation problem is an *instance* of the vision problem. Putting all the start states into one "generalized start state" s', a vision problem has the form $\mathcal{P} = \langle K, T, s', G, C \rangle$.

Vision Algorithms: Given a vision problem, we would like to have a method that can solve all of its solvable instances.

We may define a *state-space-search-based vision algorithm*, $\mathcal{A} = \langle K', T', s', G, C, h \rangle$, as a system comprising a set K' of "generalized states" of the state space K; T', a subset of T; a generalized start state s' that corresponds with the set of possible input images; the goal nodes and the cost function of the vision problem; and a heuristic evaluation function h that is used to evaluate nodes in the course of the search. Normally h estimates the remaining distance between a given node and the closest goal node. (This explains our choice of the letter h rather than f for this purpose.)

The set of generalized states is defined as follows: s' is a generalized state. If k'_i is a generalized state corresponding to a set $K_i \subset K$ of states of $\mathcal{M}$, and $t \in T'$, then k'_j, corresponding to the image of K_i under t, is a generalized state; in such a case we say that t maps k'_i to k'_j.

The Algorithm Graph: For any vision algorithm $\mathcal{A}$, there is a (possibly infinite) graph (called the *algorithm graph* for $\mathcal{A}$) whose set of nodes corresponds to K' and whose arcs are labelled with members of T'. An arc (k'_i, k'_j, t_l) exists if t_l maps k'_i to k'_j. Note that there may be more than one arc connecting a pair of nodes. This may be drawn as a single arc with two labels.

Relationships Between Algorithms: It would be helpful if we had a clear notion of when one algorithm is more powerful than another. Putting the issue of speed aside for the moment, let us construct a basis for deciding when one algorithm is more general than another.

An SSSB vision algorithm $\mathcal{A}_1 = \langle K'_1, T'_1, s'_1, G_1, C_1, h_1 \rangle$, is an *extension* of another, $\mathcal{A}_2 = \langle K'_2, T'_2, s'_2, G_2, C_2, h_2 \rangle$, if the following criteria are met:

1. $K'_2 \subseteq K'_1$,

2. $T'_2 \subseteq T'_1$,

3. $s'_2 \subseteq s'_1$,

4. $G_2 \subseteq G_1$,

5. $(\forall k'_i, k'_j \in K'_2) C_1(k'_i, k'_j) = C_2(k'_i, k'_j)$, and

6. $(\forall k' \in K'_2) h_1(k') = h_2(k')$.

We would expect that if $\mathcal{A}_1$ is an extension of $\mathcal{A}_2$, then $\mathcal{A}_1$ would be capable of seeing any object that $\mathcal{A}_2$ could see and therefore would be more general. This is not entirely correct because it is possible for the values of C_1 and h_1 to be so low for the portions of the state space of $\mathcal{A}_1$ that are outside the state space for $\mathcal{A}_2$ that $\mathcal{A}_1$ never gets a chance to see the objects that $\mathcal{A}_2$ does, even though the appropriate goal states are reachable. By placing some additional restrictions on C_1 and h_1 we could ensure that $\mathcal{A}_1$ would actually be capable of seeing anything that $\mathcal{A}_2$ could.

As a rough rule of thumb, however, we can say that there is a good chance that $\mathcal{A}_1$ is more general than $\mathcal{A}_2$ if the algorithm graph for $\mathcal{A}_2$ is a subgraph of the algorithm graph for $\mathcal{A}_1$.

5   An Example

Most of the definitions and concepts discussed above can be further clarified with an example. We now examine one.

5.1   Informal Description

Let us imagine that a factory vision system takes in images that may contain hex-nuts and bolts. The images are 256^2 arrays of 8-bit pixels and contain gray-scale information. The vision system has a number of operations available to it, and it must use these to make interpretations of the images. The contents of the images are not very predictable; objects may occur in arbitrary positions and orientations, the imaging process introduces noise, there may be extraneous objects or no objects, and by a quirk in the imaging system, each image having objects may either have light objects on a dark background or vice versa.

Sketches of possible input images that this system should be able to interpret (in some way) are given in Figure 6. The ways in which these could be interpreted are discussed later.

5.2 Formulation as a Vision Problem

A more precise formulation of this problem specifies its components in more detail using the previously introduced form, $\mathcal{P} = \langle K, T, s', G, C \rangle$.

State Space: We specify the state space K for this problem as

$$K = k_0' \cup k_1' \cup \cdots \cup k_5'$$

where

$k_0' \;=\; \{256^2 \times 8 \text{ images }\}$

$k_1' \;=\; \{256^2 \text{ binary images }\}$

$k_2' \;=\; \{256^2 \times 8 \text{ images marked with "complement" }\}$

$k_3' \;=\; \{256^2 \text{ 1-component binary images }\}$

$k_4' \;=\; \{x \mid 0 \leq x \leq 1\}$

$k_5' \;=\; \{ \text{"nothing significant", "bolt", "hex nut", "background" }\}$

Operators:

$$T = t_1' \cup \{t_2, \ldots t_8\}$$

where

$t_1' \;=\; \{\text{threshold}_\theta \mid 0 \leq \theta \leq 256\}$

$t_2 \;=\;$ complement-8-bit-image
$t_3 \;=\;$ erode-with-cross
$t_4 \;=\;$ dilate-with-cross
$t_5 \;=\;$ extract-largest-component
$t_6 \;=\;$ extract-2nd-largest-component
$t_7 \;=\;$ compute-relative-number-of-1s
$t_8 \;=\;$ classify

Here t_1' is a large set of operators that are similar; they can all be computed using a single subroutine that takes a parameter, in this case θ.

The morphological operations t_3 and t_4 use cross-shaped structuring elements (five pixels with origin at the center). It would be possible to parameterize these operators and incorporate a large family of morphological operators into this problem. However, we can demonstrate a substantial degree of richness in possibilities by allowing multiple applications of these two operators.

t_7 accepts a binary image with a single connected component and it returns the fraction of pixels that have value 1.

t_8 performs a mapping from numbers in the range $[0, 1]$ to elements of k'_5. The mapping is given in the following table:

input range	output
$x < 0.01$	"nothing significant"
$0.01 \leq x < 0.03$	"hex-nut"
$0.03 \leq x < 0.2$	"bolt"
$0.2 \leq x$	"background"

Generalized Start State: This is k'_0, the set of possible input images.

Goal States: $G = \{$ "bolt", "hex-nut" $\}$.

The Distortion Cost Function: We now face the difficult problem of formulating how paths should be penalized for employing each applicable transformation. The distortion cost along an arc of the state-space graph is to indicate or at least estimate the relative degree to which the relevant information about the contents of the input image is being changed or corrupted along the arc.

One basis for designing methods to determine distortion costs is the notion of approximation error. Many of the operators can be viewed as computing approximations of their inputs. By measuring the difference between input and output, the error of approximation can be obtained, and this may be suitably normalized and used as the distortion cost.

In the case of thresholding, each input pixel is being approximated by one of two values. If we regard the 256 possible input values as evenly distributed through the closed interval $[0, 1]$, and the output values as $\{0, 1\}$, then the distortion cost involved in thresh-olding image $P(x, y)$ at θ, obtaining image $B(x, y)$ can be defined as

$$\frac{1}{256^2} \sum_{x,y} |B(x, y) - P(x, y)|.$$

With a poorly chosen threshold and an input image that is uniformly 0 or 1, it is possible to reach the maximum distortion cost of 1.

Because taking the negative of an image is a reversible operation, there is no loss of information, and we assign all t_2 arcs a constant distortion cost of zero. In order to prevent this operator from being repeatedly applied (a hazard with certain operators of zero cost), the state space has been specified so as to permit at most one application of it during any search process.

To compute the distortion cost along an erosion or a dilation arc, one may simply determine the proportion of pixels in the image whose values change. This scheme is not entirely consistent, because some images may undergo no net change when dilation is followed by erosion, and yet there would be a net charge (strictly positive cost), because the dilation and erosion taken separately do cause pixels to change.

The distortion cost for extracting a connected component is more difficult to formulate in a manner that seems reasonable. Because the act of selection is normally an act of asserting that the selected item is the main item of importance, we should not charge too much for what is in effect approximating the unselected items with 0. Whatever charge there is should reflect the existence and magnitude of any evidence that the item being selected is not correct. For example, if the operator selects the largest region, but the largest region is not much larger than the second largest region, there is a chance that the largest region in the original scene got relatively smaller in the image because of noise in the camera or distortions along the path to the current node. In such a case a charge should be made to the arc in accordance with the likelihood of a mistake, as evidenced by such features of the current state.

The distortion cost at the classification step can be specified in terms of the ranges of values used in the classification. An input value of 0.04 falls in the 0.03 to 0.2 range for bolts. However, the value is far from the mean for the range, and it is close to one endpoint. The cost can be made a function of the distance of the input value from the mean value of the range that contains the input value.

Aside from the problem of formulating distortion cost functions for each operator, there is a problem in balancing the magnitudes of this diverse set of cost functions. One aims to make each cost function play its appropriate role in the overall scheme for assigning distortion distances to paths. Cost functions that are too high or too low relative to those for other operators (or relative to their own values when applied to other states) lead to undesired interpretations; the system would say it sees while a human would say the system hallucinates.

5.3   Algorithm Description

Simplified Algorithm Graphs: With the definition for generalized states given above, it is easy for a small number of operators to generate a very large number of generalized states most of which are very similar but have very slight differences among them. A simple example of this is the system of generalized states generated by the Peano successor operation σ with a generalized start state Ω which is the set of natural numbers. The generalized state space consists of an infinite chain of generalized states $\Omega, \sigma(\Omega), \sigma(\sigma(\Omega)), \ldots$ where the ith generalized state corresponds to the set $\{i-1, i, 1+1, i+2, \ldots\}$.

In order to simplify drawing the graph for this generalized state space, we may elect to lump all of these generalized states into a single node. We call such a node a "lumped state." The decision of when to lump a group of generalized states together and when to keep them separate should give primary consideration to the problem of presenting the algorithm graph in a comprehensible form. It is desirable, however, not to lump together generalized states if the sets of operators applicable to those generalized states differ.

Example Graph: A simplified algorithm graph for the hex-nut/bolt problem is shown in Figure 5.

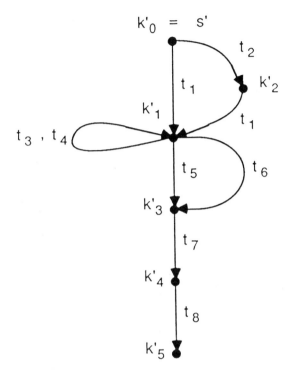

Figure 5: A Simplified Algorithm Graph for the Hex-nut/bolt Problem.

In this graph, we have lumped many distinct generalized states together in k_1'. The distinctions are due to the fact that the functional image of a domain of a morphological operator is not identical to the domain; there are some binary images which are meaningful as inputs to the erosion operator which could never be produced as outputs of that operator.

However, the self-loop on k_1' suggests that t_3 and t_4 can be applied as many times as desired and in any order desired (the results may be different, of course). This allows a richness in the possible behavior of the algorithm that partially compensates for the fact that t_3 and t_4 are not parameterized.

Evaluation Function: By taking h to be uniformly zero, we would simplify the presentation of this example and still have an algorithm that could solve the hex-nut/bolt problem (at least in theory). However, coming up with reasonable heuristic evaluation functions is a major challenge of the state-space approach to machine vision, and that would be missing an important opportunity.

In a highly diverse state space such as the K we are discussing here, any h which ignores this diversity is unlikely to be meaningful. A good way to take the diversity into account is to relate h in some direct way to C. The purpose of h is roughly to approximate C on various as-yet-unexplored parts of K.

A general way to approximate the cost of getting to a goal node is to approximate a path to a goal node and then estimate the cost of that path. This is a form of "planning" [3,1]. Methods for planning typically use search in simplified versions of the state space, usually with a modified set of operators.

Planning with Static Estimates: It is sometimes possible to use the algorithm graph for an elementary form of planning. By computing the expected distortion cost for each operator once and for all, the algorithm graph may be augmented with extra labels on its arcs carrying these average costs. These expected costs are static. Each node of the graph can then be labelled with its static distance from the closest generalized state that contains a goal state.

Then while the vision algorithm is running, $h(n)$ is computed by finding the generalized state k' that contains n, and looking up the static distance associated with it. This form of planning is not effective for this problem, because most of the actual states map into generalized states that lie on the same path in the algorithm graph, and so the h values will fail to assist in ordering the alternatives. In an algorithm graph with more branching, this method might be effective.

Planning with Resolution Reduction: With more computational effort, more useful values of h can be obtained. Let us define h in terms of a new search space called the "planning space." The states of the planning space are reached by applying a reduction operator t_{red} to a state in K and by applying "reduced versions" of the operators of T' to other states in the planning space. We may define t_{red} as a resolution reduction operator mapping 256^2 images to 128^2 images (by sampling every other pixel in every other row) for all states which are images and as an identity operator for all other states. In general, the goal states of the planning space are obtained by applying t_{red} to the members of G; in the present example the goal states of the planning space are the same as the normal goal states.

In this method of planning, a value of $h(n)$ is obtained by performing a search for a goal node in the planning space. The distortion cost along the path from $t_{red}(n)$ to the closest goal node is then taken as $h(n)$. Distortion cost functions for the reduced versions of the operators are identical to their full-resolution counterparts.

5.4 Possible Interpretations

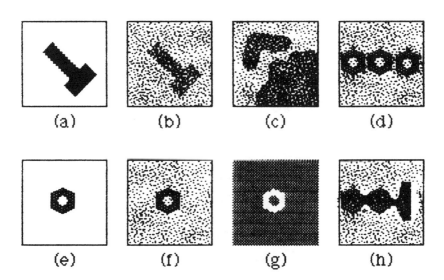

(a) (b) (c) (d)

(e) (f) (g) (h)

Figure 6: Sketches of some Possible Input Images for the Hex-nut/bolt Problem.

The input images sketched in Figure 6 can each be interpreted as a
hex-nut, a bolt, or both. Since the interpretation depends ultimately
on the area of the selected region being in the right range of values,
shape plays only a small role, and the small blob in (c) can be interpreted as a bolt as readily as the bolt-like region in (a). After only
one or two steps of dilation, the three nut-like regions in (d) merge
into one connected component whose area allows it to be interpreted
as a bolt. The white nut on a dark background in (g) is no more
difficult for the system to see than the nut in (e), since operator t_2,
which takes the negative of the image, has been defined with a constant distortion cost of zero. The bolt-sized region in (h) is readily
broken up by erosion, so that one of the pieces can be interpreted as
a hex-nut. Actually, because the erosion and dilation operators can
decrease or increase the area of a region arbitrarily (given enough iterations), any blob that this system can see as a hex-nut can also be
seen (at least hallucinated) by the system as a bolt, and vice versa.
However, there will always exist a preferred interpretation, except in
the unusual event of a tie where two paths to different goal nodes
both achieve the minimum cost.

6   Conclusion

This article has attempted to clarify the view of machine vision as
heuristic search. By treating vision as path finding through a state
space, it is hoped that generality and robustness can be combined
with the qualities of speed and precision to yield more useful vision
systems.

The difficulty in achieving these goals can be attributed to the diversity of the state space and the operators needed and the difficulty
of defining distortion cost functions, and especially, the difficulty of
identifying good heuristics that guide the search through the combinatorial quagmire.

7 Acknowledgements

The author wishes to thank Ronald Blanford and Richard Rice for constructive comments related to this paper. The support of the National Science Foundation under grant number IRI-8605889 is gratefully acknowledgement.

Bibliography

[1] D. H. Ballard. Model-directed detection of ribs in chest radiographs. *Proc. Fourth International Conf. on Pattern Recognition*, Kyoto, Japan, p. 907–910,1979.

[2] D. H. Ballard and C. M. Brown. *Computer Vision.* Englewood Cliffs, NJ: Prentice-Hall,1982.

[3] T. Garvey. Perceptual strategies for purposive vision. Technical Note 117, SRI AI Center, Menlo Park, CA,1976.

[4] A. Martelli. Edge detection using heuristic search methods. *Computer Graphics and Image Processing*, Vol. 1, No. 2, p. 169–182,1972.

[5] A. Martelli. An application of heuristic search methods to edge and contour detection. *Communications of the ACM*, Vol. 19, No. 2, p. 73–83,1976.

[6] A. Newell, J. C. Shaw and H. Simon. Empirical explorations with the Logic Theory Machine. *Proceedings of the Western Joint Computer Conference*, p. 218–230. Also, reprinted in Feigenbaum, E. A., and Feldman, J. (eds.), *Computers and Thought.* New York: McGraw-Hill, 1963,1957.

[7] N. J. Nilsson. *Problem-Solving Methods in Artificial Intelligence*, New York: McGraw-Hill,1971.

[8] J. Pearl. *Heuristics: Intelligent Search Strategies for Computer Problem Solving.* Reading MA: Addison-Wesley,1984.

[9] L. G. Shapiro and R. M. Haralick. Structural descriptions and inexact matching. *IEEE Trans. Pattern Analysis and Machine Intelligence*, Vol. PAMI-3, No. 5, p. 504-519,1981.

[10] S. L. Tanimoto. *The Elements of Artificial Intelligence: An Introduction Using LISP*. Rockville MD: Computer Science Press,1987.

[11] A. N. Whitehead and B. Russell. *Principia Mathematica*, Second Edition, Vol. 1, Cambridge University Press,1935.

Directions for
Future Research
— A Panel Discussion

Chairman: Herbert Freeman, Rutgers University

Panelists: J. K. Aggarwal, University of Texas
Nelson R. Corby, General Electric Co.
John Jarvis, AT&T Bell Laboratories
Steven Tanimoto, University of Washington
Wayne Wiitanen, General Motors Research Labs

The theme of the workshop was "Machine Vision - Where are we and where are we going?" Most of the presentations were concerned with the current state of machine vision and its near-term prospects. Because of the strong research interests of the participants, it seemed fitting to conclude the workshop with a panel discussion dedicated to the question *"What are the Directions for Future Research?"* Participating in the panel were, in addition to the chairman, five individuals who had spoken about their work in the workshop. To maintain fair balance between academe and industry, three of the panelists were chosen from industry and the other two, together with the chairman, from universities. Presented here is a general summary of the panel discussion, together with position statements by the panelists.

In listening to the presentations and informal discussion groups during the workshop, one could not avoid being impressed by the rampant spirit of optimism. In spite of the fact that many of the participants had been working in the field for 15 or more years and had relatively little in the way of commercial applications to show for it, there was a feeling prevalent that the many years of toil would soon be rewarded, that success was just around the corner. The basis for the optimism most heard was that we finally appeared to have an appreciation of what machine vision really involves, what appli-

299

cations are appropriate for the present and which would have to be deferred for perhaps another decade, and, possibly most important, that we finally have the computer power to cope with the enormous computational burden, which we so recklessly underestimated in the past.

Two major directions for future research appeared to stand out: *human visual perception* and *parallel processing.* If machine vision is ever even remotely to approach the capabilities of human vision, we must have a better comprehension of how human visual perception works. There are many ways for sensing objects in our environment, but when we speak of machine vision we are clearly thinking of electronic analogs to human vision. The study of human visual perception, a subject until recently of only peripheral interest to most machine vision researchers, must take a more prominent place in our research activities.

Also, there is today fair agreement among researchers in the field that any significant increase in machine vision performance will require vastly more computing power, and that this computing power can be realized only by using *special-purpose* computer architectures of the parallel-processing type. Much current research is focused on the design of such new architec tures using pipelining, vector processing, array processing, multi-connected processing and pyramidal structures to achieve the necessary low-cost, ultra-fast processing that will clearly be required. We must recognize - and most researchers, application engineers, and venture capitalists have already done so - that the amount of computer processing required to perceive (i.e., "understand") the content of a scene is massive, and that machine vision will not be universally practical until we can perform such massive processing with MIPS/$ figures that are a couple of orders of magnitude higher than is possible today.

As the performance/cost ratio of machine vision systems continues to increase, new areas of application will open up. This in turn will motivate more R&D activity, with further improvements in performance and costs. In every technological development there is a threshold in the performance-to-cost ratio which much be passed before development can shift from narrow-based to broad- based.

In computer graphics this techno-economic feasibility threshold was passed in the late 1970's, after nearly 20 years of "incubation"; explosive expansion followed. There is every reason to be confident that machine vision - the electronic analog of human vision - will within the next five years break through a similar threshold and assume a significant role in day- to-day industrial operations - in particular in the area of inspection; however, much remains yet to be done to bring this about.

J. K. Aggarwal

During the course of the work several issues were raised. From my perspective, the important issues include the following:

- Compute Power

- Representation

- System Integration and Competitiveness

I shall address each of them briefly.

Compute Power. It appears that significant compute power is already available in the form of single processors such as the Intel 386 or multiprocessor systems such as the NCUBE hypercube and the Connection Machine. No doubt this additional compute power allows us to implement a number of algorithms which would have been unthinkable in the immediate past. An example is the recent announcement of the two chip set by RCA for the playback of compressed, full-motion video in real time. However, compute power alone is not going to solve all our problems! Availability of images at all resolutions may make it easier to accomplish a particular task but certainly does not give us the prescription how to do it. We still have to find the right algorithm to accomplish the task at hand. Segmentation is a simple example. The increase in data is approximately 33images at all resolutions. The additional data is really not overwhelming but the increased complexity of processing for segmenting an image is substantial. Another example is the task of the recognition of a three-dimensional object and its relative position. The argument that an exhaustive search will find the correct object and its orientation from a library of three- dimensional objects is really not tenable. Tracking all views of an object by itself is a monumental task. Matching several objects would make the task almost intractable. One has to prune the search tree in an intelligent and meaningful fashion. As usual, sheer compute power is not the solution but its intelligent use provides us the avenues for a solution.

Representation. Representation is still a serious problem. No representation is universal. It is unlikely that we are going to find a universal representation. More likely we shall keep several copies of the same piece of information in several forms. Also, we shall learn to transform efficiently information from one representation to another. Certain representations are efficient and are compact with respect to their storage requirements whereas another representation may be more amenable to processing. A rectangular parallelepiped representation is certainly more compact and less time-consuming to obtain in comparison to an octree representation. However, I believe the octree representation will be more amenable to parallel processing to obtain a single view of an object, given the view point and the source of the illumination. It is difficult a priori to know which representation is the one to use for a given application. At times it is only after considerable experience and use that one is able to determine the desired representation.

System Integration and Competitiveness. System integration and the competitiveness of the machine vision solutions for industrial problems are nothing new that we are facing in the context of machine/computer vision. Other technologies have had to face similar challenges. The slowness with which machine solutions have been adopted in the industrial environment may be attributed to a variety of reasons, including the delays as a consequence of system integration and lack of the competitiveness of the machine vision solutions. It is useful to recollect that it is only recently that we have been blessed with easy acquisition of images and equally easy display of processed results. The relatively cheap CCD cameras and the IBM PC with its acquisition and display cards have been around only a few years. I do not feel disheartened by the slowness of the progress. However, it goes without saying that machine vision solutions must compete in the market place and be competitive with other technologies. This competitiveness has to transcend the entire range of issues including economics, reliability and changing environment. I believe that as we learn more about system integration we shall become more adept at it.

On the whole, I am very optimistic about the future of machine/computer vision. With the advent of significant computing power and the improvements in acquisition and display technologies coupled with CCD cameras, I feel the future of machine/computer vision is bright in industrial inspection applications and in a host of other applications, including medicine, defense, and monitoring.

Nelson R. Corby Jr.

Machine vision research has captured the imaginations and efforts of many researchers world-wide over the last thirty years. This work has revealed how ambitious a task machine comprehension of images really is. Many avenues of research are being explored and in many cases vision researchers have moved from investigation to application.

A major problem facing the vision community is finding ways to capture and build cooperatively upon its discoveries. In many ways, too much emphasis is placed on novelty of approach, with not enough emphasis on systematic investigation and thorough comparisons. Although it may be more personally rewarding to develop a novel approach to solving a problem, in many cases the more valuable long-term work consists of exploring, understanding, extending and modifying approaches that have already been proposed. In particular, thoughtful and insightful comparisons and analyses of existing approaches and results can be very valuable.

Experiments in machine vision can benefit from the concept of the reproducible experiment. The goal of the research should be clearly defined along with specific assumptions, simplifications and domain knowledge. The source data should be documented and the results reported in such a way as to encourage analysis, comparison and verification by other researchers.

Standard image libraries and benchmarking tasks can aid in cooperative comparisons. Library images have been used for many years in image enhancement, image quality assessment and bandwidth compression. Well-documented and carefully described image libraries (temporal and spatial sequences of luminance images as well as explicitly sensed "range" images) can significantly advance the progress of current research in image understanding of scenes drawn from a three-dimensional environment by comparing the results of a given approach with the library description, as well as by allowing comparisons among the results of "competing" approaches. Also, because of the difficulty of constructing effective range sensors, the availability of range data library scenes would allow research participation by potentially many more researchers.

Most of the problems associated with less successful applied vision systems have been caused by lack of scope, robustness and flexibility. Failures can be caused by not anticipating a wider range of potential scenes as well as by sensitivity to noise and clutter. Proposed approaches should attempt to confront these factors directly, rather than assume that at some point the problems will disappear. The availability of standard images will allow for reasonable comparisons of approach with respect to the above factors.

John F. Jarvis

Industrial machine vision, either inspection or machine control, is an engineering discipline distinct within the more general computer vision community. Industrial machine vision is performance-oriented: throughput, cost and accuracy constraints must be met. The industrial visual environment can be manipulated to enhance performance in a particular task with respect to almost any requirement. There is a strong preference for the simplest solution meeting the task requirements. Usually, there is not a significant benefit to be gained from greatly exceeding the task requirements. All of these considerations lead to one prominent characteristic of functioning machine vision systems: they are specific solutions to specific problems.

Computer vision research typically proceeds by stretching constraints with little regard for resources used: whatever computer resources are used now will be suitably inexpensive in a few years. Generality of result is a principal goal for research. This research thrust has not served the industrial machine vision community well. Several 10-year-old projects were represented as current or typical during the workshop. If references to archaic hardware were removed, it is likely that much 10-year-old work could still be presented and accepted as good or perhaps even state-of-the-art. Generality, although an appropriate topic for research in vision, has costs of its own and has not significantly aided the industrial vision community.

What would be useful to the industry-applications community? New low-level features, both global and local, encoding useful parameters as scalars or small vector quantities are desirable. Projection, connectivity, moment and transform techniques have proven their utility. Expanding this set can only help. Quantitative results are key to many industrial applications; consequently, advances in methods for subpixel resolution, calibrations, and working with non-ideal geometries will be useful. Dedicated hardware for low-level vision is needed. Hardware "subroutines", that is, hardware modules that can be configured into a system as easily as software modules, are needed. Architectures, interfaces and algorithms all need work to achieve this.

During the last 15 years we have witnessed the introduction of the single-board computer and its development into potent subsystems exceeding the processing capability of all but the largest "minicomputer" systems. Parallel processors add another dimension for increasing system performance. In spite of orders- of-magnitude increases in processing, the apparent functionality of computer vision systems has not increased proportionally. This suggests fundamental problems exist that are not well understood. Determining why computer vision advances as slowly as it does is itself a research problem worthy of study.

Steven L. Tanimoto

Although there are a number of technological factors that limit the application of machine vision today, I believe that the primary obstacle is a general lack of understanding of the existing technology of machine vision throughout our society. This lack of understanding exists in all aspects of the field: theory, practice and general intuition. I believe that there are things that can be done to improve the situation, and when the general level of familiarity with machine vision grows, we should start seeing the number of applications increase.

It is instructive to compare the field of machine vision today with that of computer graphics about 15 years ago. Around that time, the cost of good-performance graphics equipment was getting low enough to cause the number of people working with computer graphics to grow significantly. As the number of people familiar with graphics technology grew, the number of applications grew until today, graphics is a standard part of most computing environments (at least at the level of bit-mapped displays or spreadsheet-style graphics). The cost of machine vision systems has finally come down to the cost of mid-70's graphics systems. If other factors are equal, we should expect to see machine vision now take off as graphics did then.

However, while I think that the vision field will grow, I do not believe that it will grow as rapidly as graphics did in the 70's. I see two reasons for this: (1) vision is a technology whose final product is unglamorous in comparison with that for graphics. With graphics, we see the end result, and the results are often dazzling. With vision, the system's end result, if it is output for human consumption at all, may be of the form "I see it" or even more tersely, "OK; ...; not OK; OK; ...". Vision just does not have quite the same appeal that graphics has. (2) The mass-market applications for vision have been harder to identify than those for graphics. Graphics has been widely integrated into the communications industry— television, film, and publishing. The main market for vision has been in manufacturing, where it has played a relatively minor role. Vision has also played a role in medicine, but that again is mostly out of the public's eye.

If we wish to stimulate the growth in the field of machine vision, there are several possible things we might do. One of these is to try to raise the level of awareness about vision by getting more people involved with the technology. There are probably a large number of potential vision amateurs who would make machine vision a hobby if more of the technology were made available to them. There is an army of graphics hackers out there now, and there could be an army of vision hackers in the future. While "hacking" sometimes means sloppy or irresponsible programming, much of it is the kind of play and creative activity that builds up excitement and new ideas in the field.

In order to encourage hobbyists, low-cost vision systems with exciting possibilities have to be made available. I believe that much of this will follow from the dramatic improvements in computing power at the PC-level (e.g., the power of the Macintosh II). The same kinds of systems that will help the hobbyists can help students: low-cost, high-potential laboratory facilities with interesting software.

Machine vision will probably get a boost from the same application area that has given graphics its biggest boost: graphic arts in support of business, education, and technical communication. Electronic painting systems are already incorporating capabilities to scan images and perform simple enhancement operations on them. In the future, much more sophisticated image stylization techniques are likely to be included as well. These techniques will probably make extensive use of computer vision methods.

I am sure that other factors will contribute to widening the range of vision applications; these factors include better parallel architectures, better programming methodology, automatic programming, and machine learning. However, the keystone of a vision revolution, if there is to be one, will be making masses of people with talent and imagination aware of the techniques and possibilities for machine vision and helping them get access to appropriate experimental environments.

Wayne Wiitanen

I would suggest that indications exist for fruitful directions in future research in machine vision. These indications come from what we know about animal vision. I have confidence that what we find in animal vision, at least for low-level processing, tend to be 'universal' operations well-suited to a general visual environment because the same operators are found in at least two evolutionarily disparate phyla: mammals and arthropods (in the latter specifically in the honey bee, Apis mellifera). The large repertoire of visual behaviors found in the honey bee (whose brain is smaller than a lentil!) reassures one that it does not take a lot of hardware to do significant visual preprocessing. Based on some findings of visual physiologists in studies of mammalian vision, certain suggestions can be put forward. One finds that the primary receptors (rods and cones) of a primate retina show a hexagonal packing. This maximizes the use of the available space in the retina. In addition, the receptive fields subserved by these receptors have sizes that increase as one goes peripherally from the fovea.

The difference-of-Gaussians receptive field model is a good representation of the "computation" occurring at the retinal level and is the principal output seen in optic nerve fibers. Light intensity undergoes a log-linear compression, providing the mechanism whereby primates are able to see in an environment where light intensities can vary by as much as six orders of magnitude. Primates move their eyes to bring regions of interest into the fovea, and humans appear to use a foveally centered polar coordinate system. This intrinsic coordinate system is anatomically mapped onto the visual cortex by a close approximation to a complex log transformation. This, combined with the increasing size of the receptive fields as one moves away from the fovea, provides a mechanism for transforming dilations and line-of-sight-centered rotations into simple translations. Primates tend to classify line rotations into 10 or 11 classes, and appear to have different levels of resolution, much like Gaussian pyramids. Signals from the same regions of visual space appear in the visual cortex in adjacent slabs of tissue (the details of precisely how these signals interact are not yet known and this is an area in which machine vision can contribute suggestions to visual physiology!).

Although much is known about animal vision, there is little synergistic activity between visual physiologists and machine vision researchers. This, to my mind, is where the future lies for machine vision research.

Index

A* algorithm, 279
Adelson, E. H., 29
Aggarwal, J. K., 299, 193, 219,
    220, 253, 255, 256
Agin, G. J., 251
Agrawal, A., 93
Altschuler, M. D., 219
Ambler, A. P., 255, 270
Anderson, C. H., 29, 30
Anderson, R. L., 251
animal vision, 308
Asada, H., 253
AUTOPASS, 185
B-splines, 229
Baird, M., 158
Baker, H. H., 90
Baldwin, E. C., 184
Ballard, D. H., 297
Barrow, H. G., 270, 90
Batcher, K. E., 56
Bavarian, B., 187
Beaudet, P., 147, 251
Beetem, J., 56
Bertero, M., 90
Besl, P. J., 158, 221, 252
Bezier patches, 229
Bhanu, B., 252, 254
Bil, G., 253
Bin-picking problem, 175
Binford, T. O., 251, 255, 90
Bjorklund, C. M., 255
Blelloch, G. E., 90, 93
Bolles, R. C., 252
Boyer, K. L., 219
Boyter, B. A., 252
Brady, M., 253, 271, 91
Brain, S., 56

Brennemann, A. E., 185
Brown, C. M., 255, 297
Bulthoff, H. H., 91
Burstall, R. M., 270
Burt, P. J., 1, 29, 30
Canny edge detection, 70
Canny, J. F., 91
Cass, T., 93
Chen, D., 158, 253
CLIP4, 31, 7, 31
coarse-to-fine analysis, 14
color encoding, 207
component verification, 173
Connection Machine, 57, 63, 106
Connel, J. H., 271
Consight, 150
controlled resolution, 5, 15
Corby, N., 299
Cornog, K. H., 91
Crawford, G. F., 255
data parallelism, 65
DeFoster, S. M., 184
Delleva, M. L., 256
Delp, E. J., 252
Denneau, M., 56
depth cues, 79
depth map, 222
depth perception, 222
Derin, H., 253
difference of gaussians, 157
differential geometry, 225
distance doubling, 65
distortion cost, 290
Dohi, Y., 56
Drazovich, R. J., 255
Duncan, J. H., 95
Durmheller, M., 91

Edelman, E., 91
ego-centered coordinates, 157
Elliot, H., 253
Fan, T. G., 253
Faugeras, O. D., 253
filament inspection system, 120
fine-grained parallel machine, 57
Fischler, M. A., 252
Fisher, A. L., 56
fluorescent penetrant inspection, 123
Flynn, A. M., 92
Flynn, M. J., 56
Fountain, T. J., 103, 31, 56
fovea, 3, 17
foveation, 9, 13
FPI, 123, 133
Freeman, H., 218, 299
Frisby, J. P., 94
Frobin, W., 218
Fu, K. S., 147
Gamble, E., 91
Garvey, T., 297
Gaussian pyramid, 19, 27
Geiger, D., 91
Gelade, G., 95
Geman, D., 91
Geman, S., 91
GF11, 39, 56
Goetcherian, V., 56
Golub, G. H., 253
graph matching, 258
grid coding, 201
Grimson, W. E. L., 92
Hall, E. L., 219
hallucinating, 286
Haralick, R. M., 187, 253, 297
Harris, J. G., 92
Hausen, K., 94
Hebert, M., 253, 254
Henderson, T., 252, 254
Herman, M., 254

heuristic search methods, 278
heuristic search, 202
hexagonal packing, 157
Hierholzer, E., 218
Hildreth, E. C., 93, 92
Hillis, W. D., 92
Hishop, G., 185
Ho, C. C., 252
Holland, S. W., 158, 184
Hollis, R. L., 185
Horaud, P., 252
Horn, B. K. P., 254, 92
Houseman, E. E., 251
Hu, G., 219
hypergraph, 258
IBIS, 123
Ikeuchi, K., 254
Inokuchi, S., 254, 254
Ittner, D. J., 254
Jain, A. K., 254
Jain, R. C., 158, 187, 221, 252
Jarvis, J., 299
Jarvis, R. A., 217
Jayaramamurthy, S. N., 256
Julesz, B., 92
Kak, A. C., 219
Kanade, T., 253, 256
Kanal, L., 271
Koch, C., 92, 92
Kruskal, C. P., 91
Kuan, D. T. K., 255
Kung, H. T., 56
Land, E. H., 92
Laplacian pyramid, 12, 24, 29
Lavin, M. A., 161, 185, 187
Lee, S., 252
Leiserson, C. E., 93
Li, H., 185
Lieberman, L. I., 185, 185
Lim, W., 93
Lin, C., 255

Little, J. J., 57, 93
Loan, C. F. van, 253
Lowe, D. G., 93
Lozano-Perez, T., 92
Lu, S. W., 270
Maggs, B. M., 93
Mahoney, J. V., 93
Mallot, H. A., 91
Mandeville, J. R., 184
Maresca, M., 185
Marimont, D. H., 271
Markov random fields, 82, 89
iconic processing, 20
integrated measures, 10, 18
lattice pipeline, 22
lobula scheme, 78
local autonomy, 31
logarithmic Sobel operator, 152
Marr, D., 271, 93
Marroquin, J., 92, 93, 94
Martelli, A., 297
Masaki, I., 159
Matsuday, F., 254
Mayhew, J. E. W., 94
McCanny, J. V., 56
McPherson, C. A., 218, 219
McWhirter, J. G., 56
Medioni, G., 253, 255
mesh-connected systems, 100
Michalski, R. S., 271
middle vision, 68
Milgrim, D. L., 255
MIMD, 22, 31
minimum cost path, 277
Mitiche, A., 219, 220, 253, 255, 256
Mitter, S., 93
model-based guidance, 13
Moigne, J. L., 219
Monier, L. M., 56
MPP, 34
multi-resolution representation, 15

Mundy, J. L., 109, 147, 184
Musits, B. L., 185
Nakayama, K., 94
Nekludova, L., 93
neural modeling, 153
Nevatia, R., 253, 254, 255, 255
Newell, A., 297
Nilsson, N. J., 297
Nishihara, H. D., 271
Nita, T., 254
Nitzan, D., 184
optical flow, 72
Oshima, M., 255
PAPIA, 104
parallel region growing, 241, 244
Pauchon, E., 253
Pearl, J., 297
Peet, F. G., 255
Pennington, K. S., 218
peripheral alerting, 13
Perry, M. J., 255
Petkovic, D., 187, 184
Pieroni, G. G., 187
pipeline architecture, 20
pipeline pyramid machine, 20, 30
Poggio, T., 90, 91, 93, 93, 94, 95
polymorphic-torus architecture, 180
Ponce, J., 253, 254
Popplestone, R. J., 255
Porter, G. B., 147
Posdamer, J. L., 219
Potmesil, M., 218, 219
PPM, 22
primate vision, 153
programmable systolic chip, 51, 56
pyramid architecture, 2, 104
pyramid machine, 1
pyramid transform architecture, 30
R-tree learning, 269
R-tree, 260
range image, 222

range image segmentation, 221
range sensor, 130
ray tracing, 53
real-time vision, 171
Reddaway, S. F., 56
region iteration, 243
Reichardt, W., 94
relational tree, 260
relaxation, 206
Requicha, A. A. G., 217
retinotopic mapping, 61
Riley, M. D., 94
robot vision, 111
Rosen, C., 184
Rosenfeld, A., 187, 97
Rossol, L., 158, 184
routing, 66
Rudolph, L., 91
Russell, B., 298
Sahota, T. S., 255
Sakurai, Y., 254
Sanz, J. L. C., 184
scanning, 67
Schunck, B., 185
seed region extraction, 237
Segen, J., 257, 271
Seitz, C. L., 94
sensor-based robot control, 152
sequential region growing, 244
Sethi, I. K., 256
Shafrir, A., 94
Shapiro, L. G., 270, 297
Shaw, J. C., 297
Shirai, Y., 255, 256
Sight-1, 150
Silverman, G. H., 94
SIMD, 20, 31, 64
Simon, H., 297
Sinniger, J. O., 30
Sklansky, J., 187
smart sensing, 2, 5, 17

smart surveillance, 26
Smith, D. R., 256
Snir, M., 91
spatial coherence, 223
spatial labeling, 205
spatial parallelism, 69, 88
SRI Vision Module, 166
Srihari, S. N., 217
state-space search, 275
stereopsis, 195
Stockman, G., 219
structural primitives, 259, 260
structural properties of shape, 257
subjective contours, 86
Sugihara, K., 219, 256
surface fitting, 239
surface type labeling, 236
Suwa, M., 256
Syllie, J. C., 96
syntactic analysis, 117
Tanimoto, S. L., 273, 298, 299
Taylor, R. H., 185
Tenenbaum, M., 90, 96
Terzopolous, D., 95, 256
Thomason, R., 187
time modulation, 204
Tio, J. B. K., 219
Tomita, F., 256
Torre, V., 90
transputer, 56
Treisman, A., 95
Tsai, R. Y., 185
turbine castings inspection, 121
Ullman, J., 95
Ullman, S., 92, 93, 95
Vemuri, B. C., 256
Verri, A., 95
vision algorithms, 286
Vision Machine, 59, 61
visual inspection, 112
visual perception, 300

Voorhees, H., 95
Wal, G. S. van der, 29, 30
Walker, H., 56
Wang, P. S. P., 187
Wang, Y. F., 193, 219, 220
Ward, M. R., 158, 184
Watson, L., 253
Waxman, A. M., 219, 95
Weingarten, D., 56
Wesley, M. A., 185
West, M. A., 184
Whitehead, A. N., 298
Whitman, R., 94

Wiitanen, W., 149, 184, 299
Will, P. M., 218
windows of interest, 8
Winston, P. H., 270
Witkin, A. P., 95, 96
Wong, A. K. C., 270
Wong, K. Y., 184
Xu, Xingping, 30
Yen, Chinsung, 30
Young, R., 159
Yuille, A., 253, 92
Ziegler, R. A., 184
Zuk, D. M., 256

Perspectives in Computing

Vol. 1   John R. Bourne, *Laboratory Minicomputing*

Vol. 2   Carl Tropper, *Local Computer Network Technologies*

Vol. 3   Kendall Preston, Jr., and Leonard Uhr, editors, *Multicomputers and Image Processing: Algorithms and Programs*

Vol. 4   Stephen S. Lavenberg, editor, *Computer Performance Modeling Handbook*

Vol. 5   R. Michael Hord, *Digital Image Processing of Remotely Sensed Data*

Vol. 6   Sakti P. Ghosh, Y. Kambayashi, and W. Lipski, editors, *Data Base File Organization: Theory and Applications of the Consecutive Retrieval Property*

Vol. 7   Ulrich W. Kulisch and Willard L. Miranker, editors, *A New Approach to Scientific Computation*

Vol. 8   Jacob Beck, Barbara Hope, and Azriel Rosenfeld, editors, *Human and Machine Vision*

Vol. 9   Edgar W. Kaucher and Willard L. Miranker, *Self-Validating Numerics for Function Space Problems: Computation with Guarantees for Differential and Integral Equations*

Vol. 10   Mohamed S. Abdel-Hameed, Erhan Çınlar, and Joseph Quinn, editors, *Reliability Theory and Models: Stochastic Failure Models, Optimal Maintenance Policies, Life Testing, and Structures*

Volumes 1–12 were published as **Notes and Reports in Computer Science and Applied Mathematics.**

Vol. 11   Mark G. Karpovsky, editor, *Spectral Techniques and Fault Detection*

Vol. 12   Selim G. Akl, *Parallel Sorting Algorithms*

Vol. 13   Azriel Rosenfeld, editor, *Human and Machine Vision II*

Vol. 14   Y.C. Tay, *Locking Performance in Centralized Databases*

Vol. 15   David S. Johnson, Takao Mishizeki, Akihiro Nozaki, Herbert S. Wilf, editors, *Discrete Algorithms and Complexity: Proceedings of the Japan-US Joint Seminar, June 4–6, 1986, Kyoto, Japan*

Vol. 16   J. Duane Northcutt, *Mechanisms for Reliable Distributed Real-Time Operating Systems: The Alpha Kernel*

Vol. 17   Gerd Bohlender, Christian Ullrich, Jürgen Wolff von Gudenberg, and Louis B. Rall, *Pascal-SC: A Computer Language for Scientific Computation*

Vol. 18   D.M. Miller, editor, *Developments in Integrated Circuit Testing*

Vol. 19   Ramon E. Moore, editor, *Reliability in Computing: The Role of Interval Methods in Scientific Computing*

Vol. 20   Herbert Freeman, editor, *Machine Vision: Algorithms, Architectures, and Systems*